Making Sense of Statistical Methods in Social Research

Making Sense of Statistical Methods in Social Research

Keming Yang

Los Angeles | London | New Delhi
Singapore | Washington DC

First published 2010

SAGE Publications Ltd
1 Oliver's Yard
55 City Road
London EC1Y 1S

SAGE Publications Inc.
2455 Teller Road
Thousand Oaks, California 91320

SAGE Publications India Pvt Ltd
B 1/I 1 Mohan Cooperative Industrial Area
Mathura Road, New Delhi 110 044
India

SAGE Publications Asia-Pacific Pte Ltd
33 Pekin Street #02-01
Far East Square
Singapore 048763

Library of Congress Control Number: 2009931921

British Library Cataloguing in Publication data

A catalogue record for this book is available from
the British Library

ISBN 978-1-84787-286-9
ISBN 978-1-84787-287-6 (pbk)

Typeset by C&M Digitals (P) Ltd, Chennai, India
Printed in India at Replika Press Pvt Ltd
Printed on paper from sustainable resources

To Charles, Marie and Lixin

Contents

Lists of Figures, Tables and Abbreviations

Figures

Tables

Abbreviations

ANOVA	analysis of variance
BHPS	British Household Panel Study
CFA	confirmatory factor analysis
CFI	comparative fit index
CLA	cluster analysis
COA	correspondence analysis
CPI	consumer price index
DA	discriminant analysis
DE	design effect
df	degrees of freedom
EFA	exploratory factor analysis
ESS	European Social Survey
GSS	General Social Survey
HLM	hierarchical linear models (also the name of software)
ICC	intra-class correlation coefficient
IQR	inter-quartile range
IQV	index of qualitative variation
LATE	local average treatment effect
LGCM	latent growth curve models
MANCOVA	multiple analysis of covariance
MANOVA	multiple analysis of variance
MDS	multidimensional scaling
PCA	principal component analysis
PSID	Panel Study of Income Dynamics
PSU	primary sampling unit
QCA	qualitative comparative analysis
RMSEA	root mean square error of approximation
RMSR	root means square residual
s.d.	standard deviation
s.e.	standard error
SEM	structural equation models
SES	socio-economic status

SNA	social network analysis
SRS	simple random sampling
SUTVA	stable unit treatment value assumption
UKHLS	UK Household Longitudinal Study

Preface

This book is written for senior undergraduates, postgraduate students and junior researchers who have learnt some introductory statistics but are new to the practice of applying statistical methods in social research projects. I hope to help them not only to select the most appropriate method for their own research but also to be able to identify potential pitfalls. To achieve this, I offer a critical account and overview of the concepts that underlie the statistical methods popularly used in social science research, focusing on the logic for making sense of these methods in answering substantive research questions.

This book is a result of my experience of learning, teaching and using statistical methods in social research during the past 15 years. Although I earned a postgraduate degree in statistics and the title of 'Chartered Statistician' from The Royal Statistical Society, I am not — and I have no plan to devote myself to becoming — a methodologist who does research mainly on statistical methods. I am a sociologist who often finds statistical methods very useful. Numeric data usually cover a large sample of cases that represent an even larger population, the data are usually of high quality and available free of charge and finally, we can analyse them in many different ways and submit our analysis to some well established procedures.

The use of statistics in social research, however, has been highly controversial. At one extreme, statistics suffer many severe critiques: quantitative analysis is shallow since it does not touch the meaning of social actions; it cannot even scratch the surface of the richness of cultural values; it assumes people behave simply because of their attributes; it overlooks social interactions; it pretends to make causal arguments but actually it cannot and so on. It sounds as if we should stop using statistics and try something else, although no one has openly said that. At the other extreme, there are many 'quantitative researchers' who simply ignore these critiques and use statistical models as a routine. Such divided opinion is also reflected on the two sides of the Atlantic. While many social scientists in the USA take statistics as their default method, their British counterparts usually keep away from it, except for a handful of institutions. Courses of introductory statistics are compulsory in the American social science curriculum, while the UK's Economic and Social Research Council has long recognized the lack of statistics training among the British graduates.

So, what shall we do with statistics? First, statistics may not be everyone's cup of tea, but nor should anyone who wants to apply statistical methods in social research be discouraged. Second, applying statistical methods in social research clearly demands far more than just being comfortable with numbers, maths or computer software. It is the sensible logic that counts. The key question is: How can we make sense of statistical methods in social research? I do not think that we can reach a satisfactory answer simply by using variables related to social issues, a popular practice in statistics textbooks written for social science students. Statistical methods will remain statistical even after we rename variables or cases with popular sociological terms. If we want to better understand and apply statistical methods, then we need to closely examine the logic of each method and think hard why and when each of them will make sense. This book is about such logic.

A few words on what this book is not about. First, it is not about the philosophy or the epistemology of social research. Second, the reader should not expect a full coverage of the technical details of statistical analysis. The book can be used as a textbook for senior undergraduate students or postgraduate students in any social science discipline, but it is not the same as *Social Statistics: An Introduction Using SPSS for Windows, Statistics for the Behavioural and Social Sciences* or *Statistics: A Tool for Social Research*, etc., which offer a very good introduction to elementary statistics and popular statistics software such as SPSS. This book does not do those things. We will discuss specific techniques and we may even look carefully at some equations and models, but it is the logical and conceptual foundation of statistical methods, not merely these methods per se, that we shall focus on. Third, this book does not cover methods for analysing experimental data. It is for people who do observational studies, that is, there is little that they can do to intervene or control the phenomena under study.

Finally, let me take this opportunity to thank the people who have helped me deliver this monograph. I must firstly thank my editor, Patrick Brindle, for his encouragement, patience and critical comments. This book will not come out without his efforts. Jeremy Toynbee polished the whole draft by making many useful modifications and corrections, for which I am extremely grateful. I also very much appreciate the specific comments and suggestions, both complimentary and critical, of the nine anonymous reviewers of my book proposal. Roberto Franzosi, David Byrne and Malcolm Williams provided some valuable comments on the book proposal as well. Gareth Williams read the whole draft and provided many excellent suggestions, for which I am extremely grateful. My colleague Juan Morillas read the chapter on time-related methods, and I thank him for his useful comments.

As always, I see the value of my work in the eyes of my wife Lixin, my daughter Marie and my son Charles. They have made great contributions to the production of this book by allowing me the time to work on it. I dedicate the book to them as a token of my appreciation.

ONE

Introduction

The Status of Statistics in the Social Sciences

The history of social sciences after the Second World War can easily lead people to believe that statistical methods have enjoyed not only legitimacy but popularity (Raftery, 2001). First of all, some social scientists have made significant contributions by employing and developing statistical methods, for example, Paul Lazarfeld, Hubert Blalock, Otis Dudley Duncan, Leo Goodman, to name only a few of the most influential. For the past few decades, statistical methods have become so popular that, for some, it is the only tool in their research toolbox. In addition, some leading academic journals regularly publish papers based on sophisticated statistical methods. Institutionally, nearly all sociology, political science, and business departments in American universities now make learning statistics compulsory.

Nevertheless, there has always been a voice of caution, if not utter objection, to using statistical methods in the social sciences. Back in the mid-1950s, Hubert Blumer (1956) pointed out several problems with quantitative methods in general when used to understand group processes and cultural values. However, he did not offer an attractive alternative to statistical methods for constructing powerful models built on a large amount of data. More recent critiques have been highly specific and therefore more compelling, many coming from quantitative methodologists themselves, including Otis Duncan, Aage Sorenson, David Freedman, and Richard Berk.

At the core of the controversies is the connection between social theories and statistical models. A widely criticized bad practice is to turn every theory into a variety of linear regression models and to take the results as proof or disproof of the theory. We shall learn the details of such models in Chapter 7. For now, the reader may want to take a note that we need to exercise care when using statistical models and be cautious about what we can say based on the results.

Furthermore, social researchers can find many better uses for statistics other than just running models to support theories. Identifying what statistical methods are good at and not good at will be the task of this chapter.

The controversial status of statistics in social research is evident in the UK. Initially, the quantitative wave seemed not to have spilled over to British social sciences – academic publications are highly discursive and qualitative, and only a handful of sociology departments make the learning of quantitative methods compulsory. Although it is not true that all British social scientists shy away from statistical methods, I believe it is safe to say three things about 'quantitative social researchers' in the UK:

(1) Most researchers are clustered in a handful of institutions, including Essex, Lancaster, Manchester, Oxford, and Surrey.
(2) Instead of being sociologists or political scientists, many are 'policy researchers'. They work on issues that are connected to government policies, such as education, poverty, employment, ethnicity, election turnout and so forth, and are concerned more with the implications of their research results for policies than for the growth of knowledge.
(3) Most are specialists on the collection and management of a large data set, such as the British Household Panel Study, British Social Attitudes Survey, British Crime Survey.

What all this means is that although there are some strongholds of quantitative methods in the UK, in most institutions such methods are not integral parts of sociology. Consequently, when voices lamenting the lack of quantitative skills in British social sciences are raised, such as those of the Economic and Social Research Council (ESRC) and Royal Statistical Society (RSS),[1] most often they are those of statisticians. It would be much easier to improve the quality of statistical analysis if sociologists themselves joined the debate.

Institutional initiatives assume that this is purely an issue of training. It is unclear, however, how social scientists in the UK view statistics in the first place. It will be very hard to improve the situation if it is an attitude problem. Why do most British social researchers shy away from statistics? Is it because they know that they are not mathematically competent and are put off by the difficulties of learning statistics? If this is the case, then it is simply a training problem. There is another possibility, however, that they believe that the limitations of statistics are too serious for it to be useful. The most perilous situation, in my view, would be one in which established social scientists in the UK discourage their students from learning and using statistics *for reasons other than the accepted limitations of statistics*, such as rejecting statistical methods as an example of positivism, thereby depriving social science students of the opportunity to learn how to use statistics carefully and thoughtfully.

All in all, the status of statistics in social sciences is not as secure and widely accepted as it initially appears. It is important to point this out at the beginning,

---

[1] In its First Report of Session 2004–05 to House of Commons Science and Technology Committee, ESRC was 'deeply concerned by the skills shortages afflicting, in particular, the quantitative branches of social science' (p. 33). The current Chief Executive of ESRC, Ian Diamond (2006), expressed his personal concern in a cover report of *RSS NEWS*.

especially for those who are about to learn and use statistical methods seriously. It may sound disheartening, but it is more helpful to tell a sad truth than a happy lie. Most importantly, we should address the question of what statistical methods can (or cannot) do for social research.

Before doing that, it is important to point out that the limitations of statistics should never be confused with problems that are caused by bad practices. Improper use of a tool should not lead to the judgment that the tool is useless. It is not fair to ask statistics to do something that it is not designed to do, and it is even more unfair to claim that it is the fault of statistics while the researcher is a fault. It is counter-productive to focus only on the limitations of statistical methods, ignoring situations in which these methods are of great utility. Such a negative attitude can easily lead the novice to believe that statistics is ill suited to social research and should not be used at all. To completely dismiss statistics from social research is not the solution. Let us think about the limitations and the utilities of statistical methods in specific terms, and then we shall know how to use them properly and responsibly.

My Approach

I take a pragmatic view to the application of statistical methods in the social sciences. To my mind, social researchers should not spend much time on philosophical or epistemological issues. Some may object, feeling that I am distracting students from 'the deeper issues'. My reply would be to let us do some research before talking about philosophical problems. If it turns out that we cannot proceed without sorting out those abstract issues, then it will not be too late to consider them; otherwise, it takes an unnecessarily long period of time to reach any useful results. Social researchers should spend more time developing new skills and trying them out in real research than they spend considering the philosophical background to those skills. We come to philosophical issues only when we have to.

In empirical work, I believe that social researchers should adopt a more balanced attitude towards statistical methods. Statistics should not be used automatically but carefully and appropriately. This means that we must consider the context in which the data were produced and the implications of our statistical analysis for the substantive conclusions that we can make. For this reason, it is very hard to be a social scientist, because it is a considerable challenge for one person to produce creative research designs, to be well read, to be competent in employing statistical methods, and to be able to make sharp observations based on the data gathered. Similarly to any other method, statistical methods have their limitations, but I seriously doubt that one can understand – let alone criticize – their limitations effectively without actually having used them in real research. It is only through careful learning and working with statistics on specific problems that we can identify the limitations and benefits of using statistical methods.

My students usually make two general complaints about statistics: first, statistics is not relevant, and, second, statistics is too hard. Both are understandable, but they can be easily countered. For relevance, just browse the large number of publications on social issues. Is statistics hard? Yes, and it will remain hard forever if you keep telling yourself and everyone else that 'I am not a math person' or 'I am not here to learn statistics'. What I have found absolutely unacceptable is to connect the above two points together: 'statistics is irrelevant because it is hard'. If you are not prepared to learn statistical methods, please apply qualitative methods – many prominent social scientists have made great contributions without using statistics at all. However, it is unfair to claim that statistics is useless or too hard to learn for the sake of justifying your choice of qualitative methods.

Overview

While planning this book, I have tried my best to employ a logical structure, gradually moving from simple topics to the more complicated ones, more specifically:

- from general issues to more specific topics;
- from data collection to data analysis;
- from univariate (one variable) to bivariate (two variables) to multivariate (three or more variables) statistics;
- from descriptive statistics to inferential statistics;
- from one-level models to multilevel models;
- from cross-sectional (one time point) to longitudinal (multiple time points) models;
- from variable-oriented methods to case-oriented methods;
- from manifest (observed) variables to latent variables.

The reader is strongly recommended to read the whole book in its present order unless you feel absolutely confident of selecting or skipping any particular chapter. Most people should have no difficulty of understanding the first five chapters, but for those without any background in statistics it is a good idea to read an introductory statistics text before moving on to Chapters 6–11.

After this general introduction, we shall discuss a few more specific issues pertinent to the status of statistical methods in social research in Chapter 2. What can they do? What can they not do? What general principles must we follow in order to use them properly?

From Chapter 3, our journey of learning specific concepts and techniques starts with the target of statistical analysis, that is, the case-by-variable data matrix. It is crucial to have a proper understanding of cases and variables before learning any special method for analysing them. The most important issue here is a variable's level of measurement. We should not be obsessed with it, but it is nevertheless true that many statistical tools are created by considering the level of measurement. Therefore, our choice of a particular tool will often heavily depend on it. Later in the Chapter 4, I offer an overview of statistical methods based on our discussion of variables. The final section of Chapter 3 will contain some basic but important rules for using statistics in social research.

Where do the data come from? We cannot analyse data until we examine the data collection process. As most data for social research are collected from sample surveys, we shall take a closer look at the idea of sampling in Chapter 4. The difference between population and sample might seem obvious, but many researchers are not really aware of the effects of sampling designs and sampling errors. We will spend some time on sampling issues, but the key objective of Chapter 4 is to help the reader understand how sampling procedures affect subsequent statistical analyses.

Knowing the effects of sampling is also a first step toward learning the logic of statistical inference – saying something about the population based on the information collected from only a part of it (the sample). Using the example of measuring and estimating one important phenomenon, we will learn in Chapter 5 why we can say something about the population parameters with statistics produced from only one sample.

Today, social researchers are rarely satisfied with estimating the magnitude of a single variable, no matter how important it is. They study several variables at the same time in order to say something about their relationships, such as looking for the direction of the relationship and measuring its strength, and testing the robustness of the relationship across different situations. Things can appear quite complicated due to the demand of using a specific method for each combination of two types of variables. The relatively large number of ways of describing and representing relationships often perplexes students. Which method should be used? In Chapter 6, I identify the situations in which a particular method should be used and discuss the logic of why that particular method is the right choice.

In Chapter 7, by looking at the relationships among three or more variables, we enter the world of multivariate statistical methods. Perhaps the most popular method is multiple linear regression and its generalizations. Although statisticians have tried to invent flexible models so that we can always have a model suitable for a particular situation, there have been growing criticisms of using such models in social research. Again, a key issue centres on the function of these models: what are they supposed to do? Most users would say that the models should 'explain' the relationship between the variables that we are interested in. But is that the right thing to expect from the models? Even if it is, what do we mean by 'explain'?

All the above methods are used to analyse data collected at one particular time point. Time, of course, is significant in social research. The challenge, however, is to incorporate the temporal dimension explicitly and meaningfully in our analysis. In Chapter 8 we shall learn a few methods that in one way or another take time or temporary order seriously. Without going into technical details, this chapter presents the similarities and differences between these methods by clearly laying out the situation in which the social researcher may find it useful to apply one of the selected methods.

There has been a call to move away from variable-oriented to case-oriented methods in social sciences. In Chapter 9, I show that in addition to qualitative methods there are 'case-oriented' statistical methods. I use the word 'oriented' purposefully because I believe that cases and variables are interdependent on each other and that we should not create another artificial division between research methods. The major difference is that case-oriented methods look more carefully at the relations among the cases, while variable-oriented methods pay special attention to the relations among the attributes of the cases. It would be simplistic to say that one is better than the other.

Most of the methods discussed in Chapters 4 to 9 are designed, or will only work properly, for manifest (observed) variables. Many variables, however, cannot be directly measured, or even when they can be measured, there is a large amount of error. The source of such errors can be either conceptual or practical, or both. In Chapter 10, I introduce some methods that are exclusively designed to analyse latent (unobserved or unobservable) variables. The first thing to keep in mind is the appropriateness of the variables that are deemed as 'latent' before any of the methods is to be used. It would be pointless to apply these methods if the variables were incorrectly identified as latent in the first place.

In the final chapter we come to the most difficult topic of this book – causal analysis in observational studies. It is relatively straightforward to demonstrate causal relations in controlled experiments as we can manipulate the initial conditions so that the effect of the interested cause will stand out. Most social science studies are observational because such manipulation is almost always infeasible. Therefore, in social sciences, causal relations are proposed first of all based on theories, knowledge, logic and even common sense. Then, evidence is collected to support these causal arguments. Many criticisms have focused on the practice of using linear regression and structural equation models to make causal inference, so we shall try to identify what these problems are. To go beyond those models, some statisticians have developed counterfactual statistical methods for inferring causal effects in observational studies. We cannot sufficiently cover the details of these methods in a single section of one chapter, but the basic ideas will be introduced.

TWO

The Use of Statistical Methods in Social Research

What Statistics Is Not Good At

Describing Unique Phenomena in Great Detail

Statistics is a tool for discovering meaningful information from a large amount of numeric data. It is most useful for obtaining concise and precise information about a large number of cases. Cases may come in many different forms: groups of human beings, buffalos, crops, microchips, accidents, web pages and so forth. When it is more important to know the characteristics of these cases as a whole than to learn about each particular unit, statistics starts to shine. It is simply too hard for human brains to detect any meaningful patterns in a large matrix of numbers. Statistics comes to the rescue with a few numbers and equations that summarize the patterns.

Conversely, statistics is a very clumsy tool when the interest is in the details of one or very few unique cases the idiosyncrasies of which can be represented in many different aspects. For example, anthropologists try to understand the uniqueness of a very small number of cases in a particular context. They routinely carry out this kind of work by staying in a unique community for years, taking extremely detailed field notes, and finally writing up what Clifford Geertz calls 'thick description' (1973: 5–10). In sociology, beginning with Max Weber, there has been a long tradition of understanding meanings, interpretations, values and contexts. Comparative studies on a small number of cases – the so-called 'small-N' studies – have been an attractive research method to many students of social, historical and political sciences.

For example, why have some former communist nations been successful in transforming their economies while others failed? There are not many former communist nations in the world, and not all of them have tried to transform their economies. Moreover, each nation's economic development is unique because it is a product of the combined effects of many factors, including history, ideology, leadership, international relations, cultural values, its citizens' educational levels, political structure and so forth. Here, we have many complicated variables the values of which are hard to define and very few cases within which to show any pattern; this is a situation in which statistics is not of much use.

Representing Relations and Networks

Obviously, social relations are of considerable importance for understanding social phenomena. In the mid-1940s, Harvard University established the interdisciplinary Department of Social Relations under the leadership of Talcott Parsons. Nevertheless, it was not until the late 1970s that social scientists started to be able to study social relations directly and rigorously. Beforehand, social relations were discussed in abstract terms or through analogies. Following development over the past three decades or so, social network analysis (SNA) has become a very effective and popular method (Scott, 2000; Carrington et al., 2005).

The mathematical foundation of SNA is graph theory, which is different from the foundations of statistics: probability and matrix algebra. A graph consists of vertexes and edges (or arcs) that connect the vertexes. When used in social sciences, the vertexes can represent individual human beings or larger groups, and the edges can represent a variety of social relations. With statistics, we study the attributes of the vertexes, not the relations among the vertexes. That is, statistics cannot help us represent and analyse the overall structure of social relations among a group of individual units. To social scientists, this is a serious limitation, because in many situations it is structural positions, not attributes, that account for people's actions. To study social structure directly, you need to employ SNA, not statistics.

However, this does not mean that statistics has no part to play in the studying social networks. First of all, statistics can do a good job of measuring the quality of social relations. Even after years of development, many measures used in SNA remain crude, such as naming friends, having lunch, playing for the same sports club, sitting in the same board of directors, etc., measures which are barely able to capture the subtleness and complexity of the quality of social relations. In my opinion, SNA researchers should make use of statistical tools such as latent variables or indexes to obtain more refined measurements of social relations and incorporate these measurements in their analyses. Recent developments in SNA show that some statistical methods are highly useful for advanced analyses of social network data (Koehly and Pattison, 2005; Snijders, 2005).

Identifying Causal Relations

We shall come back to the difficult subject of causal inference in Chapter 11. Here we discuss it in light of the limitations of statistical methods. Broadly speaking, making a causal argument involves not one but several tasks: identifying causal relations; modelling complex causal relations; verifying the causal relations; and measuring the size of causal effect. The most serious limitation of statistics lies in its inability of identifying causal connections, but it can be of great value for measuring and modelling.

It is important to recognize that the establishment of causal relations is a cognitive process. The idea of the existence of a certain causal relationship comes to our mind in different ways: the observation of regular connections among several phenomena, the discovery of unusual phenomena, the deduction of axioms and so forth. In these activities, we need heuristics, not statistics (Abbott, 2004). This is so because the function of statistics is to describe numerically what has already happened, not to speculate, hypothesize or theorize some unobservable processes that may be at work. Statistics can help us to evaluate how well a piece of numeric evidence would support a perceived causal process, but it is not able to offer an explanation for that process. What we should observe and what we can say about unobservable processes are beyond the capabilities of statistics.

This also explains why statisticians have been extremely cautious of moving from association to causation, especially for non-experimental studies. Most recently, techniques drawing on the idea of counterfactuals have made some progress in confirming the causal effect of candidate causal factors (Morgan and Winship, 2007). No matter how sophisticated these methods are, however, the candidate causal factors arise from theories and current knowledge; they cannot come from statistical methods. What statistics can do is to measure and model the proposed causal connections when conditions (research design, quality of data and so on) permit. Deriving causal statements completely based on statistical models is to manipulate statistics beyond its capabilities.

Modelling Nonlinear Dynamics

There are at least three things about nonlinear dynamic processes that statistical methods will find very hard to cope with. First, the data underpinning statistical analysis do not contain sufficient information about the dynamic entity, be it a group of human beings, a social movement or any other social phenomenon. The information underpinning statistical analysis is *the attributes* of the entity, not the records of *how the entity's behaviours have evolved over time*. In certain circumstances, the temporal changes of these attributes may represent the changes of the entities themselves, but there is always a gap between the two, and in some situations the attributes may give a distorted reflection of the dynamic process. Therefore, it is at best clumsy and at worst inadequate to take the attributes as proxies of the process. The objective of statistical methods is to study the varied distribution of the attributes across cases, not the changes that the targeted entity has gone through. This inability to study dynamics derives from the restricted structure of the statistical analysis data. Statistics is good at representing the variation of variables across cases rather than any actual processes.

In relation to that, there is a limit to which statistical methods can incorporate time, an essential element of dynamic processes. Data collected from standalone cross-sectional surveys are inherently static. Although the whole data collection process may take a long period of time, such as a year, it is assumed that the data refer to the situation at one particular time point. Data collected in repeated, cross-sectional social surveys do reveal situations at different time points. Nevertheless, because the respondents differ from one time point to another, that is, the entities under study have changed, the data simply cannot show any dynamic processes of the same thing unless it can be established that all the samples represent the same population. Data collected with longitudinal designs are best suited for statistical analyses of temporal processes, but even here the analysis of dynamics is seriously limited owing to the restricted structure of the data matrix. As we shall see later in Chapter 8, longitudinal models tell us the probability that a variable's effect changes across time points rather than models the dynamic directly. Such studies are useful for exploring the patterns within the data, but they constrain our theoretical imagination because our theories of a particular dynamic process may not be properly represented by the attributes. Statistical methods may be of great use for measuring the actual change of some important quantities, but they cannot supply a specific functional relationship that links the interested entities at different time points. The specific function that models the dynamic should be backed up by a strong theory, not derived from fitness to a particular set of data.

This brings us to another limitation of statistics: it is very likely that functions that model dynamic processes and are supported by a theory involve nonlinear relationships, because changes are rarely constant, universal or stable. As they are inconstant, specific and unstable, dynamic processes usually pass different phases. To represent these phases with a single mathematical function is very hard, and it cannot be done without a specific theory. Statistical methods, designed to explore and represent the regular patterns in the data collected in a specific context, have to rely heavily on linear models and their transformations because that is the most convenient form for specifying relationships. Although efforts are made to ensure that the linearity assumption is reasonable, the modelling process rarely begins with a nonlinear idea.

What Statistics Is Good At

To many social scientists, causal explanation is the most important objective (Stinchcombe, 1968; Abbott, 2004; Cartwright, 2007). There should be no doubt that social researchers should make every effort to achieve causal explanation whenever they can. Nevertheless, I would take a softer line than that. I would not even claim that it is *the most important* purpose. There are many other things social researchers should aspire to achieve, and statistical methods can make valuable contributions to these seemingly less honourable undertakings. The uses listed and discussed below are for illustration only and are not meant to be exhaustive and mutually exclusive.

Establishing the Target Phenomenon

While planning his prefatory paper for the 13th issue of *Annual Review of Sociology*, Robert K. Merton (1987) gave the editors a list of 45 topics on which he could write focused discussions. The space allocated to him, however, could accommodate only three. The three selected, being each ranked 1 of 15, indicate the importance of those topics. Of the three selected, 'Establishing the Phenomenon' came first. The reason cannot be clearer: social scientists would waste a huge amount of resources if they reached the end of their research only to find that the phenomenon they have planned to explain actually does not exist or exists in a different form. As Merton shrewdly reminds us:

> In the abstract, it needs hardly be said that before one proceeds to explain or to inter-pret a phenomenon, it is advisable to establish that the phenomenon actually exists, that it is enough of a regularity to require and to allow explanation. Yet, sometimes in science as often in everyday life, explanations are provided of matters that are not and never were. (1987: 2)

He then illustrated such careless practice in both natural and social sciences.

How could such embarrassing incidents occur in the first place? Why do people rush to explain something even before checking out the existence of what they are trying to explain? Although it is likely that some do it on purpose, let us believe that the majority of researchers maintain a high level of intellectual integrity. And alternatively, assume that they simply forget to verify the existence of their phe-nomena before explaining them, how can they forget? This is not a simple matter of bad memory.

Here is a more plausible explanation. The researcher is in an exciting process of justifying or illustrating the power of a theory with a piece of information obtained from a particular source. The main worry is that information will slow down the whole research process, and worse, if the information turns out to be incorrect, then the whole project will crumble. Consequently, the researcher wish-fully assumes the establishment of the phenomenon. Another possibility is that the researcher may find little value in fact-finding activities because the main interest is in theorizing, explaining or interpreting. Fact-finding is something of low academic value and can be easily done by others.

To avoid these embarrassing and wasteful incidents, it would be useful to require that all research questions be preceded with a statement about the factual existence of the phenomenon under study. Pertinent to the subject of this book, although not all facts are numeric, reliable statistics can supply the evidence for establishing the phenomenon. Using statistics is not the only way of establishing the phenomenon, of course, and it can be a highly contro-versial process: the definition of the phenomenon, the theoretical as well as empirical boundaries, the trustworthiness of the evidence and so on. How to resolve these disputes is beyond statistical analysis, but regardless how they are resolved, producing statistics is perhaps the best way of establishing the phenomenon.

Detecting Patterns among a Huge Amount of Information

Most statistical methods are data reduction tools, most useful when the amount of numeric information tends to overwhelm our cognitive capacity. With a few numbers, equations or graphs, statistical analyses can reveal patterns hidden in a data matrix of thousands of cases by hundreds of variables, or even several such matrices. With statistical procedures properly followed, not only can researchers establish the phenomenon in question, but they can discover patterns that they may have never thought about before. The phrase 'data mining' best expresses such exploratory process: we may have a vague idea of what we shall find based on our common sense – and it is a commendable practice to keep common sense in our mind – but we can never be completely certain about exactly what we shall find until we see the results. I personally find it the most exciting experience of using statistics to challenge the status quo with numeric results, an excellent opportunity to show the value of statistical work. A large amount of money has been invested in social surveys, which then have generated a huge amount of numeric data. It is an academic sin not to maximize the use of this freely available source of information.

Comparing Groups (Broadly Defined)

Human beings differ along many dimensions: gender, age, race and ethnicity, wealth, cultural values and so on. To describe, understand and explain these differences constitutes a major research activity for statistical analysis (Harkness et al., 2002; Liao, 2002). Statistical methods cannot help us explain *why* people are so different, but they are good at describing *how* they are different. Again, it is presumptuous to think that all 'the why questions' are necessarily answerable, worth answering and more important than 'the how questions'. In social reality, many 'how questions' with regards to human groups are much more important than 'why questions' because their answers provide the starting point for actions, *regardless of whether we know why people are so different*. Clearly, it is one of statistics' specialties to measure the magnitude, the scale and the scope of group differences, and further to connect these differences with other interested factors. One particular contribution that statistics can make is to assess the comparability of measurements used across different groups, such as communities, organizations or nations. For example, results from different social surveys may not be comparable even though the wordings of the original survey questions are exactly the same. Some other factors, such as people's different understandings of the questions, may render the results incomparable. By carrying out a few statistical tests, we may make our comparisons more reliable.

Measuring the Unique Effects of Risk (or Contributing) Factors

Often researchers have several factors in mind that they believe have at least some partial causal effects on the target phenomenon. The causal effect is established not through experiments but through what John Goldthorpe (2000) calls 'robust association' in observational studies; that is, although we cannot make causal arguments purely based on observed associations, if the association exists in almost all the situations that we have examined, then there is at least no clear evidence against the proposed causal relationship. We may not have sufficient evidence to show that a few factors are really the causes and how they work, but if their effects persist, we must pay careful attention to the size of these effects. This is the logic followed by medical doctors who are able to explain why it is more likely for a particular type of people, say females above the age of 60, to get a particular disease, but they would be well prepared to take these 'risk factors' (gender and age) very seriously.

Evaluating and Assessing the Impact of Policies, Actions or Events

Statistical methods can help us evaluate the impact of policies, actions or events (Rossi and Wright, 1984; Freudenburg, 1986). Will the introduction of speed cameras make drivers slow down? How many peoples' financial and marital lives will be affected, desirably and undesirably, by the building of a casino centre? Questions such as these abound in policy-related issues, and statistics can offer valuable help in answering them. Perhaps this is why Andrew Abbott claims that the only place where statistics can find itself of some use is in social policy while condemning the practice of employing statistics to make causal arguments (2004: 40). The contribution by statistics is widely deemed to be legitimate and helpful because policy-makers and researchers are usually content with the discovery of regularities as a reasonably good basis for taking actions. 'The point was to decide whether to take some action, not to understand mechanisms' (Abbott, 2004: 38).

Types of Statistical Methods

Univariate, Bivariate and Multivariate

The first distinction refers to the number of variables involved. An analysis is 'univariate' if it is focused on only one variable. An analysis of two variables is 'bivariate' and one of multiple variables 'multivariate'. It is very rare for any serious analysis to completely focus on only a single variable, but knowledge of one variable is necessary for understanding more complicated situations with multiple variables.

Numeric versus Graphic

Numeric methods produce exact and meaningful numbers, while graphic methods visualize the data with charts or plots to show patterns, unusual cases, clustering and other features in the data. It is too big an exaggeration to say that 'a graph is worth more than a thousand words'. If it is true, all statistical studies should be presented with graphs rather than numbers. Graphs can reveal things that are hard to see in numbers, but they are much less accurate and precise than numbers, and there are situations in which graphs struggle to show anything meaningful that is not difficult to show with numbers. For example, a table can be much more effective than a graph because the reader does not have to go back and forth between the graph and the key. Besides, graphs produced with advanced statistics may be hard to understand. The bottom line is to use both types of methods in a complementary manner in order to achieve clarity and accessibility.

Cross-sectional versus Longitudinal

This is a research design issue. Most studies collect data on the same group of respondents at only one time point. They are 'cross-sectional' because their aim is to cover the situations in different sections of the population. Obviously, these studies are static by design. If the main objective is to study changing situations temporally, then the same group of respondents must be followed and contacted at each one of several time points. This type of study is longitudinal, which is technically more difficult and financially more costly.

The distinction between 'cross-sectional' and 'longitudinal' is, however, not as clear-cut as it appears. Some cross-sectional social surveys are repeated at multiple time points. The participating respondents are different from one time point to another, but the operation and the contents of the study (sampling schemes, instruments used, administration) remain the same. This type of study is not as good as completely longitudinal studies for the purpose of studying change because it is hard to tell whether the observed changes are effects of the interested factors or of the differences among the respondents. In contrast, sometimes longitudinal studies may have to incorporate elements of cross-sectional design. For example, attrition, the loss of some respondents from one wave to another, is a constant problem for longitudinal surveys. To make up the loss, researchers usually recruit new respondents in a particular wave in order to maintain a desired sample size. As a consequence, the group of respondents do not remain completely the same. Different statistical methods will be needed depending on how the data were collected. The general principle is to incorporate features of the design into data analysis.

Descriptive versus Inferential

To make the last distinction, we need first to make the distinction between a population and a sample. The population is the ultimate target of our investigation, which must be defined before any empirical work is conducted. For most large-scale sample surveys, the target population is usually all the adults living in private residences at a particular point of time, but one must think the specific population carefully for a particular research purpose.

For various reasons, either because we cannot study the whole population directly or because there is no need to do so, we draw a sample from the population in the hope that the information drawn from the sample would still allow us to say something about the population. If we make conclusions about the population based on our analysis of the sample data, then we are doing inferential statistics; that is, we are inferring from the sample to the population. In contrast, if our analysis focuses on the sample or the population alone, then we are doing descriptive statistics. A bad practice commonly seen in social research is not clearly stating whether the study targets a particular population, and if there is an interested population, how it is defined. Alternatively, little attention is paid to the connection between the population and its sample. This is a very important issue because it determines the kind of statistics – descriptive or inferential – used.

Ten Rules of Using Statistics

During the past years of learning, using and teaching statistics, I have built up a set of rules of using statistics in social research. I have found it very important and useful to keep them in mind.[1]

Rule No. 1 – Understand the Subject Matter

The raw material for statistical analysis is the data matrix. On appearance, a matrix is just a set of numbers, and statistics is mostly concerned with the procedures that process the numbers. The numbers do carry meanings, of course, and they are produced in a particular context. It should be common sense now that data must be understood and interpreted in relation to a particular subject matter and its specific context (van Belle, 2002: 4). But this point is still worth repeating, especially for novice users, because the subject matter and its context are not directly attached to the data, so researchers tend to forget them when their attention is focused on the data. Without intensive training, our human brain is simply not good at considering things that are out of sight. Researchers must realize that the process of turning every piece of information into a number has further separated the data from its subject matter.

In contrast, for 'qualitative data' such as documents, conversations and photos, the data and their meanings are tightly intertwined, thus forcing us to go back to the data's context and meaning. Researchers using statistics need to avoid becoming buried so deeply in statistical procedures that they lose sight of what they plan to argue substantively. An effective method is to repeatedly ask yourself: 'What can I say based on the data and my analysis?'

Rule No. 2 – Learn How the Data Were Collected and Examine Their Quality

It is safe to say that most researchers no longer collect their own large numeric datasets. Today, many researchers analyse secondary data, that is, data that were collected by others. Even when they are involved in collecting primary data, this is not a one person job, and consequently they have to accept that at least a part of the

---

[1] I may not be able to identify the original source of all these rules, so I apologize that I couldn't give credit to the person who initially suggested them.

data collection process has to be carried out by their co-researchers. This rule is thus valid not only for researchers using secondary data but for all researchers.

To follow this rule, try to answer the following questions. An answer may not be always available for every question listed here, but researchers should try as hard as they can to find them. First, there are a series of questions about the nature of the study from which the data were collected, and researchers should keep in mind the implications when conducting subsequent analysis. Is it an experimental, quasi-experimental or an observational study? Is time an essential element in the research design? Answers to these questions may indicate how far the researcher can go in making a causal argument.

Next, are there a population and a sample? How is the population defined? If there is a sample, how is it drawn? The answers will determine whether statistical inference can be appropriately made, and the answers will affect weighting and statistical estimates as well.

We also need to consider the method of data collection: How was the data collection administered, by telephone, personal interviews, post or email? What were the sample size and the response rate? Information about these issues will highlight the quality of the data. Even for a study with a high response rate, there are usually many missing values. But the data matrix usually appears to be very clean when one is analysing a secondary dataset. How was it cleaned up? This is a highly difficult issue, but we should try at least to answer the following three questions when reporting the results so that our reader can have a good sense of the data quality:

(1) Why were some data missing – was it failure of contact, refusal, lack of knowledge of the subject matter?
(2) How have the missing data been handled – ignoring them, imputing from available data with an average, or nearby values or other method?
(3) What are the effects of the previous strategy on the final results and conclusions?

The final issue relates to variables: How many variables are there to estimate the same phenomenon or concept? What was the original rationale of creating those items? What were the options from which respondents chose? How were they worded? Answers to these questions will affect the choice of statistical procedures and interpretations of statistical results.

Rule No. 3 – When Studying a Single Variable, Analyse and Report Statistics of Both its Centre and its Spread

Most people are satisfied with statistics that describe the centre of a variable, such as the mode (the most frequent value), the median (the value in the middle) or the mean (the arithmetic or the weighted average), as they offer a quick and clear summary of the variable's values.

For at least two reasons, any of these alone is not sufficient for depicting the whole picture of a variable. First, our real interest should be *the overall distribution* of a variable's values, of which the centre is only a part. There are several other things we must look at, such as the number of modes, cyclical patterns, whether there is a skew to one side and so forth. At the minimum, we should know the degree of variation of the values. 'A measure of centre alone can be misleading', as McCabe and Moore have reminded us, 'The simplest useful numerical description of a distribution consists of both a measure of centre and a measure of spread' (2006: 44). The measure of spread includes index of variation, interquartile range and variance. We shall learn the exact meaning of these terms in Chapter 5, but the reader should keep this general rule in mind from now on.

Another reason that we should not be satisfied with a measure of centre alone is that it varies from sample to sample. One can easily see this in the results published by different polling agents. Which one should we trust? None of them, because they are all from a sample, and sample results are always different from the true but unknown value in the population. Loosely speaking, we call the uncertainty of sampling results 'sampling errors'. There are other types of errors, but the sample error alone should be sufficient to make the point that one should not be concerned with the specific statistics itself. What we should be concerned with are the procedures that have been adopted to produce the statistics and the possible range of variations from sample to sample.

Rule No. 4 – Use Both Numeric and Graphic Methods as Supplementary Tools

Words and graphs serve different functions and thus have different utilities. Graphs are intuitively appealing and effective of showing relative positions in a single picture. However, these advantages come with some conditions. For example, it is unnecessary and perhaps a waste of space to produce a graph when there are very few pieces of information. Van Belle listed two situations in which it is not useful to graph data: 'when there are few data points, or when there are too many relationships to be investigated. In the latter case a table may be more effective' (2002: 159). Therefore, he suggests that we use 'sentence structure for displaying 2 to 5 numbers, tables for displaying more numerical information, and graphs for complex relationships' (2002: 154). A table may be clearer and more informative than a graph when all variables are categorical and we want to compare the groups defined by these variables. No matter how we will present the data, it will be a trail-and-error process, not a one-off activity.

Rule No. 5 – Refrain from Using a Pie Chart or a Bar Chart (Especially a Stacked or Three-dimensional Bar Chart)

The reader may be perplexed by this rule, as pie charts and bar charts are widely used in all sorts of publications and are standard functions in statistical software, why should we not use them? Actually, van Belle suggests that we not use pie and bar charts at all (2002: 160–7). I think it is a bit too radical to ban pie and bar charts once and for all; therefore, I suggest to refrain from using these charts.

The best way of making sense of this rule is to do the following: put a pie chart (or a bar chart) and the data table on which the chart is produced side by side, examine them and ask yourself: 'What is the added value of the chart?' The answer would be 'very little, none, or even negative'. When there are a limited number of categories in the data table, there is no need to put them in a chart – in this situation our brain is capable of recognizing the information in the original data. If we use a pie or bar chart, we will have to use a key, thereby forcing our eyes to go back and forth between the chart and the key. We may also have to put the value for each category in its corresponding slice in order to know the exact value – we are not that good at recognizing which slice is larger when two have very similar values, which repeats the information in the table.

In addition, when there are a large number of categories in the data table, the chart simply cannot handle so much information – it will look very crowded, especially so when some slices are too tiny to be clearly recognized. Similarly, in a bar chart, bars for categories whose values are very small will be suppressed by categories of much bigger values, making it very hard for us to figure out exactly how small they are. Some would say that an advantage of a bar chart is to sort the categories so that we can detect a descending or ascending trend. This, however, can be easily and more effectively achieved by a table with all categories being sorted in order.

That said, I think that in one situation pie and bar charts can be very useful, that is, when we try to compare several groups with a pie or bar chart representing each of them, and each pie or bar chart can show the information clearly. A single pie or bar chart is of little value.

Rule No. 6 – When Creating a Table or a Graph, Draw it by Hand on a Piece of Paper before Producing it on a Computer

I realized the value of this rule from my own experience: there are so many times that I produced a table or a graph directly on a computer, only to find that I needed one more row or column, some parts were not necessary, the direction should have been reversed, or there was a better way of presenting the same information. We all know that a good practice of time-saving is to prepare a shopping list before shopping in a supermarket, because we know much better what we exactly want when at home. We should follow a similar practice in creating a table or a graph. The increasing power of computers should not preclude manual alternatives. Before making a table or a graph, we had better ask ourselves: (1) What do I really want to show in this table or graph? (2) What are the expected values or patterns? (3) What will it make me able to say about the substantive issue?

Rule No. 7 – Do Not Cut and Paste All Outputs Generated by Computer Software

In order to make computer software popular, computer programmers want to satisfy as many different demands as possible, so that all sorts of people can find what they want. An advantage for the software's marketability, it may not be desirable for a particular user. As a user, you should know exactly what *you* want from the software and what the software has produced for you. You must be able to know which pieces of information in the outputs are exactly what you want, which are relevant and which can be discarded. Learn as much as you can about what a particular piece of computer software can do for you, so that you know as much as you can about what you can delegate to the computer to do and what you have kept back for your independent thinking.

Rule No. 8 – Edit the Outputs that You Want to Include in Your Report

Similar to deleting redundant words or breaking up a long sentence into easily under-standable short ones, editing is no less important for presenting statistical work. For example, one of my statistics teachers at Columbia University, Andrew Gelman, used to ask us to keep only two decimal digits. Many statistical software programs, however, automatically produce numbers with four or even six decimal digits, which is both unnecessary and distractive for most purposes. More generally, decimal num-bers may not make sense at all for some variables, such as sex, ethnic groups or cities. For another example, after producing a table, you may find some cells empty, so you may think whether it is necessary and sensible to merge some of them with others. There are some issues of style as well: lines under the categories should be darker than others, and many academic journals require that no vertical lines be used in a table, some numbers must be flagged up with asteroids to signal statistical signifi-cance, and a note of resources may be needed under the table.

Rule No. 9 – No Cheating in Making Causal Statements

One thing you must never forget after reading this book or taking any statistics class, no matter how elementary, is that correlation is not causation. Perhaps you have learnt it or have heard it somewhere, but it is still worth emphasizing. Statisticians are extremely cautious about making causal statements. There is even a legendary story about this. A well-known statistics professor was dying, but he could not close his eyes before checking one thing with his students. Summoning them to his deathbed, the professor prompted them by saying: 'Correlation is …' Fortunately, his students did not let him down.

Albeit common sense now, this rule has been manipulated by many researchers for the purpose of claiming a discovery of causal connections among some social phenomena. Indeed, it is very tempting *to* make such claim when you see strong and statistically significant correlations in the results. Being aware of the embarrass-ment of confusing the two, many researchers would not explicitly use the term 'cause' or 'causal', but it is very clear that nothing but causation is in their mind. Such disguised causal statements come in a variety of forms, for example, 'A has happened, consequently, we have witnessed B', 'the statistical results indicate a strong and significant impact of A on B' or 'given the statistical significance of this coefficient, it is no wonder that we observe such a big magnitude of B'.

Rule No. 10 – Translate a Statistical Model into Words and Ask: Do Those Words Make Sense?

As a human device for representing a connection or a process in reality, models come in a variety of forms: verbal, graphical, numerical or visual. Very often, each can be transformed into another, and such transformations help us gain extra knowledge and insight that cannot be easily seen in an alternative form. Statistical methods usually present models with mathematical equations, which we can submit to independent procedures, not only making our analysis more rigorous but also producing some results that we can hardly expect to see beforehand.

Nevertheless, for us as social researchers, mathematical operations are not the ultimate concern. Rather, we want to say something substantively fresh and important. Presenting our model in a verbal form can help us ensure that we have not lost contact with the background, the meaning and the relevance of the statistics. Most social researchers know that they must address their substantive research question with statistical analysis. My observation is that most of their attention is given only to *the results*, but we must know what the model says before we estimate its parameters and interpret its results. A statistical model is not just an equation with symbols on each side; it says something about what the model builder believes. However, these beliefs, assumptions and understanding are usually implied in the model, hidden from direct observation, and we need to talk them out if we want to understand and use the model meaningfully.

THREE

Cases and Variables

The data for statistical analysis are usually organized in a matrix, with cases (the units of measurement) in rows and variables (the attributes of the cases) in columns (Table 3.1). Therefore, each cell shows a particular case's value for a particular variable.

We start with such matrix for two reasons. Practically, a proper understanding of this matrix is of critical importance for choosing the right statistical method. More fundamentally, the data matrix implies our approach to analysing social reality; therefore, the matrix has been a main source of controversy over the use of statistical methods in the social sciences. What is a variable? What does it represent? Are cases more important than variables in social research? Spend some time thinking over these questions and you will better realize what exactly you are doing when you analyse a data set.

Cases

As the target of social science research is normally human beings, a case is usually an individual person or a group of persons such as a household, a family, an organization, a community or a nation. There are no rules, however, on what the case must be for a particular study; it is the nature of a particular research question and practical considerations in data collection that determine what an appropriate case is. Sometimes you need to think more carefully and imaginatively about what kind of case will best serve your research purposes. The general principle is that the case must illuminate the phenomenon to be studied. For example, if we are interested in voting behaviours, it is appropriate to take an individual person as a case.

Table 3.1   Case-by-variable matrix[1]

	Variable 1	Variable 2	Variable 3	Variable 4	......
Case 1	1	23 290	2	3.4	......
Case 2	2	32 980	5	5.6	......
Case 3	2	12 690	4	7.8	......
Case 4	1	45 900	5	1.2	......
......	......	......	......	......	......

However, if we are interested in energy consumption, then it does not make much sense to collect data on individuals – aside from single person households or those sharing a rented property, who pay their energy bills separately, people consume and pay for electricity or gas collectively in a household rather than individually, so household should be a case. In other situations, our interest is in what has happened to human beings rather than the human beings themselves. A case can be an event, such as protest, divorce or bankruptcy. Sometimes, what constitutes a case is determined by how the data were produced. An example of non-human cases is text, such as newspaper reports, textbooks or meeting minutes. They are about human beings, or they are products of human beings, but it is not on human beings that we take our measurements. In short, although most often the cases are individual human beings, particularly for data in social surveys, there are some other units of measurement that we can take as cases.

In social research, it is often infeasible to collect data on our own, either because we do not have sufficient resources, it is unethical to carry out the study or we do not have access to a set of private documents. We have no choice but to use the data collected by someone else. Today, most of such 'secondary' data were collected in large-scale sample surveys and stored electronically, with the Inter-University Consortium of Political and Social Research (ICPSR) in the US and, in the UK, Data Archive being the largest collections. Although free of charge for university students and faculties, we do have to pay a 'price' for using such data; that is, we have no control over what the cases should be. The time and money saved by not having to collect such data should be reinvested in thinking about how we can make sensible use of them: Do we really want to study all members in a household or will it be sufficient to study the heads of household? Can we take a particular geographic area as our case? The principle is that our selection of the case must be justified.

Relations among the cases are another issue we have to consider. Most of the secondary data have been collected in large-scale sample surveys. This means that very likely the samples were drawn in multiple steps and each step was related to a particular unit. For example, regions may be the primary sampling unit (PSU), followed by states (or counties), then followed by cities (or towns, or rural areas), then districts and neighbourhoods, and finally households and individuals. The

---

[1]The numbers in the cells of this table are hypothetical and for illustration only. We shall see more complicated data structures when we analyse multilevel or longitudinal data. However, the simple case-by-variable matrix serves a good starting point.

hierarchical relationship among the cases is very clear during the sampling process but it tends to get lost in the data matrix: what we see are only individuals and variables. It appears that all individuals were selected at the same time and all variables are at the same level, which is clearly not the case.

A hallmark of effective methods is that they take into account as much available information as possible. At this point, we must take the relations among the cases seriously as they have an impact on the quality of our statistical analysis. Cases selected in different steps of a sample were usually selected with different probabilities, which will heavily influence our estimate of a population value. Furthermore, factors at a higher level (or 'contextual factors') affect those at a lower level. For example, people living in the same household tend to be in the same socio-economic class and vote for the same political party, and organizations selected at the national level tend to be more powerful than those selected at local levels. More generally, cases belonging to the same higher level unit may share some similarities. It may take a while to grasp all the technical details required to analyse such a 'clustering' effect, but this is an issue we need to keep in our mind.

The above discussion brings us to a more general issue: inter-dependency among the cases. Most statistical methods are created with the assumption that the cases are independent of each other. That is, the attribute of one case has nothing to do with that of another, so we cannot know what a particular case looks like by knowing anything about any other cases. The most commonly used example is rolling a die – we cannot tell what will show up in a particular roll based on what showed up in the previous roll. Human beings are not dice, of course. Either accepting or rejecting their parents' views, children simply cannot escape from the influence of their parents. Also, a person's answer to a particular survey question may be heavily influenced or even determined by the person's knowledge of how others have answered the same question.

In practice, it is next to impossible to know whether people's answers are connected to each other, how many of their answers are connected and in what way they are connected. This is why survey interviewers must ensure respondents are not influenced by other people when answering the questions, and they should urge their respondents not to base any answer on their previous answers or other people's answers. To ignore the effects of relations and assume no interactions among the cases is unacceptable to many social scientists. Nevertheless, it is unfair to say that statisticians are ignorant of them. For statisticians, most of the time it does not do much harm to assume independence of the cases – how often do we find that people talk to each other when they answer a questionnaire, especially when they are interviewed in person or by telephone? At least, we can take independence as a starting point. If we think this assumption is seriously violated in the given situation under study, such as in the cases of social movements, collective decision making or intensive networking activities, then we should not use statistics in the first place and choose methods specially designed for dealing with dependent relations, including social network analysis and social choice models.

Finally, it is important to realize that those cases not included in the data set play no smaller role in our statistical analysis. This is the missing-value or non-response problem in statistics. The decline of response rate has afflicted almost all major social surveys.[2] To be a bit more precise, there are two broad types of non-response: item non-response and case non-response. The former refers to the situation where the respondent *did* participate in the survey but would not or could not answer one or more questions; therefore, responses to some survey items are missing. Most people are thinking of case non-response when they talk about non-response – the selected respondents did not or could not participate in the survey at all. Case non-response is our main focus in this section, because we are concerned with whose responses are missing and, most importantly, whether our statistical results will be biased due to those non-responses.

To minimize non-responses, researchers have spent an enormous amount of time figuring out how to maximize the chance of making selected individuals participate. The question is, should refusal itself be taken as a response? As John Goyder has asked: 'If people ignore calls by interviewers or solicitations through the mail by considered choice, should their wishes not be respected?' (1987: 116). There are different strategies and techniques for dealing with non-responses and their consequences – missing data – and the interested reader can consult specialized texts (Little and Rubin, 2002; McKnight et al., 2007). Those who have experience of editing survey data will have no problem understanding the issue here. However, for those without such experience or having analysed only secondary data, please keep in mind that the data were not so clean at the beginning and it is always wise to learn what missing values have been replaced and how.

Variables and Probabilities

In mathematical statistics, the proper term for variable is 'random variable'. To define 'random variable', we need 'sample space'. A sample space is the set of all possible outcomes of a particular event. The event is the variable, and the possible outcomes or values constitute the variable's sample space.

An event would not be of much interest to us if it has only one possible outcome or if multiple outcomes are equally likely to occur; statistics is of little use in such situations. A random variable usually represents an event that has two or more outcomes that have different probabilities of occurrence. Here, the word 'random' suggests that we have no way of determining which of the possible outcomes will occur in a particular event. The most widely used example is flipping a fair coin, which has two possible results (values), heads and tails. The fairness of the coin is a necessary condition for ensuring the randomness of the results – if it is not fair, then the lighter side of the coin will be more likely to show up, making the results non-random.

A more important question is: what is the probability that a particular outcome takes place? This is important because our answers constitute our statistical knowledge

---

[2]In March 2006, Susan Purdon gave a presentation on the decline of response rates at Royal Statistical Society in London. For a published report on this issue, see Stoop et al. (2008).

about how a variable behaves, and this knowledge will help us make decisions and take actions. If we know there is a 0.9 chance (an informal word for probability) that it will rain tomorrow, then we will bring an umbrella with us. If female employees know that the chance of them getting promoted is very low if they take maternity leave and they do not want to give up the chance of being promoted, then they will not have children or will have children only after they have already been promoted to a desired position. In short, the probability of each occurrence is behind many human choices.

So how do we find out the probabilities? In the discipline of statistics, there have been two major approaches to answering that question, one 'objective' and the other 'subjective'. The first is objective because it does not allow our judgements, opinions or expectations to get involved in determining the probabilities. Rather, it is what happens in reality that shows the probabilities. This approach is therefore 'empirical' in the sense that we have to observe the occurrences in order to calculate the probabilities, and the probability of a particular outcome is defined as the ratio of the number of occurrences of this outcome to the total number of events. As this approach builds on the frequencies of values, it is also called 'the relative frequency approach'.

Practically, it is, however, not so easy to follow this approach, because a different outcome may show up each time we observe the event. We cannot determine the probability by watching a limited number of events: it is very premature to say that the probability of getting heads is 100% after observing three tosses, as it is very likely the next toss will result in tails. The solution is the following phrase frequently used in statistics: 'in the long run'. We note down the value (e.g. side of a fair coin) in each event (tossing the coin), and we do this for thousands of times.[3]

The question is: how long is long enough 'in the long run' so that we can stop and say 'we have found the probabilities'? This is a really hard question to answer, so hard that I do not think statisticians have come up with an agreed answer. In theory, we should keep observing for an infinite number of times. In practice, we have to stop at a point, of course, but how do we know when we should stop? A general strategy is to observe for long enough that the probabilities 'stabilize' around a certain value. It is true that in most situations we do observe such stabilizing tendency, but still it may not be exactly the probability that the tendency is pointing to. Furthermore, how do we know the trend will not change its direction if we observe for a bit longer?

In contrast to the objective approach, the other approach – Bayesian statistics, attributed to Thomas Bayes (1702–1761) – takes human beings' assessment of the probability into account, which is why it is subjective. In essence, it points out that, despite the difficulty of determining objective probabilities, even if they do exist, what matters in reality is not objective probabilities but

---

[3]A few people did toss a coin for thousands of times, including the French nationalist Count Buffon, the English statistician Karl Pearson and the South African mathematician John Kerrich (Moore and Notz, 2006: 353).

the probabilities held in people's mind. Bayesian statisticians define probability as a subjective assessment of uncertainty, and such probability has enormous implication for predicting other following events. The main advantage of Bayesian statistics, as I see it, is its power to analyse the interrelations of probabilities that can be put in temporal or logical order. However, this is not the place to go into the details.[4]

The debates over probability between the frequentist and the Bayesian approaches can be highly philosophical as well as technical. The Bayesian approach has gained much popularity in the past two decades, particularly in the social sciences, mainly due to the fact that prior and subjective probabilities play important roles in human behaviours. Nevertheless, the frequentist approach still enjoys relative dominance, although some have called for a complementary approach. My purpose here is to raise your awareness of such a distinction, and our following discussions will follow the frequentist approach.

Levels of Measurement

A variable has two or more values, each having a corresponding probability of occurrence. For example, the variable gender has two values (male and female),[5] the variable education has several ordered values, and the variable of the exact amount of time a person spent on watching television yesterday has numerous values. A variable's level of measurement refers to the nature of its values.

Social researchers may be very interested in the meanings of variables and their values, but statisticians are more interested in the level at which a variable's values are measured, because the level of measurement determines the distribution of the values, which then determines the appropriate method to be used. Therefore, before learning specific statistical methods, it is crucially important to know what the levels of measurement are and how they relate to statistical methods.

Strictly speaking, there are five levels of measurement: nominal, ordinal, interval, ratio and absolute. In social science research, however, the distinctions between the last three levels do not make much difference; therefore, they are usually grouped together into one category, loosely referred to as 'continuous', 'quantitative' or 'metrical' variables. A distinctive feature of variables of this type is that they have many different values. In contrast, nominal and ordinal variables have only a limited number of values that refer to a set of categories. For the sake of simplicity and consistency, in the rest of the book we shall use three levels of measurement: nominal, ordinal and metrical. A 'categorical' variable can be either nominal or ordinal, and a 'metrical' variable can be either interval, ratio or absolute, whose meaning we shall explain below.

---

[4]For the interested reader, I would recommend starting with Jeff Gill's (2007) *Bayesian Methods: A Social and Behavioral Sciences Approach.*
[5]There are people who have changed their sex, but the number of those exceptional cases is very small so usually such cases are ignored.

Nominal Variables

By definition, the values of this kind of variable are purely names or labels. There is no meaningful way of putting them in a ranking order and no mathematical operations can be conducted on them. There are two further requirements on assigning the values of a nominal variable: (1) exhaustive, i.e. they must include all the possible values that each case carries; (2) mutually exclusive, i.e. a particular case belongs to one category only; otherwise, a case belonging to two or more categories will be counted more than once. There are situations when we do not know all the possible values. A solution is to create a 'residual' category, such as 'Others', 'Not applicable' or 'Don't know'. Obviously, such residual values are not informative to our statistical analysis, and unless we have missed something important in our respondents, the number of cases belong to these categories should be very small.

Note that *the equal footing of all values is not a statistical notion but an ideological one*. To illustrate, take the example of gender again. In societies where liberty and equality are basic human rights, it would be politically incorrect to declare the superiority of one gender over the other. This clearly illustrates that a variable's mathematical and social characteristics are intertwined. When we call a variable 'nominal', we assume that the researchers and their readers agree on the irrelevance of ranking order among the values of that variable.

The values of these nominal variables should be represented as words. Nevertheless, if you look at a real dataset, very often you will not see any words – all values are numbers. This is because all categories have been recoded with numbers. For example, 1 means female and 2 means male. It is important to keep in mind that these numbers should be treated as labels that are of no difference from the original words. We cannot say male is superior to female simply because 2 is larger than 1; we can easily make males inferior to females by assigning 0 to them and 1 to females. Recoding the labels with numbers is purely for the convenience of inputting and analysing data. Do not take the face value of the numeric categories, and make sure that you understand what they mean in the original coding scheme.

Ordinal Variables

For these variables, it makes sense to put one value above another, thereby forming a ranking order among the values. Survey questions designed to measure people's attitudes and opinions are good examples. Usually, a statement is shown to the respondents, such as 'People who have come to live in this country should be given the same rights as everyone else', and respondents are asked to indicate whether they 'strongly agree', 'agree', 'neither agree nor disagree', 'disagree' or 'strongly disagree' with the statement.

Note, however, we cannot measure the exact distance between any two consecutive values. How much stronger is 'strongly agree' than 'agree'? There is no clear and meaningful answer. If the distance can be determined, then the variable is at a higher level in terms of measurement because we have more information about the values. Due to the lack of such information, mathematical operations do not make sense either – we can assign 5, 4, 3, 2 and 1 to each of the above five categories, respectively, but that does not mean that the distance between any two consecutive categories is exactly 1. Any set of numbers will do as long as they keep such order intact, such as 9, 7, 5, 3 and 1. What we can do is to examine any possible orderly pattern among the values. For example, does the proportion of respondents for each value become larger and larger? The discovery of patterns is important for analysing ordinal variables.

Metrical Variables

Interval variables are one level higher than ordinal ones in that the distance between any two values can be measured. But the difference between the interval and the ratio variables is a subtle one, which is why most statistics books put them together as 'interval–ratio variables'.

The usual way of distinguishing interval and ratio variables is to identify whether multiplication and division are meaningful or not. If it is meaningful, then the variable is ratio, and if not, the variable is interval. This is also related to the meaning of the zero point – if the zero point is only an arbitrary number, that is, 0 does not actually mean 'nothing', then the variable is interval; otherwise, if 0 does mean something then the variable is measured at the ratio level.

In social life, it is difficult to find pure interval variables. The most commonly used example is temperature. The temperature 0°C is assigned by human beings, and it does not mean there is no temperature; there is a temperature, at which water turns into ice. Most are ratio variables, such as amounts of money, years of schooling and so on. For these variables, the number 0 does mean that there is no money in a bank account or a person has never gone to school. In this book, we shall not trouble ourselves with such differences.

This is a proper place to clarify the meanings of 'discrete', 'continuous' and 'categorical' variables. A variable is discrete if we cannot find a meaningful value in between any two consecutive values. If we can always find a meaningful value in between, then the variable is continuous. For example, most variables in the natural sciences are continuous variables, such as length, weight and speed. Note that, income in terms of an amount of money is a discrete variable – there is no smaller unit than pence (or cent), so we cannot find a meaningful value in between one penny and two pence.[6]

The count of units is a special type of variable, called 'absolute variables', such as the number of people in a city, the number of abortions or crimes. Although in practice they are often treated as continuous variables, it is clearly meaningless to talk about 2.3 people (abortions or crimes), unless one is referring to an average.

Table 3.2 summarizes the above discussions and should help the reader understand the relations among these terms.

Why should we care about a variable's level of measurement? The first reason is that it determines what meaningful things we can say: it does not make sense, or it is not politically correct, to impose an order on a nominal variable such as ethnicity,

---

[6]In exchanging currencies, units smaller than pence (or cent) are used because most transactions involve thousands or millions of pounds (or dollars).

Table 3.2   Levels of measurement and their relations

Grouped level of measurement	Level of measurement	Discrete or continuous?	Examples
Categorical	Nominal	Discrete	Gender, ethnicity, etc.
	Ordinal	Discrete	Education, class, etc.
Metrical	Interval	Either discrete or continuous	Temperature, etc.
	Ratio	Either discrete or continuous	Income
	Absolute	Discrete	Number of people

nor would it make sense to talk about the exact distance between undergraduate and postgraduate degrees. Most statistical methods have been invented based on the level of measurement of the variables under study, so our choice of a particular method is largely determined by whether the variable is nominal, ordinal or metrical.

Conversely, we should not be obsessed with the level of measurement. The correspondence between a level of measurement and a statistical method does not always hold. Some methods can handle variables of more than one level of measurement, and especially when we analyse several variables at the same time, we usually have different types of variables. In addition, variables in social sciences are rarely measured at levels higher than the interval. Therefore, statistical techniques most useful for categorical variables are of great use in social sciences (Goodman, 2007).

Finally, transformations from one level to another can be easily made. Variables measured at higher levels can be easily transformed into ones at a lower level, but the reverse is not true. Income, a ratio variable, is often transformed into an ordinal variable with a hierarchy of bands of income. The downside is that *we lose the more refined information contained in the higher level variable* – we do not know a person's exact income if the band 'under 50,000' was ticked. The benefit is that the question becomes less sensitive, so survey researchers will have fewer refusals. In the end, this comes down to the issue of how much we care about such loss of information, which is not a statistical question.

Working in the opposite direction, although we cannot transform a variable at a lower level into one at a higher level, we can construct a variable measured at a higher level based on several variables measured at lower levels. Many scales and indices are created in this way. Suppose we would like to measure a respondent's involvement in political activities. We can begin with 10 questions that have binary answers (yes/no), such as 'Did you contact your political representative in the past seven days?', 'Did you have a conversion with anyone on political issues during the past seven days?' and so on. Using these 10 categorical variables, we can create a metrical variable with values ranging from 0 to 10 (coding yes = 1 and no = 0).

Variables versus Cases?

In the 11th edition of *The Practice of Social Research*, perhaps the most popular social research methods book in the world, Earl Babbie claims that:

Social research, then, involves the study of variables and their relationships. Social theories are written in a language of variables, and people get involved only as the 'carriers' of those variables …. The relationship between attributes and variables forms the heart of both description and explanation in science. (2007: 15)

For students who are about to use statistics in their own research, it is important to note that not all social scientists share this view. Some prominent social scientists have found not only the use of variables but also variables per se highly problematic. Learning what these controversies are will keep students alert to the substantive meaning of their statistical analyses and ready to defend their conclusions.

Let us start by thinking about where variables come from. Most directly, they come from instruments of data collection, such as questionnaires used in sample surveys, documents and observations. As our main concern here is with statistics rather than data collection, we focus on the data collected from sample surveys. The direct connections between survey questions, variables and values constitute the key source of data for statistical analysis.

For questions about the respondent's demographic characteristics, such as age, gender, race and ethnicity, there is not much difficulty of connecting survey questions and variables – the meanings of these terms are relatively clear, and so are the answers. Most of the time respondents should not have much difficulty of reporting their attributes; therefore, the quality of their answers should be quite high.

Few social scientists, however, would be satisfied with finding out simple facts. Often, they would like to do two more things: to measure variables whose values are not so limited and stable, and to explain the values of one variable with the values of another, such as to explain the commitment of crimes with unemployment. In these research activities, the connections between survey questions, variables and their values are not so clear-cut, and as a result, controversies arise. This section focuses on the first issue, and we reserve the difficult issue of establishing causal connections among variables for the later chapters.

More than half a century ago, Herbert Blumer pointed out at least three major problems with what he called 'variable analysis'. First, the easiness of turning almost every target of research into a variable has reduced 'human group life into variables and their relations', thereby producing a chaotic situation with 'a conspicuous absence of rules, guides, limitations and prohibitions to govern the choice of variables' (Blumer, 1956: 683). Second, nearly all variables were 'localized and non-generic' (1956: 585); therefore, he lamented 'the disconcerting absence of generic variables, that is, variables that stand for abstract categories' (1956: 684). A third problem is that '[t]he variable relation is a single relation, necessarily stripped bare of the complex of things that sustain it in a "here and now" context' (1956: 685); consequently, variables 'conceal or misrepresent the actual operations in human group life' (1956: 688).

As a matter of fact, Blumer did not completely dismiss the use of variables. 'Variable analysis is a fit procedure', he claimed, 'for those areas of social life and formation that are not mediated by an interpretative process' (1956: 689). The question is: which areas of social life are not mediated by interpretations? I guess what he meant to say was that the gap between the richness of social life, especially the richness of people's interpretations of all sorts of symbols in their lives and the limited meanings and values represented in variables, is unbearably big; that is true. However, the gap between meanings and numbers should not mean that we have to stop using statistics. It is not reasonable to expect variables to reveal all the rich details of people's thoughts, narratives and stories. If you want to know those things, then you have to use methods such as interview, ethnography or content analysis.

Blumer's critiques were unable to curb the use of variables in American sociology. On the contrary, variables and statistical models flourished in recent decades. That does not mean, however, that the controversy is over. Forty years after the publication of Blumber's paper, Hartmut Esser pointed out three other problems with 'variable sociology': 'it is … *not explanatory*, it is *incomplete*, and it is in a specific way *meaningless*' (1996: 159, emphasis in original). The three problems are interconnected as they are all about the same question: what can variables do in sociology? It is a complete misunderstanding that statistical models, which connect variables together mathematically, can explain anything on their own. They *represent* the explanation, which is supposed to be already achieved *before* the models are constructed. As such, they are incomplete by definition. *Statistical models tell us what we could expect the relations of the interested variables to look like if the underlying explanatory theory, from which the models are derived, is true.*

To have a sense of how far the critiques can go, let us learn the views of Andrew Abbott. He has been the editor of *American Journal of Sociology* for many years, so his views exercise substantial influence on sociological publications. Abbott illustrates the problems of statistics with 'the cycle of critiques' in Table 2.3 of his book *Methods of Discovery* (2004: 66). The cycle shows how the four main methods (ethnography, historical narration, standard causal analysis [SCA] and formalization) criticize each other. As our interest here is in statistics, there is no need to know the problems with other methods and it would be beneficial to humbly learn what complaints others have about statistics.[7] Ethnography has argued that statistics 'uses worthless or meaningless data; assigns meanings arbitrarily' (2004: 66) and treats 'social facts as "variables" on universal scales (where a given fact has a given meaning irrespective of the other facts in its context)' (2004: 68). Historical narration has made a similar complaint: statistics 'ignores contingency; lacks account of action; cannot represent "history" of its variables' (2004: 66); in addition, statistics 'has no account of action and reaction whatsoever' (2004: 71). Furthermore, Andrew Abbott himself points out that statistics 'denies context':

> because contextualism is a major inconvenience to the statistical methods it [SCA] uses. The whole idea of variables is to remove particular attributes of particular cases from the contexts provided by other attributes of those cases. Realism is likewise a strong assumption of SCA, since it presumes fixed and given meanings. (2004: 57)

---

[7] Abbott did not tell us who made those critiques, but I assume he can easily supply a list of names and publications representing each school of critiques. For the sake of clarity, whenever I can I shall use statistics rather than SCA.

For social researchers, meaning and context are of vital importance. Indeed, it is by paying serious attention to meaning and context that social sciences distinguish themselves from national sciences. Attributes of natural phenomena can be defined and measured universally, but the meanings and contexts of social phenomena vary from one place to another. So, if variables fail to capture such variation, what can they do for social research except for producing insensible results? It should be very clear to the reader now that if this line of arguments is to be accepted, then the whole enterprise of using statistical methods in social research should be abandoned once and for all.

Shall we ignore those critiques and keep using statistics, or shall we give up on statistics and switch to 'qualitative methods', which it is argued are far more effective of analysing meanings and contexts? I personally think this question is itself wrong, because it assumes the necessary contradiction between statistics, on the one hand, and meanings and contexts, on the other. We shall come back to this point later. Now, suffice it to say that while social researchers must take greater notice of the effects of meanings and contexts on their interpretation and analysis of variables, it is nevertheless too radical to claim that variables – and therefore statistical methods – have reached the end of their usefulness in social sciences.

I appreciate the call for making our analysis more directly related to social realities. Indeed, it does not make much sense, especially when the target of our research is human beings, to believe that variables themselves are forces. Further, if it is people's actions, not variables that do the acting that drives social processes, why do we not study the actions directly? This is one of the general principles adopted by qualitative comparative analysis (QCA) (Ragin, 1992, 2000, 2008).

Certainly, cases (human beings), not variables, do things. But that does not necessarily mean that we cannot learn about what human beings do by studying variables. Not only variables can describe actions but relations among variables can represent a theory of social actions as well. For example, a statistical model may show a strong and negative correlation among adults between age and the number of text messages sent out from mobile phones. Obviously, it would be a joke to conclude that age has sent out the messages, people do. But how could we find out who uses this technology without studying the variables that represent their actions and socio-economic attributes? The function of a statistical model is to represent a theory behind it: that young people are keen on using the most fashionable technologies at minimum cost and sending out text messages turns out to be the solution.

More generally and importantly, we simply cannot study cases without variables and vice versa – cases constitute the basic elements of our analyses, while we cannot achieve any analysis without analysing some attributes (variables) of the cases. We may want to focus on either of them for a particular purpose, but that should not mean we have to study one of them by sacrificing the other. Therefore, I cannot agree more with Caramani, who has just published a monograph on QCA, on the relationship between variables and cases:

Comparison can take place only when one compares case's values of shared properties or attributes, that is, variables .... Reasoning in terms of 'variables' is thus not specific to a 'variable-oriented' approach, but rather is a common feature of both the variable- *and* case-oriented approaches ... (2009: 89–90)

It is not variables and statistics that have made social science research lose contact with meanings, contexts and the many other things that social scientists want to analyse. The real source of the problem is the researcher! If certain conclusions do not make sense, that is not because of the use of variables but because the researcher has failed to use the variables properly.

FOUR

The Logic of Sampling

The Idea of Sampling

Often we want to know something about a group of cases, which we call *a population*. However, its size is so large that we cannot afford to collect data from every case. Therefore, we plan to study only some of them, which constitute *a sample* of the population.

A series of difficult questions arise from this seemingly simple process: What kinds of cases are eligible for being included in the population? Do we have access to all of them for collecting the data we need? Which cases shall we select for our sample? There are many ways of selecting the cases, which one shall we follow? As any particular sample is only one out of many possibilities, how reliable is it? Clearly, to say something about the population by analysing the results from a single sample is quite a big analytical jump, involving some fundamental and hard decision-making.[1] To ensure the safety of the jump is the business of sampling design and statistical inference. These two tasks are connected because statistical inference relies on high-quality data and one aspect of the quality is sampling. Without good data, no matter how sound the inference procedure is, the results would be wrong or even misleading. There are many things that influence the

---

[1] In this chapter we shall develop an intuitive understanding of sampling schemes without going into the technical details of statistical estimation. Readers interested in these techniques can consult more advanced mathematical texts such as Cochran (1977), Kish (1965), Lohr (1997) and Thompson (2002).

quality of the data, including sampling, questionnaire design, mode of data collection, fieldwork administration, data processing and editing. This is why sampling is a critical and initial step of statistical inference; therefore, this and the following chapters are closely connected.[2]

It seems straightforward that a sample is the only option for collecting information from a large population – it would be too expensive and time-consuming to administer a census, i.e. to enumerate every case in the whole population. However, is the sample 'good value for money'? While it is much cheaper to run a sample survey than to do a census, not all samples are worth the invested resources. The low cost and the high speed of a sample survey are desirable *only when we are satisfied with the level at which the sample represents the population*, a task not so easy to achieve. Low cost and high speed cannot completely establish the value of samples without a more important but less obvious reason: if properly managed, they can do a *better* job than a census. The key advantage of a sample is *the gain of accuracy through keeping things small*. In contrast, the major advantage of conducting a complete enumeration (census) is the elimination of coverage error – very few cases have been missed out, but that is only one of the several factors that affect the quality of data. That is, a census's advantage of having a small coverage error is achieved at much higher costs in other respects: total operation costs, total amount of time required by data collection, organizational complexity, errors made in processing the results and the subsequent delay of the availability of data. Errors and the subsequent disputes from the UK 2001 Census are only a recent example.[3] Even the problem of coverage error cannot be completely resolved – homeless people, people abroad, people living in remotely accessible areas and so forth may never be reached. In contrast, a sample is more desirable because good coverage can be achieved with smart sampling schemes and effective organization of fieldwork. In the meantime, the small scale of a sample makes the whole process less prone to errors.

Today, most social researchers rely on data collected by institutions in large-scale and carefully designed sample surveys. When planning to use any of these 'secondary data' – secondary only in the sense that the user was not involved in collecting the data, not that the data are of secondary quality – one must carefully consider *how the population is defined for the particular research project under consideration*. This does not mean that clearly defining the target population is not an issue if researchers intend to organize their own surveys; on the contrary, the responsibility of using the resources properly will demand the researchers to define the target population more clearly.

When using secondary data, as the survey was already completed, the researchers may unwittingly develop a sense that the task of defining the population is not an issue anymore or there is nothing they can do about it. Social researchers must put this task at the top of their agenda and spend time thinking carefully what *their*

---

[2]It is beyond the scope of this book to cover the effects of other things on data quality and statistical inference, but at the very least the reader should keep in mind that *statistical inference will not be effective unless some conditions of data quality are satisfied*.

[3]For example, it was claimed that the census massively underestimated the total population of Manchester ('Census "Errors" could cost city £18m', BBC News, 12 December 2002).

target population is and whether their population is congruent with that of the original survey. Most large surveys have multiple purposes (hence the phrase 'omnibus surveys'). It is not true that they do not have a particular target population in mind; they do, but it is a general one, such as 'adults and children aged 12 and over, civilian and non-institutionalized' (National Crime Victimization Survey), 'non-institutionalized adults in the coterminous US' (Surveys of Consumers), 'all persons aged 16 and over resident in Great Britain' (Labour Force Survey). There are so many surveys now that researchers must carefully look for the one the target population of which is the same or the closest to the one they would like to study. A part of a large survey can be used if that part happens to represent the population of interest.

The importance of the distinction between a population and a sample should not be taken lightly, as it is the crucial starting point for understanding the ideas of sampling and statistical inference. When researchers work on the data from a sample, they need to ask *what is this a sample of?*; otherwise, it is pointless to analyse the sample if our ultimate interest is not in the population. For example, after drawing the sample, some researchers tend to focus their analysis on the sample alone, without making any attempt to derive any inference about the population. It seems that their main interest has turned to the sample itself, rather than the population. This very likely happens because not enough attention is paid to the connection of a sample to the population. As a consequence, researchers have ignored some important issues in conducting statistical analysis on sample survey data.

This point is closely connected to our use of statistical methods because a major utility of statistical methods is their ability of assessing the level of uncertainty of how results from a sample represent those in the population. In principle, all sample statistics should be accompanied by statistics of sampling uncertainty, but that rule has not been consistently followed. Often statistics about the sample alone (means, coefficients, etc.) are reported or highlighted; statistics representing the uncertainty of the results, such as confidence intervals, measurement errors and power, are either ignored or presented without discussion. Even when researchers tend to report these issues, many of them are put off by the conceptual and technical difficulties.

What is a good sample and how should we draw one? First of all, we need to be very clear about the distinction of two types of samples: probability samples and non-probability samples. If we know the probability that each case in the population will be selected into the sample, we have a probability sample, and if we do not know the probability, we will have a non-probability sample. Put simply, results from probability samples allow us to measure the uncertainty of referring to the value of the population with sample results, but we cannot do that with results from a non-probability sample. This is why probability is so important for statistics in general and statistical inference in particular. Because our ultimate goal is to know something about the population rather than the sample, we are very interested in how accurate or uncertain the sample results are in terms of representing the population value. Therefore, we prefer probability samples to the non-probability ones, but before introducing how to draw a probability sample we should know what is wrong with non-probability samples.

Problems with Non-probability Samples

Non-probability samples are still widely used in many research projects. Why? One reason is that to make reliable statistical inference based on probability samples is not what motivates the researcher to draw a sample. One condition for drawing a probability sample is to know the probability of selecting each case of the population. That knowledge does not seem to worry some researchers. Rather, it is some practical issues that occupy the researcher's mind, particularly having access to the respondents and to the information for drawing the sample, such as the sampling frame (the list of the cases in the population).

Researchers have many reasons for studying only those accessible to them, such as being incapable of drawing a probability sample but still having to produce at least some results for a thesis, meeting a conference deadline or simply being lazy. I believe most researchers realize that to stand on the street or in front of a shopping mall and to beg the passers-by to fill out a questionnaire does not look like a professional practice. It is not professional not because of standing on the street but because we have no idea of how representative and reliable the results will be. Results are not reliable if they change when we conduct the same investigation at another time or in another setting. We cannot expect the results remain the same every time The main problem with such samples, usually referred to as 'convenient samples', is that we have no way of finding out how changeable they are.

To better understand why non-probability samples are not desirable, let us consider a hypothetical situation. Suppose that all people are the same with regard to their characteristics of interest to our research and they have the same reason for taking a particular action. If that is the case, then neither the way the sample is drawn nor the sample's size matters, because everybody is the same, so it would be sufficient to select anyone of them. Unbelievably to social scientists, many natural scientists do work on phenomena at least close to such extreme. For example, it does not matter where an apple falls to show the force of gravity. It does not matter what kind of apple it was and it does not have to be an apple at all. Anything on the earth, perhaps except for things such as balloons, will fall. Apples and other things do differ, of course, but the differences do not matter for the research purpose at hand. Sampling is rarely an issue in such situations.

Now back to the reality: people – the research target for the social sciences – are not apples. They are not the same with regard to the characteristics of our interest and more importantly, their differences may represent the reasons for their different behaviours. To disentangle the relations among these differences and to identify the key difference at work are the ultimate goals of social research. Therefore, we must do something to ward off the effects of other things that may interfere our reasoning when we concentrate our analysis on a particular factor. This line of logic is not followed if we simply stop people on the street to participate in a survey. Without knowing who has provided information to us, we have no way of knowing anything for sure about the population. *In drawing these convenient samples, it is assumed that it does not matter who will participate in the study because the participants and the non-participants are treated as if they were all the same.* They are not the same, of course. So, if we ignore these differences, we will not be successful in understanding why they have behaved differently. This is the inherent problem with non-probability samples and why social researchers should avoid them. The only acceptable justification that I can think of for using a non-probability sample is that the population is so important that *any* results about it, including those derived from a convenient sample, will be valuable. In other words, these are populations of great practical importance, whose elusive nature defies sampling with a known (and non-zero) probability.

Probability sampling clearly demands stronger conditions than non-probability sampling, one of which is a good sampling frame. It would be ideal if every case we want to study is included in the list and no ineligible cases are included. But this is rarely the case in practice: some eligible cases are missing while alien cases are listed. Therefore, we say that a sampling frame is 'good' if it has no *systematic* distortion of the complete list, for example, a whole group of cases is absent. For some populations – homeless people, criminals, newly arriving immigrants, travellers – it is very hard even to obtain a 'good enough' list. When you are studying these populations, probability sampling is clearly unfeasible. Note, however, that the foundation that makes the research valuable has changed: it is not the way in which the research is designed and conclusions are drawn but the importance of the population that makes the study worthwhile.

Even when we truly have no other choices but to draw a non-probability sample, we can do a much better job than drawing the sample purely based on convenience. It would be very rare that there is nothing we can do to improve the representativeness of our sample. We may not have a good sampling frame, but we should try our best to learn as much as we can about the population.

Take the example of illegal immigrants in a metropolitan city such as New York or London. Due to their very nature, it is very difficult to find illegal immigrants, let alone to compile a sampling frame. But you can hardly justify the value of your work if you just interview a dozen of them through personal connections, unless your purpose is not to say something about this group of people in general. What is so important about that dozen, especially compared with those you did not happen to know? We must do some preparatory work learning about these immigrants in the city from other sources: the police department, newspaper reports, neighbourhoods, labour-intensive factories and restaurants, which have the reputation of hiring illegal immigrants. There is no doubt that if our sample is drawn based on our knowledge gained from these investigations, it will be much more informative and representative, albeit still not probabilistically, than the dozen immigrants we happened to know. We can select a certain number of immigrants from each particular type or subgroup to learn about the variation of their experiences. Better still, our knowledge will enable us to locate the extreme cases, which are of particular value for learning about the range of the phenomenon under study (Stinchcombe, 2005). This strategy is sometimes called 'purposive' or 'judgemental' sampling, but perhaps the term 'intelligent sampling' is more appropriate as the sampling procedure is determined by our intelligence about the elusive population.

The above strategy of classifying the cases of the target population and sampling from each subgroup follows the logic of quota sampling, which has been very popular even among polling institutions.[4] Its popularity comes from the proportional match of the sample structure to that of the population at a low cost and a high speed, offering a miniature of the population. Here, the structure of the population refers to the proportional distribution of cases in a table that is constructed with several categorical variables, and the information is usually available from government statistics agency. For example, Table 4.1 was published by the Census Bureau on the population structure in the year 2000 with regard to three variables: age group, gender and the number of races.[5]

Table 4.1   US population structure by age, gender and the number of races, 2000

	One race (%)		Two or more races (%)	
Age	Male	Female	Male	Female
Under 18	12.7	12.0	0.5	0.5
18–64	30.1	30.5	0.6	0.6
Above 65	5.1	7.2	0.1	0.1

In Table 4.1, age has three groups, sex has two and the number of races has two. Therefore, there are $3 \times 2 \times 2 = 12$ types of people. Each number is the proportion (or percentages) of a particular type of people out of all the people contacted in the 2000 Census. For example, there were 35,608,943 males under the age of 18 who chose only one race, which is 12.7% of the total number of people in the Census, 281,421,906.

The idea of quota sampling is to draw a sample whose results would produce the same percentage in each corresponding cell, thereby reflecting the structure of the population in a small scale. Once the sample size is determined, the number of cases to be studied for each subgroup will be the product of each percentage multiplied by the sample size, from which we shall obtain the quota frame. For example, if we plan to study 1000 cases (people), then we need to have 12.7% × 1000 = 127 cases who are male, under the age of 18, and think themselves belonging to only one race. The same can be done for other cells as well.

In practice, it is the interviewer's job to complete the required number of valid questionnaires for each subgroup (or cases for each cell). From their perspective, the difficult part of the job is to find the required number of respondents who carry those characteristics, but that is a practical rather than a statistical matter. The easy part of the job is that once the criteria are satisfied, the interviewer has the

---

[4]For a more detailed discussion on quota sampling, see Moser and Kalton (1971: 127–37) and Lynn and Jowell (1996).

[5]Table 1 of 'Race and Hispanic or Latino Origin by Age and Sex for the United States: 2000 (PHC-T-8)' at http://www.census.gov/population/www/cen2000/briefs/phc-t8/index.html. I calculated the percentages based on the numbers in the table.

freedom of choosing whoever they want among the eligible respondents for an interview. From the statistical perspective, however, it is this easy part that makes the following analysis subject to biases because interviewers may choose a particular type of respondents, willingly or inadvertently, which will damage the representativeness of the sample. For example, most interviewers are female, who might not choose to interview tall and rough men who appear threatening. But they would have to interview them if these rough guys happened to be selected randomly in a probability sample. Survey administrators have to consider the safety of interviewers, of course. If, however, the interviewer chooses her respondents randomly, i.e. not picking up a particular type of respondents, then the danger of getting a biased sample is somehow controlled. The problem is, it is not always clear whether interviewers have followed the randomization procedures, and sometimes it proves unfeasible to follow such procedures in practice, as randomness can be achieved only when it is feasible for the interviewer to compile a list of the individuals for a particular type and to choose the required number of them in a random manner.

There are two further problems with quota sampling, one minor and one major. The minor issue is that the quota frame is usually produced based on results from population census, which is usually administered centennially. When a research project is conducted a few years after a census, census statistics may not be a very good guide. The major issue concerns the function of quota sampling. The ultimate purpose of drawing a quota sample has never been simply to mimic the population structure in the selected variables, such as age, gender and race. Rather, it is to model and predict people's behaviours and attitudes, for example, for which party they would vote, or with which opinion they agree. Data from quota sampling only help to make a prediction when the variables can be taken as contributing factors of people's behaviour; otherwise, it is pointless to represent the population structure along these dimensions.

Here is a rule of thumb: do not draw a non-probability sample unless you can make a strong case for it. And simply saying 'This is an exploratory study' is not good enough. I do not mean that exploratory work should not be carried out; obviously, it is sometimes necessary and desirable to explore. What I have found unacceptable is to shy away from the difficult but important task of designing a project rigorously, with probability sampling being a special case, by taking exploration as an easy way out. What kind of sample to use is a decision to make, and we must have a convincing logic for making a choice.

Randomization

All non-probability samples suffer from the same problem: the probability of selecting some of the cases is higher than that of selecting others, and more importantly, we have no idea of who have higher probabilities and how much higher those probabilities are. For example, those with a more approachable appearance are more likely to be given a questionnaire than others, people with stronger opinions are more likely to participate in order to get themselves heard and individuals the researcher knows personally are more likely to be interviewed if a snowball sampling scheme is adopted. The differentiation of probabilities may not be a problem if any difference between the selected and those not selected is not related to the subject matter of interest to the researcher. The trouble is that there is no way for us to know the extent to which this is true.

Consequently, the risk of generating biased results by selecting the cases with distinctive attributes is always there. The first thing we must do in order to minimize any potential bias is to make the process of selecting the cases subject to something beyond the control of the cases as well as the researcher. We should also make the probability of being selected for each case known so that we can estimate its effect. A common strategy is to make the probability not only known but equal as well, usually labelled with the acronym EPSEM for 'equal probability selection method'. That is, every case has the same probability of being selected into the sample, which is usually defined as the ratio of the sample size (n) to the population size (N), but it can be quite a complicated matter if the sampling procedure involves several steps. Also, it is sometimes desirable to purposefully apply a higher probability for selecting a particular group, such as ethnic minorities. Note that this is different from non-probability sampling. Here, the higher probability can be determined and thus known, while the probability is unknown in non-probability sampling.

To strictly follow this rule in practice is no easy matter. How can we ensure that every case of a population has the same probability of being selected? The idea is that since *it is this intervention by human beings in the selection process that makes equal probability impossible*, we therefore must eliminate any conscious choice in order to obtain equal probability. But if neither the researcher nor the respondents should make the selection, who should? Here comes the crucial idea of randomization. Its objective is to sever the connection between those involved in a study and those to be selected into the study. It does that by submitting the selection process to something free (or almost free) of human control.

As a matter of fact, randomization is widely used in our life to avoid disputes over possible biased selection. For example, two football (soccer) teams toss a coin to decide which team will kick off a match. This is done with the following assumptions: (1) each team is represented by one side of the coin and one side only; (2) the coin is fair, i.e. both sides have the same probability of turning up. For selecting a large number of cases from a huge population, a coin's limitation becomes obvious – it has only two sides. To choose from a large number of values, we can imagine a die with several thousand sides. In practice, it is next to impossible to produce such dice, of course. Statisticians and mathematicians thus use machines and computers to generate a large number of random numbers. In theory, these numbers are not completely random, which is why I said 'almost free', as the generating process has to follow a particular algorithm, which is an artefact of human intervention.[6]

Drawing a sample randomly is only a first step toward obtaining a good sample. A sample is good when it achieves at least two things: first, it well represents the

---

[6]Social researchers, as applied users of statistics, do not need to worry much about these issues; the numbers at the back of statistics textbooks or at some websites (such as http://www.random.org) are random enough for most of purposes.

population structure, and, second, an estimate made based on the sample enjoys a high chance of being very close to the population value. We shall specify what we mean by 'well represent', 'a high chance', 'very close' in the next chapter when we discuss specific statistics. For now, it should be clear that equal probability of selecting cases into a sample through randomization is an effective way of minimizing the chance of drawing a biased sample.

Bias, Precision and Errors

If we know the probability that each case of a population is to be drawn into a sample, we have a probability sample. There are many ways of drawing such sample, and a standard textbook will cover the most widely used sampling methods: simple random sampling (SRS), stratified sampling and cluster sampling.[7] We will discuss these methods, but our discussion will focus on the following questions: What do these sampling methods want to achieve? On what ground can they claim they have achieved their objectives? What are the issues we need to keep in mind when we apply these methods in practice? In the next and final section, we shall discuss how these methods will affect our analysis after the data are collected.

Bias and Precision

All samples aim to achieve two main objectives: to represent the population structure accurately and to obtain a precise estimation of the value of any interested attribute of the population.[8] If the sample has failed to represent the population structure well, then it will render our estimate of the population value biased. Naturally, the discrepancy between our estimate and the true population value indicates the precision of our estimate. There is no necessary connection between the two dimensions, so we have the four possible scenarios presented in Table 4.2.

Table 4.2   Scenarios of bias and precision in probability sampling

		Precise?	
		Yes	No
Biased?	Yes	(1) A precise but wrong estimate	(2) The worst scenario
	No	(3) The ideal scenario	(4) A correct but rough estimate

Obviously, scenario (3) is the ideal – not only our sample represents the population structure very well but our estimate based on the sample is very close to the population value as well. In contrast, scenario (2) is the worst situation; for example, the sample represents only one particular group of the population, missing out the

---

[7]See the three textbooks cited in footnote 1. For texts at a much lower mathematical level see relevant chapters in Moser and Kalton (1985) or Fink (2003).
[8]In statistics, such an attribute of the population is called 'parameter', which we do not know and will estimate based on sample data.

attributes of other groups, and even for that particular group the derived estimate is too far away from the true value of the interested parameter.

Let us take an example to understand scenarios (1) and (4). Suppose we are trying to estimate the strength of people's support of a new immigration policy. Further, suppose that women and men in the population hold very different views on this issue – most women are strongly opposed to the policy while most men either welcome the policy or have no strong opinion at all. We create an 11-point scale to measure each individual's level of support, with −5 meaning 'most strongly against', 0 'no opinion', and +5 'most strongly welcoming'. Finally, suppose the true mean scores for the whole population, men and women are 2, 4 and −2, respectively. It is very likely that our sample represents the gender structure of the population very well – the respective proportion of females and males is about the same as that in the population – but our calculation based on the sample indicates that the mean score is 0, rather than 2, therefore, we are in scenario (4). In contrast, if most people included in our sample are men and the sample results generate an average score of 3.8, which is very close to the true value of 4, then we have a highly biased sample toward men but it has very precisely estimated the true value; in short, we are in scenario (1).

Sampling and Other Errors

A series of errors make it very difficult to achieve high levels of accuracy as well as precision. In *Survey Methodology*, Robert Groves and his colleagues (2004: ch. 2) specify the errors that may arise in the survey lifecycle from the perspective of quality control. Here, the word 'error' does not mean mistakes but refers to the discrepancy between what the survey is supposed to achieve and what it has actually achieved. Coverage error occurs if we fail to include some cases in the sampling frame. We have sampling error if the particular sample we drew does not happen to represent the population structure. In addition, some people simply refuse to participate. For those who agree to participate, our questions may have failed to capture what we really want, or the respondents understand them in different ways, thereby causing measurement errors. After the data are collected, errors may occur during the processing and editing processes. Some of these errors, coverage and processing errors in particular, are due to practical constraints, which are relatively easier to control with greater care and administrative support. Others, however, are much more fundamental, especially sampling and measurement errors. Below we will have a brief discussion on how different sampling methods may reduce sampling errors. The issue of measurement errors will be dealt with when we learn about the logic of measuring a concept and structural equation modelling.

Sampling errors occur not merely because a sample is only a part of the population. The intrinsic disadvantage of a sample comes more from the fact that the individuals of the population may hold different values on the attributes that we are interested in. If, for example, all people earn the same amount of money, then we can pick up any individual person and get the correct answer. Statistics will be of no use at all in such situation. The reality is that individuals do have different values and the more varied these values are the more difficult it will be for our sample to capture the variation in the population, so the bigger the sampling error will be.

Optimizing the Sample Size

As the difficulty mainly comes from the limited size of our sample, our natural reaction would be to increase our sample size so that more varied values will be included in the sample, which is why larger samples, if financial support permits, are often desirable. If the size of our sample is about the same as the size of the population, then the sampling error would be very small, but then the whole point of drawing a sample will be lost – why did we simply not conduct a census? In short, our ultimate goal is to draw a sample of an *optimal* size that is big enough for representing the variation in the population but is still small enough to be affordable.

As Salant and Dillman (1994: 55) have shown, the relationship between population size and the required sample size is not a linear one. More precisely, *a large population does not necessarily demand a large sample*. A larger population demands a larger sample only when the population size is below 25,000. Beyond that, no matter how large the population is, a sample of more than 1000 will do a very good job in terms of precision of estimation. This is the case under the conditions that the sampling error is very low (3%) and the population is believed to be evenly split on the interested characteristic. If we relax these conditions – larger sampling error and uneven split, then the required sample size could be even smaller. In general, how large a sample should be depends on how precise we want our estimate to be and how much we know about the population. Clearly, the more precise we want our estimation to be, the larger the sample size has to be; the more we know about our population, the more effective we will be of selecting the sample elements to capture the variation in the population, thus the smaller the sample size will be.

Note that this refers to the *valid* sample size, that is, the number of returned questionnaires with valid answers. The *actual* sample size should be much larger as we have to compensate for the loss arising from non-response. To obtain the actual sample size, we need to divide the required valid sample size by the expected response rate.

Finally, sample size is only one of the factors that affect the accuracy and the precision of our estimation. Also very important is how the sample is drawn, so we need to discuss the logic behind each sampling method.

Different Ways of Drawing a Probability Sample

Simple Random Sampling (SRS)

Most statistical methods have been created under the assumption that the data have been collected by SRS, which would allow statisticians concentrate on the statistical question and not to be distracted by sampling issues. There are procedures for samples drawn by other methods, but they build on those for SRS. The irony is that SRS is mathematically simple but practically can be quite clumsy. It is mathematically simple because it assumes no structure in the population; therefore, there is no need to incorporate any relations among the cases in the sampling procedures and later statistical analyses. The population is presumably consisted of N number of independent cases, from which we shall draw n of them as a sample.

To draw the sample, we must have a good sampling frame – the list of all the eligible cases in the population with no alien entities. We label each case with a unique identification number. Then we find n random numbers, which is determined beforehand as the sample size, that have the same number of digits as the identification numbers. It does not matter whether we get them by computer or from random number table. Those cases whose identification numbers match the random numbers will be selected into the sample. Note that here we are drawing a 'non-replacement sample'; that is, we do not put an individual case back to the population after it is selected because we do not want to waste our time selecting the same case repeatedly.

We can draw many such simple random samples, all of the same size. In general, for a population of size N, we can draw $\binom{N}{n} = \frac{N!}{n!(N-n)!}$ number of samples of the size n.[9] Take a very simple example. Suppose the population size is 100 and we plan to draw a sample of the size 10, here is how to find out the number of all possible samples:

$$
\begin{aligned}
\binom{100}{10} &= \frac{100!}{10!(100-10)!} \\
&= \frac{100 \times 99 \times 98 \times 97 \times 96 \times 95 \times 94 \times 93 \times 92 \times 91 \times 90!}{10! \times 90!} \\
&= \frac{100 \times 99 \times 98 \times 97 \times 96 \times 95 \times 94 \times 93 \times 92 \times 91}{10 \times 9 \times 8 \times 7 \times 6 \times 5 \times 4 \times 3 \times 2 \times 1} \\
&= 17,310,309,456,440
\end{aligned}
$$

You must be shocked by this huge number. Please do not be. In real surveys, the number could be much larger because N is usually more than several hundreds of thousands or even millions, while n is more than a thousand. You can imagine how many possible samples of the same size we can draw, and ours is only one of them! There are so many out there; very likely you will get a different one next time.

Despite its simple logic, SRS is not simple at all in practice, and nor is it the most desirable method from a statistical perspective. Practically, the size of the target population in most real social surveys is usually very large (tens of thousands, if not millions or even more). It is very unlikely that a reliable sampling frame exists for such large populations. Examples of typical target population will be all private

---

[9] For readers unfamiliar with the notation, $n!$ reads 'n factorial', which equals the product of n and all the following integers till 1. That is, $n! = n \times (n-1) \times (n-2) \times \ldots 2 \times 1$.

households or all adults aged 16 or over living in private households. It is only in a handful of countries, such as Sweden, Singapore and the Czech Republic, that a list of all eligible households or individuals exists. Even if we have such sampling frame, selecting the required number of cases randomly is a tedious task.

Stratified Sampling

A statistically better and practically more feasible strategy is to break the population into some subgroups ('strata') and then to draw an SRS within each subgroup ('stratum'). Note that although it is usually called 'stratified sampling', *the strata do not have to constitute a hierarchy*; they simply mean groups. For example, each state in the USA or each county in the UK may have their own list of private households, but there is no hierarchy, at least not in terms of status, among the states or counties. You may rank the states in a way, such as by size of population, but that does not have any effect on the sampling process. Usually, the sample size for each stratum is the product of the total sample size, which should be determined beforehand, and the proportion of each stratum of the total population size, which should be available from government statistics agency or from any other survey. Such strategy can be used further for smaller strata, depending on the availability of information.

Sometimes, we may not want to use the same proportions in the population to draw our sample. For example, the proportion of one stratum may be so small that if we use it, then the total number of cases in the sample will be too small to allow for a precise estimation. For example, as an ethnic group, the Chinese population constitute only 0.8% of the total population of the UK. If we plan to draw a sample of 2000, then we should select only $0.008 \times 2000 = 16$ Chinese respondents, which is obviously too small to produce any reliable statistics about the Chinese population as a whole. In this situation, higher proportions could be applied in order to boost the number of proportionally smaller groups, hence the term 'booster samples'.

It is important to note that, although stratified sampling is effective of representing the strata, this is achieved *only in the way the strata are classified*. The population can be classified in many different ways, such as age, race and ethnicity, level of economic development, political orientation and so forth. From these 'stratification factors', survey investigators usually choose the one for which information is conveniently available from official statistics. Stratification is only useful, however, when *the stratification factors are relevant to the interested research question*. For example, if you think gender and socio-economic status are the most important factors for predicting which political party people will vote for, then the population should be classified into six strata (assuming three classes, lower, middle and upper): male lower, male middle, male upper, female lower, female middle and female upper. An SRS then is drawn from each stratum.

The trouble is that the factors with available information may not happen to be the factors that we plan to use for explaining the target phenomenon. Therefore, when analysing the data collected from a stratified sample, researchers should carefully examine what stratification factors have been used and whether they are of any relevance to the research purpose at hand. Most stratification factors are basic demographic characteristics, so it would be surprising if they happen to be exactly the variables that researchers intend to use for predicting or explaining purposes. Actually, if a factor important to the researcher is not one of the stratification factors, then the researcher should be very cautious in using the data as the sample may actually undermine the estimation of the interested attribute.

Cluster Sampling

Cluster sampling can be easily confused with stratified sampling. The confusion comes from the fact that both involve the process of classifying the elements in the population into subgroups. The key is to remember that *these subgroups are the units to be sampled in cluster sampling, but they are not in stratified sampling*. In other words, in cluster sampling, there are at least two steps: first, select some of the subgroups; and, second, select some elements in each selected subgroups. This is why cluster sampling is a multi-stage sampling method, and the subgroups are labelled as 'primary sampling units' (PSU), 'secondary sampling units' (SSU) and so on, according to the stage in which they are sampled.

To illustrate further, let us take a look at the two charts in Figure 4.1 that respectively represent the two procedures. In both cases, there are nine subgroups to sample from. They are called 'strata' in stratification sampling but 'clusters' in cluster sampling. In the chart on the left-hand side representing stratified sampling, cases in all strata are selected, which is why we see dots (selected cases) in all squares (strata). In contrast, cases cannot be directly selected in cluster sampling on the right-hand side. *We must select clusters as the first stage before cases in the selected clusters are to be selected*. In this illustration, clusters (1), (3), (5) and (9) are initially selected,

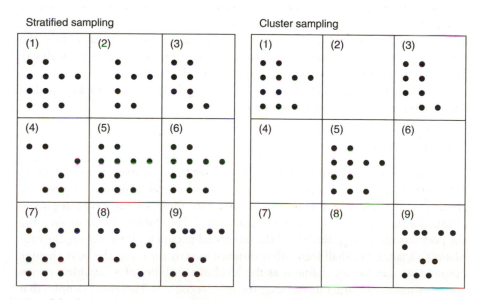

Figure 4.1   Distinguishing cluster sampling from stratified sampling

while others are not. Then in the second stage, some cases are selected in each of these four selected clusters. In real surveys, there can be many stages of selection, depending on the structure of the population and the available information about them.

Statisticians can prove that stratified sampling will generate better results than cluster sampling – 'better' in the sense that our estimates of values about the population have smaller errors. Intuitively, this is not surprising at all if we compare the two charts in Figure 4.1. The population structure is much better covered by stratified sampling than by cluster sampling, as the latter completely misses out the subgroups that were not selected in the first stage.

Shall we give up cluster sampling and all choose stratified sampling? The answer is, not necessarily, because cluster sampling can be a good choice due to its lower cost level. The best thing about cluster sampling is its administrative efficiency: investigators of sample surveys can recruit and deploy interviewers in a particular geographical area so that the costs of staffing and transportation can be minimized. In fact, statisticians explicitly factor the costs into calculating the effectiveness of a sampling method. In the practice of survey sampling, the optimal design maximizes representativeness of the population while minimizing the cost of drawing the sample at the same time.

Effects of Sampling Design on Data Analysis

Sampling is a part of the data collection process, not statistical analysis of the data. Why do we need to pay serious attention to it? If our main objective is to analyse the results of sample surveys, why can we not leave the tasks such as drawing a sample, designing a questionnaire and administering the fieldwork to survey methodologists? The answer is that we may not have to do those things ourselves, but we must understand how the specialists did those things, because how the data were collected will have some effects on how the data are to be analysed. Data analysis should not be separated from data collection.

Two concepts are currently used for representing the effects of sampling on data analysis: the design effect and weighting.

Design Effect

As we learnt in the previous sections of this chapter, there are many ways of drawing a probability sample. This is especially so when several sampling schemes are applied in multiple stages. How can we compare these schemes with regard to estimating the value of the interested parameter? The statistical way of assessing the performance of an estimator of the interested parameter is examining the estimator's variance. We shall learn what variance exactly means in the next chapter. For now, we can loosely define it as the level of variability of a variable's values. For an estimate, the larger its variance, the less precise it is. Therefore, samples that could produce smaller variances are more desirable.

Let us use V_{design} to represent the variance of an estimate that is derived from a relatively complicated sampling design and V_{srs} to represent the variance of an estimate derived from a SRS. The design effect is the ratio of the two:

$$DE = \frac{V_{design}}{V_{srs}}$$

If $DE = 1$, there is no difference between the two designs. If $DE > 1$, then the sampling design used is worse than SRS; if $DE < 1$, then the used sampling design is better than SRS. Stratified sampling is more effective than SRS, so its DE is usually smaller than 1. In contrast, cluster sampling is less effective, as shown above, so its DE is almost always larger than 1. As some kind of clustering is often used in real surveys for the sake of reducing costs, DE is normally larger than 1.

It should be clear even from this brief discussion that how the sample is drawn has a direct effect on the precision of our estimates of a population value. Some statisticians have suggested that DE should be incorporated in calculating statistics related to estimating any population value, such as confidence intervals (Lohr, 1997), which we shall learn in the next chapter.

An implicit effect of sampling design on statistical analysis is on the sample size. As we shall see in later chapters, we need to use the sample size to calculate many statistics. But which sample size should we use? Normally people use the actual sample size, that is, the total number of valid questionnaires collected from a survey. However, if the questionnaires were collected with cluster sampling, then we have used an inflated sample size, because cases in a cluster tend to be more homogeneous, thereby providing less useful information than that from an SRS. This is why the design effect can also be defined as the ratio between the actual sample size and the effective sample size (Groves et al., 2004: 108):

$$DE = \frac{n_{actual}}{n_{effective}}$$

As DE is usually larger than 1 with clustering sampling involved, the effective sample size should be smaller than the actual sample size, reflecting the loss of information (effective cases) due to the homogeneity among the cases.

Weighting

The effect of sampling on the subsequent statistical analysis is also reflected in weighting. Again, this stems from the usual practice that more complicated sampling design rather than SRS is used. For example, if we find that we have overdrawn much more females than males in a sample – we know that by comparing the percentage of each sex in our sample with that in the population, which is usually available, we would increase the weight of males in order to increase their representation. Such weighting is 'post-stratification' because it is done after the sample is already drawn and based on the information of stratification in the population.

There are some other reasons for weighting cases as well. Similar to the above situation, we may find that one group has higher response rate than another and therefore has been overrepresented in the sample. The group with a lower response rate is therefore in need of a larger weight to increase their representativeness. The same logic applies to the situation in which we combine several samples together into one sample but the cases in each sample have different probabilities of being selected. For example, researchers may give higher probabilities of selection to people of ethnic minorities. When they are analysed together with whites, we may want to weight down the ethnic minorities.

Some have argued that weights should be used in all statistical analyses on data that are collected in non-simple-random samples, such as constructing a confidence interval, testing a hypothesis, and even for running a statistical model (Lohr, 1997: 228–9; Dorofeev and Grant, 2006). There should be no doubt that weights are necessary for estimating a population parameter in order to balance probability of selection and to better represent the population structure. For constructing statistical models, however, the effect of weighting has been a controversial issue. The argument for the use of weights is that statistical models need to take into account of the way in which the data are sampled, as the sampling scheme itself can be seen as a model. However, very few published studies follow such instruction, perhaps because there has been little evidence that statistical models would be seriously flawed without taking into account of weights.

FIVE

Estimating and Measuring
One Important Thing

From this chapter we embark on our journey to learn specific statistical concepts and procedures, most of which aim to measure and estimate a particular value. While estimation and measurement are important for all statistical analyses, they are especially important for univariate statistics. Apparently simple and easy estimating and measuring do not enjoy an equal status in practical social research as modelling, predicting and explaining. So I shall begin the chapter with a few comments. Then we shall start to learn descriptive statistics and move on to statistical inference, a most important procedure in statistics. The distinction between inferential and descriptive statistics stems from the distinction between population and sample. If we study either a population or a sample alone without any attempt to link the two together, descriptive statistics will be enough. If our objective is to learn something about a value in a population based on sample data, we will carry out two tasks of statistical inference: testing a hypothesis about this value and constructing confidence interval for it. The latter is more informative than the former.

Importance of Estimating and Measuring in Social Research

It is unfortunate that except for the economists, many social scientists do not seem to acknowledge the importance of estimation and measurement. Eminent scholars, such as Andrew Abbott, Arthur Stinchcombe and Nancy Cartwright have claimed that explanation is *the* purpose of social sciences. Indeed, most social science classics – Max Weber's *The Protestant Ethics and the Spirit of Capitalism*, Emile Durkheim's *Suicide*, Barrington Moore's *Social Origins of Dictatorship and Democracy* – are models of explanation. How these great thinkers measured their key concepts – the prevalence of a religious belief, the distribution of accounting practices across businesses owned by people of different religions, the rate of suicide in a particular country at a particular time point and the level of democracy – has been overshadowed by how they explained the connections of some important phenomena.

However, few would disagree that one cannot explain things convincingly without measuring them properly in the first place. If so, then we would wonder to what extent the above classics have relied on the measurement of their key concepts. Later generations of social scientists have done a lot of work on measuring. But measuring key concepts properly has seldom become a respectable mission on its own; more often than not it only serves the purpose of explanation rather than a precondition to be satisfied before any explanation can be done. No one has explicitly claimed that the concepts under study are so complicated that we are unable to make any explanatory statements about their relationships. Somehow, explanation can always be achieved regardless of whether measurement is done and how it is done and researchers simply carry on with explanation no matter whether they have properly measured what they would like to measure.

There is a price to pay, however: our explanations may become pointless if what we intend to explain is not the true representation of social phenomena because they are falsely or poorly measured. Many observed associations of phenomena are effects of measurement, not reflections of the reality. Furthermore, there have been very few key contributions in social sciences (again, except for economics) that have become influential mainly because they have measured an important social phenomenon. One reason that sociology and other social sciences have not earned a reputation on a par with economics is the shortage of social indicators that are of great concern to the public.[1] Think about how many people are waiting to hear the forthcoming figures of unemployment rate, the changing percentage of people who claimed benefits in the last quarter, consumer price index, any index of consumer confidence and many others. How many similar figures are produced by sociologists, political scientists, social work researchers or social geographers?

Most social concepts suffer from the deficit of public interest simply because they are unable to give the public a clear sense of the magnitude of a social problem or phenomenon. This is puzzling because it is not that social researchers do not have important concepts or indicators. There are many: social inequality, social exclusion, social conflict (or harmony), racial and ethnic relations, social capital and many other more specific concepts. Any claims that these are less important

---

[1] The information on The Web of Science indicates that the journal *Social Indicators Research* does not seem to enjoy a high impact factor. Perhaps the single most influential indicators sociologists have made are social classes or socio-economic status (SES) that have been widely adopted by national statistics agencies. Currently, a lot of effort has been invested in the measurement of social capital, but many issues remain unsettled.

than the unemployment rate or any other economic indicators are either ground-less or ideologically biased. Moreover, it does not make much sense to argue that social indicators are much more complicated and therefore much harder to measure. Many economic concepts, for example consumer confidence or the unemployment rate, are no less complicated. The most important reason is that for so many social scientists, explanation and understanding are far more important than measuring. Those with an ambition to explain will not let measurement – no matter how poorly it is done – prevent them from explaining.

In addition, the difficulty of measuring social science concepts has long been recognized. Here let me try to give a brief account. The concepts exist at three different levels: essential, proxy and instrumental. Essential concepts aim to capture *the essential characteristics* of the interested phenomenon, identifying the phenomenon's distinctive nature and its boundaries. Such concepts lay the foundation for all the investigations that follow. These concepts, however, are very abstract in nature, defying direct implementation of measurement. Researchers then have to find another concept that is much more accessible but can still represent the essential concept. Usually there is more than one *proxy* available, so researchers have to decide which one best represents the essential concept or how to use multiple proxy concepts at the same time. To measure a proxy concept, an instrumental concept must be used in order to render a *direct* measurement. It is this type of concepts – later transformed into variables – that eventually enter into statistical analysis.

To illustrate, take social capital as an example.[2] Despite its popularity, confusions already arise at the essential level. What are key features that define social capital? The most authoritative definitions come from Pierre Bourdieu (1986) and James Coleman (1990), and it is not easy to determine how much they agree with each other. Most of the credit for popularizing the concept should go to Robert Putnam (1993, 2000), but it remains hard to find a consistent definition in his own publications too. For example, it is not clear whether social capital consists of the features of social relations or social relations per se are social capital. With regard to the boundaries of social capital, it is not clear whether it refers to a group, either naturally or institutionally defined, or strangers on the street can also share some social capital. If social capital means several different things, then they should be clearly distinguished, and each must be defined separately in order to obtain essential consistency.

Even such consistency is obtained, it still remains unclear which proxy concepts can represent the essence of social capital. It is encouraging that most researchers have accepted the following as proxies of social capital: trust, engagement in civil organizations, social networks, social norms and practices. Nevertheless, there are not clear principles as to which one of these proxies can better represent social capital under a particular circumstance and whether they should be used in connection with each other in a single research project. It is all up to the researcher.

So far the tightest connection is between the proxies and the instrumental concepts. Many statisticians have done an excellent job in an effort to reach a

---

[2]This is not a place for even a brief review of the studies on social capital. I have provided an overview of measuring social capital in social surveys somewhere else (Yang, 2007). Interested readers could browse the social capital gateway at http://www.socialcapitalgateway.org/.

consensus on how each proxy concept should be operationalized with survey instruments. Items used in major social surveys have been relatively stabilized on a set of widely accepted questions. We should keep in mind that measuring is a human activity with an aim to make sense of the surrounding phenomena by inventing and employing intellectual tools that human cognitive capacities can handle. Obviously, there is a risk of losing contact with what is being abstracted and its context. But that is not the fault of measurement as a scientific practice. We should not give up measurement simply because of its limitations; otherwise,

> differences in measurement may lead not to doubt about the accuracy of the particular act of measurement but to doubt about the measuring instrument or even to doubt about the uniqueness of the quantity being measured. If enough people develop enough doubt, this can lead to widespread rejection of the measurement technique, to the loss of whatever benefits it might have obtained, and even to a reduction of credibility for the entire scientific enterprise. (Bradley and Schaefer, 1998: 109)

True, not all important things are measurable and not all things measurable are important. The challenge to social scientists is to figure out what is important as well as measurable. We must work hard to clarify our concepts, try to reach consensus on what they mean and how they should be measured before trying to explain their relationships. It is crucial to keep the gap between the two in mind when understanding statistics.

Describing a Variable's Centre and Variation

Often we are interested in a particular value of a variable. For example, 'voted in the last national election' is a value of the variable 'voting behaviour in the last national election'. It is important to note that we cannot estimate or measure that value very well without a good knowledge of that variable. The statistical concepts introduced below are created for describing *the distribution* of a variable's values; we must first specify the distribution before any statistics is calculated and interpreted.

To describe the distribution, it is very rare that any single statistics can do the job alone. Perhaps the only situation in which one statistic can is when all the values are the same. In that rare and uninteresting case, any single value of that variable can represent the whole set of values, and we do not need statistics anymore. In most situations, we need at least one statistic to describe the centre and another to describe the variation. Which statistics are to be used largely depends on the exact form of the distribution. Statisticians have worked for many decades in an attempt to pin down the characteristics of some commonly encountered distributions, such as the normal, the binomial, the Poison, the exponential and so on.[3] Their work is indispensable

---

[3]The meaning of the normal distribution will be explained later. I will not introduce other distributions as they are not our main concern here and the reader can find them in standard texts of mathematical statistics.

because later researchers could immediately recognize the mathematical features of a particular distribution and decide what further analyses they wanted to carry out. Recall that our choice of statistical methods largely depends on the level of measurement of the variable under study, which also dictates our discussions below.

When the Interested Variable is Metrical

The most widely used and known statistics for describing the centre of a variable's values is the mean, defined as:

$$\overline{X} = \frac{\sum_{i=1}^{N} X_i}{N} \tag{5.1}$$

Here, X is the variable that we are studying, and N is the total number of cases. Many students would be put off straightaway when they see the symbol Σ, the Greek capital letter sigma. However, you will not be intimidated anymore if you understand what it means and why it is used. Equation (5.1) is a compact version of the following:

$$\overline{X} = \frac{X_1 + X_2 + X_3 + ... + X_N}{N} \tag{5.2}$$

If X has only a small number of values, i.e. if N is small, such that we can easily write out all the Xs, then we do not need that sigma. But if N is very large, say more than a thousand, it will be very tedious to write them all out. Some other times, we do not know the exact value of N, or we simple do not care what it is, so we need a symbol to represent it. What Σ says is simply that 'Please add up all the values to the right of me'. In this case, we need to add up all the Xs. How many Xs are there? N, from 1 to N, which is why we have a little $i = 1$ under Σ and capital N above it to indicate that we are adding up all the values from the first value X_1 up to the last value X_N. After adding them up, the definition asks us to divide the total by N in order to make the final result.[4]

The calculation of the mean only involves summation and division, which everyone with a primary school education should know. To use it properly, however, is not easy. First of all, a common warning is that the mean is sensitive to extreme values. To illustrate with a simple example, here are the marks of 10 students: 48, 51, 62, 65, 65, 66, 67, 67, 68 and 72. You can find the mean to be 63.1. The professor may be happy with it as most students' marks fall into the 60s, which means '2:1', or upper second class, in the UK. If however one student did extremely badly, for instance the first one got only 15 instead of 48, then this mark will pull down the mean to be 59.8, a mark of a lower class '2:2'. Or, if the last student did extremely well by getting 100, then that mark will push up the mean to be 65.9.

---

[4]In daily language, people use the word 'average' to refer to the centre of a set of numbers, which are values of a variable. It is never clearly defined but we could assume that an average is the arithmetic mean as defined above. However, we should avoid using 'average' because, as we shall see below, the mean is not the only statistics for describing the centre of a variable.

Recall from the previous chapter that sampling has an effect on our statistical analysis, and we can see that effect on calculating the mean.[5] It is appropriate to use the above definition only when the sample is a simple random sampling (SRS). The calculation will be different for other kinds of samples. Start with a stratified sample. Suppose there are S number of strata, each having its own weight W_s, that is, the proportion of the population that it represents, and its own mean $\overline{X}_s$, then the overall mean would be:

$$\overline{X} = \sum W_s \overline{X}_s$$

(5.3)

With cluster sampling, if the sample is drawn with C clusters and each cluster has its own mean $\overline{X}_c$, then the mean should be calculated as

$$\overline{X} = \frac{1}{C} \sum \overline{X}_C$$

(5.4)

Sampling will show its effects on statistics most clearly when the three means calculated on the same sample are very different. Note that the denominator in the above two equations has gone as it is actually in $\overline{X}_s$ and $\overline{X}_c$.

In all these calculations, it is clear that the mean is sensitive to extreme values, which brings us to the general conditions for using the mean appropriately:

(1) the variable is metrical (quantitative, or interval/ratio);
(2) there is only one centre; if there are two or more centres, then any one mean is misleading;
(3) most values are evenly clustered around that centre; the mean cannot properly represent the centre of a skewed distribution, such as income;
(4) there are no values extremely far away from the centre.

Distributions with these conditions satisfied are 'normal'. In short, you should only use the mean when you have a normal or at least approximately normal distribution.

The trouble is that researchers may not check the satisfaction of these conditions before they use the mean. For example, there are many variables with values that indicate ranked levels (5 = extremely strong, 4 = relatively strong, 3 = no difference, 2 = relatively weak, 1 = extremely weak), such as how strong the support is to a policy or how much the respondent agrees to a statement. Such variables are clearly ordinal; therefore, it is meaningless to calculate the mean even though a bar chart may show a shape of normal distribution, because a mean such as 2.3 cannot be explained with the original scale – there is no such category in it! The problem with this way of thinking is that it forces the original ordinal variable into a metrical one by *assuming the existence of a continuum* from 1 to 5. It is only when such assumption is accepted that a mean can be meaningful.

A similar example is the number of children in a household. It is often reported that the average (mean) number of children is 2.3 in a country. It is obviously meaningless to have 0.3 children. Nevertheless, many people do not find such number problematic because, as they would argue, it meaningfully indicates that most

---

[5]Calculation of the mean may also be different if we have grouped data. As my main purpose here is to introduce the basic ideas, I will not take space to present those statistics.

households have *two to three* children. This statement is not acceptable because the idea of the centre is lost: is it two or three that represents the centre? As 2.3 is closer to 2, should we say there are more households with two children, not three?

A second condition that some researchers may not check is the distribution of the values. In real research, few quantitative variables are very close to the normal, bell-shaped curve. It is commonly advised that the median should be used when the distribution is skewed by one or a few extreme values. This makes sense because the median is not sensitive to these values because it does not take the values of each case directly into account; the median is identified as the middle value after all values are put in a ranking order.[6] If most distributions are not normal enough, then we should see the median to be more frequently used than the mean, but that does not seem to be the case. Or, if you are not certain about the normality of the distribution, then both the mean and the median should be found and compared in order to see how different they are.

It is worth repeating that a single statistic about a distribution's centre is not enough, because different distributions may share the same centre but some of them have very different values while others have little variation. Depending on the shape of the distribution, *a statistic describing the distribution's level of variation should always accompany the centre statistic*. If there are no signs of serious distortion of normality, then the standard deviation (s.d.) may be used. If it is clearly skewed, then the inter-quartile range (*IQR*) is preferred to go with the median. The logic is the same as that for choosing the mean or the median – the s.d. is sensitive to extreme values while the *IQR* is not. Although most statistics software packages will automatically generate these statistics, it is useful to look at their defining equations in order to have a sense of the underlying ideas.

The s.d. is the square root of variance. As variance has many more uses than s.d., let us have the definition of variance:

$$\text{var}(X) = \frac{\sum_{i=1}^{N}(X_i - \overline{X})^2}{N - 1} \tag{5.5}$$

If you understand the idea of the mean, then it should not be difficult to understand the logic of variance. First of all, keep in mind that variance is created to measure how variable (adjective) a variable's (noun) values are. It does this by measuring 'the mean distance' between each value and the mean. The values are varied, but from what? The mean $\overline{X}$ serves as a reference point so that $X_i - \overline{X}$ could measure the variations among the Xs, and it is squared up simply to avoid the zero after summing them up. Therefore, variance is always a positive number – it can only be zero when all the terms of $(X_i - \overline{X})^2$ are zero. In short, variance indicates

---

[6]Curiously, statisticians have not designated a symbol for the median. The only alternative to writing the words 'the median' is to use Q2, representing the second quartile (or the 50% percentile).

[7]It is $N - 1$ rather than N in the denominator because we will definitely know the value of the last case if we know the values of the all the previous $N - 1$ cases. When N is very large, mathematically it makes little difference to replace it with $N - 1$.

the variation of a variable's values by measuring the mean of the distances between each X and $\overline{X}$.[7]

Again, we should take into account of the effect of sampling method if it is not an SRS. Using the same notations for (5.3) and (5.4), the variance for a stratified sample is:

$$\text{var}(\overline{X}) = \sum W_S^2 \text{var}(\overline{X}_S) \tag{5.6}$$

The weight needs to be squared up due to the square of calculating the variance for each stratum. The variance for a cluster sample looks a bit different:

$$\text{var}(\overline{X}) = \frac{1}{C(C-1)} \sum (\overline{X}_C - \overline{X})^2 \tag{5.7}$$

But the principles remain the same: we need to weight the variation because cases in different strata or clusters represent different number of cases in the population or they have been selected into the sample with different probabilities.

The logic of *IQR* is also similar to that of the median. Again, if you know how to find the median, then you should know how to find out the *IQR*. After identifying the median, all the values have been broken into two parts, 50% above it while the other 50% below it. Now try to find the median for each part separately, so you will get two more 'sub-medians'. The sub-median for the upper part of the values is labelled as *Q3*, while that for the lower part *Q1*. It should make sense that the original median is *Q2*. The *IQR* is the difference between *Q3* and *Q1*, i.e. *IQR* = *Q3* − *Q1*. As all of them are based on the relative positions of the values, not the values per se, all these medians and consequently *IQR* will not be affected by extreme values.

When the Interested Variable Is Categorical (Nominal/Ordinal)

Most statistical procedures have been developed with the assumption that the variable is metrical. There are at least two reasons that statisticians pay most of their attention to this kind of variables. It is only during the past four decades or so that statistics has been widely used in social science research. Most statistical concepts and procedures were created for the natural sciences, agriculture and engineering. Variables in these fields are indeed continuous, such as length, weight, time, speed and many others. On top of this practical motivation is the mathematical properties of metrical variables that allow the use of advanced mathematics, mostly calculus and matrix algebra. In contrast, most variables in social sciences are categorical, and the mathematics for dealing with such variables, i.e. finite or discrete mathematics, has been much less developed. It is only in the past few decades that statisticians and methodologists have advanced the statistics for categorical variables, and we shall learn some of them in this book.

It does not make much sense to talk about 'the centre' of a nominal variable. What could be the centre of gender, religion or ethnicity? What we can do is to describe how the cases are distributed across the categories with a frequency table, in which we may use both absolute counts as well as relative counts (proportions

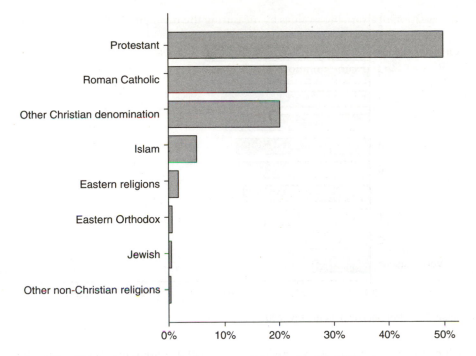

Figure 5.1   Distribution of respondents across religions in the UK, 2006

or percentages). As pointed in the previous chapter, such tables are more informative than a pie chart. However, I have found that a bar chart could be very useful for comparing the frequencies if we put them in order. The added value of such chart – Figure 5.1[8] as an illustration – is that it gives an intuitive sense of the scale of the differences across the categories.

Note that *such ordering should not be used for ordinal variables*, as some of my students have done, because otherwise we shall change the original order among the categories, making us incapable to detect *any changes along the original order*. Figure 5.2 well illustrates the point.

The bars have been reorganized to show a descending trend, but it does not make any sense as it has messed up the original categories. The only thing it does is to show which category has the largest or the smallest percentage.

In most statistics books, it is hard to find statistics for describing the variation of a categorical variable. Perhaps an exception is the index of qualitative variation (*IQV*) (Mueller and Schuessler, 1961, see also Kader and Perry, 2007, for a recent review). Obviously, one can scrutinize the proportions to get an intuitive sense of the distribution of the cases across the categories. *IQV*, however, can give us a more exact measure of a nominal variable's spread. As nominal variables are often found in social survey data, *IQV* should have been more frequently used than it is now.

The idea of *IQV* is to look at the observed variation across the categories of a nominal variable in comparison with the maximum variation. We can understand a specific

---

[8]I created Figures 5.1 and 5.2 with the data collected from the third round of European Social Survey.

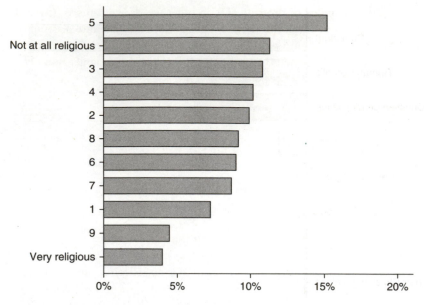

Figure 5.2　Religiousness in the UK, 2006

value of IQV as a point somewhere in the middle of a continuum. At one end of the continuum is the minimum variation, that is, all cases are in the same category while no cases at all in the other categories. At the other end is the maximum variation – the cases are evenly distributed across the categories. If the distance between the minimum and the maximum is measurable from 0 to 1, then a decimal number can represent the variability of a nominal variable. The following definition is created to represent that idea:

$$IQV = \frac{k(N^2 - \sum f^2)}{N^2(k-1)}$$

$$= \frac{k}{k-1}\left(1 - \sum_{i=1}^{k} p_i^2\right)$$

$$= \frac{k}{k-1}D \qquad\qquad (5.8)$$

where　k = the number of categories
　　　　f = the frequency of each category (from 1 to k)
　　　　N = the total number of cases
　　　　$p = f/N$

Try to understand what this equation says: the variability is measured by the difference between the square of the total number of cases and the sum of the squared frequencies of all categories ($N^2 - \sum f^2$). The second line transforms this into proportions (p) because proportions can better represent the distribution than absolute frequencies. The third line shows the definition of another related measurement of variability of a nominal variable: the index of diversity (D). In other words, we can see IQV as D adjusted by the number of categories because D itself does not take into account the effect of k. We need to take into account the effect of the number of categories as values will be more variable when they have to be distributed to a larger number of categories. Table 5.1 shows the effect of k.

Table 5.1 Effect of k on D and IQV

	$k = 2$	$k = 5$	$k = 10$
No variation	$D = 1 - (1 + 0) = 0$	$D = 1 - (1 + 0 * 4) = 0$	$D = 1 - (1 + 0 * 9) = 0$
Maximum variation	$D = 1 - (0.5 * 0.5 * 2) = 0.5$	$D = 1 - (0.2 * 0.2 * 5) = 0.8$	$D = 1 - (0.1 * 0.1 * 10) = 0.9$
Adjusted by $k/(k-1) = IQV$	$D = 0.5 * (2/1) = 1$	$D = 0.8 * (5/4) = 1$	$D = 0.9 * (10/9) = 1$

When there is no variation – all cases fall into the same category – the number of categories (k) does not make any difference: no matter how many categories there are, all cases are in one of them. When there is an extreme variability – the cases fall evenly into the categories – k matters: the larger it is, the more diverse (from 0.5 to 0.8 to 0.9) the cases are. But IQV neutralizes such effect by the factor of $k/(1-k)$, which is why the values of D in the last row all become 1 as they all represent the extreme variation. In short, D is sensitive to the number of categories while IQV is not. The advantage of using IQV is that it allows us to compare the variability of nominal variables that have a different number of categories. We can only use D for such a comparison if we have the same number of categories.

Logic of Statistical Inference

Recall the distinction between a population and a sample of it. Our ultimate goal is to know something about the population (a parameter). In the previous chapter I showed that we could draw a large number of samples of the same size from the same population. The numeric information that we derive from the sample is called 'sample statistics', or simply statistics. Consequently, the relationship between the population and a sample can be translated to the relationship between a parameter and its corresponding statistic.

There are many things that may undermine using a statistic to represent a parameter, including coverage errors, measurement errors, processing errors and so on. The gap between a population and its sample is the sampling error, and it is this error that statistical inference is mostly concerned with. Figure 5.3 illustrates the situation. It shows that statistical inference is the process of estimating the values in the population, such as the population mean μ and the population standard deviation σ with their respective sample statistics, $\overline{X}$ and s. The question is: with such uncertainty in sample statistics – very likely you will get a different statistic when you draw another sample next time, why do we still want to use a statistic to estimate its parameter? On what ground can such induction be justified?

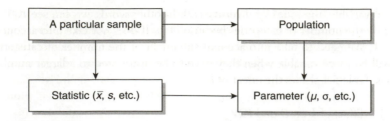

Figure 5.3   Statistic for sample as parameter for population

The answer is: it can never be completely justified. There is always some uncertainty when we jump from sample statistics to population parameters. But that should not make us abandon the whole enterprise of statistical inference; otherwise, we will not be able to estimate the attributes of the population that are so important to us. What we can do – and this is the art and science of statistical inference – is to estimate the level of such uncertainty against a stable pattern so that we know how uncertain it is.

At this point two things need to be clarified. First, the last statement in the previous paragraph follows a 'frequentist' approach in statistics, which sees probability as an objective state. As discussed in Chapter 2, other statisticians following the Bayesian approach see probability as a subjective judgement, and they have their own way of making statistical inference. I think these two approaches are complementary to each other but here I only illustrate the frequentist approach. Second, it is important to realize that estimating the uncertainty and reducing the uncertainty are two different tasks or processes. Statistical inference is about estimating the uncertainty, but it cannot reduce the uncertainty, which is a task for research design, such as drawing a representative sample and making a reliable measurement instrument.

Now back to the question of how we can estimate the uncertainty embedded in sample statistics. The idea is first to find something certain as a reference framework and then to see where the statistics from a particular sample stand in such a framework.

The framework was a major discovery made by eminent statisticians such as Carl Friedrich Gauss, Pierre-Simon Laplace, Ronald Fisher, Egon Pearson and Jerzy Neyman. What they found, intuitively speaking, is this: if we draw a very large number – in theory an infinite number – of samples of the same size from the same population,[9] then the statistics calculated from these samples will form a pattern, which statisticians call 'the sampling distribution'. In reality, none of them drew so many samples, of course, but then how did they find such stable pattern? They used mathematics, calculus and probability theory in particular.[10]

---

[9]These samples are assumed to be independent of each other; that is, results from one of them have nothing to do with those from another.
[10]It would be very nice if social researchers could learn how they proved the existence of such patterns, but I think social scientists can afford to stop here without learning all the proofs.

In the end, they organized their findings with some useful sampling distributions, such as the normal distribution, Poisson distribution, geometric and negative-geometric distribution and so on. Further, they have used two key statistics, the mean and the variance, to describe the characteristics of each distribution. The mean and variance we learnt previously in this chapter are for the normal distribution, and other distributions have their own mean and variance. Note that these are 'theoretical distributions' in the sense that no empirical data from a particular sample would show exactly the same shape as described by these distributions. Again, they are reference framework for us to use when we analyse a particular result so that we know what we can expect from that particular distribution and what statistics we can use to describe its characteristics.

Let us take the normal distribution as an example, which is the most popular among these distributions. It is popular not because people like its balanced, bell-shaped curve but because of its flexibility and its capacity to approximate some other distributions, such as the t distribution, as long as the sample size is large enough. More precisely, all the means calculated from the samples of a large size will form a normal distribution among themselves, even when the distribution in the original population is not normal. For social sciences, the sample size requirement is usually not a problem at all. The normal requirement is 30 to 100, but the size of samples in social sciences can easily exceed 1000. Its flexibility is reflected in the fact that it is not constrained by the population distribution, which is intuitively surprising but statisticians can prove this phenomenon as 'the central limit theorem'.[11] With this theoretical framework, we can evaluate the uncertainty involved in inferring the population mean based on a particular sample mean by two methods, constructing a confidence interval or testing a hypothesis.

Confidence Interval

Sample variation makes it necessary to construct confidence interval. Even without any other errors, the results from one sample – for example, the mean or the standard deviation – are bound to be different from those of another sample due to the fact that different cases are selected. The result may or may not be close to the value of the population parameter at a level to our satisfaction. The problem is: we do not know; therefore, we should not trust the result from any particular sample. Unfortunately, in reality that is the only sample we can get.

One source of the difficulty is that the sample result is only a 'point estimate'. Obviously, it is very hard to hit a point (the population parameter) with another

---

[11]The central limit theorem has its own limitations. The statistics of interest initially has to be represented as a mean. Some statistics cannot, for example, the count of events, variances, ratios and so forth. In some situations we may be able to transform the original variable so that the distribution of the transformed variable becomes normal, but then we need to remember to go back to the original distribution later one. In other situations, we simply have no other choice but to use a different, albeit less well-known, distribution.

point (the sample estimate). This being understood, then the solution should become clear: we can use a range of values, like a net, to estimate the parameter. The two values at the end of this range constitute a confidence interval of the population parameter. These end values should be of great importance for social research. We understand that it is very hard to make statistics of social phenomena very accurate, but at least we should have a clear idea of their range so that we can make proper decisions.

Note that we are not going to throw away the point estimate. It may not be very close to the parameter, but it is definitely much better than no information at all. Our task is to figure out how close or how far away it is from the parameter. We call the difference between the sample estimate and the parameter 'the error term'. Therefore, we can express the confidence interval as the following range:

$$(\text{estimate} - \text{error}, \text{estimate} + \text{error})$$

We can get the sample estimate by doing some calculations on the sample data, so now the question is to find out the size of the error.

There are three factors that determine the size of the error. To illustrate, suppose we have calculated a mean of a continuous variable from our sample $\bar{x}$. First, the error between $\bar{x}$ and its target parameter, the population mean μ, is determined by the population standard deviation σ. This makes sense because, if this variable's values in the population are highly varied, which is measured and therefore reflected by σ, then it would be harder for $\bar{x}$ to hit its target μ, so the error would be larger.

The second factor is the size of the error that we can tolerate. This has to be determined beforehand; otherwise, we cannot pin down the error term. Seen in this light, a 'confidence interval' can also be seen as an 'error interval'. The word 'confidence' is used because of our motivation of estimating the population parameter with a high level of confidence. How high is high? The answer is clearly arbitrary. The usual standard is anything above 90%, and most people have accepted 95%, hence the phrase '95% confidence interval'. We cannot use 95% directly because it is not directly related to σ. This is where the z score comes in, which tells us how many σ there are at a certain level of confidence based on the standard normal distribution.[12]

Finally, we need to consider the sample size n. The larger the sample size, the closer the sample is to the population, so $\bar{x}$ should be more likely accurate; in other words, the error should be smaller. The sample size and the error term therefore move in opposite directions, which is why we divide σ by $\sqrt{n}$.[13]

In the end, the confidence interval can be written as follows:

$$(\bar{x} - z\frac{\sigma}{\sqrt{n}}, \bar{x} + z\frac{\sigma}{\sqrt{n}})$$

---

[12] As my objective here is to show the logic of confidence interval, I will not go into the details of the standard normal distribution. The reader should be able to find its definition and illustration in all introductory statistics books.

[13] We use $\sqrt{n}$ instead of n because originally n goes with σ^2. As we are using σ now, we need to take the square-root of n as well.

Obviously, this is for the mean of a metrical variable. If the variable is categorical, we can construct a confidence interval for the proportion of one of its categories. The logic remains the same, and the only change is the representation of the error term, as shown below:

$$(\widehat{\pi} - z * \sqrt{\frac{\widehat{\pi}(1 - \widehat{\pi})}{n}}, \ \widehat{\pi} + z * \sqrt{\frac{\widehat{\pi}(1 - \widehat{\pi})}{n}})$$

where $\widehat{\pi}$ is the proportion estimated from the sample data.

To summarize, the size of the error is positively connected to the population standard deviation and the confidence level (represented by the z score) but negatively connected to the sample size. Besides the sample mean, you need the values of the three factors to calculate the confidence interval. There is a problem with σ because it is a population statistic and usually we do not know it – if we know it, it would be very likely that we know the population mean as well, and then why did we carry out the sample survey in the first place? In practice, we replace σ with the sample standard deviation s, which can be calculated on sample data. The question is: is it appropriate to substitute σ with s? The answer is positive but conditional: if we have large sample size (say, more than 60), then it is safe to do the substitution. Sample sizes in social surveys could easily pass that requirement.

What can we say after producing a confidence interval? Most commonly people say 'we are 95% confident that the mean of X lies in between so and so'. Keep in mind that this is not a word game that we simply say the same thing in a technically fancy way; our statement reflects whether we have the correct understanding of the whole procedure. The above statement is quick and easy, but it is not clear and is even misleading. The phrase 'we are 95% confident' sounds as if we have made a subjective judgement, which is not true as we know the confidence interval is produced by following the frequentist, not the Bayesian, approach. The '95%' is an objective probability, indicating the percentage of all the confidence intervals produced from all possible samples that contain the true population value. That is, the other 5% of the confidence intervals do not contain that value.

Is the confidence interval we have got one of the 95% or the other 5%? We will never know, because we do not have all the other intervals. It may be disappointing but it is true that we do not know whether the particular confidence interval we have produced contains the value of the parameter or not. We still want to use it because it is a result of a very good procedure. It is good because if we follow it, then 95% of the intervals will indeed contain the true population value. It is this procedure, not anyone of its particular results, that we trust.

In practice, few people would understand such a sophisticated notion of variability. I have come to believe that the confidence interval has not been widely used in daily life because people tend to have a different idea of the variability of a set of values. They realize that they cannot rely on one particular statistic. The basis of their distrust is, however, not because there are so many other possible samples that may generate different results, but because they want to know how different most of the other values can be from this single statistic. They want an interval of values to gain a sense of the variability of the values for a particular variable without having to draw samples.

For example, when people want to buy a used car, they would like to know how high or how low the price can be for a particular model and year of age. The standard deviation does not give them an idea that intuitively easy to understand. A confidence interval is about the population parameter and can never guarantee anything. Or we may just tell them the lowest and the highest prices, the difference of which is called 'the range' in statistics. But the range is usually very wide and thus not very helpful. So, what statistics can we give them for describing the variability of a variable's values?

I think that the buyer is looking for something like 'the percentile interval', or *PI* for short. We have learnt the concept of *IQR* in the previous section. A *PI* follows the same idea but will cover a larger range that is determined by the researcher. For example, we can produce a 90% *PI* that covers the middle 90% of the values, with the 5% of the values at each end being left off. This is especially useful for a variable such as car price, as it is unlikely to be normal. An important difference between *PI* and the confidence interval is that the *PI* concerns only the sample under study, without any attempt to make inference to the unknown population.

Test of Hypothesis

Like confidence intervals, the test of hypothesis is also about inferring from the unknown population based on one of its samples. However, unlike constructing a confidence interval, which is purely an estimating exercise without any idea of the population parameter's exact value, we now have a hypothesis about such value.

Few studies in the social sciences have been carried out to test only one hypothesis; social researchers usually test a bunch of hypotheses at the same time with a statistical model and most often the objective is to test the hypothesis that a parameter is zero. Therefore, testing a single hypothesis may not seem to be of any direct use in research but it is crucially important for understanding the logic of deriving any conclusion from a statistical model.

More importantly, social researchers must think carefully *why they want to test a particular hypothesis* and *how the result may relate to their substantive research question*, because *statistically*, where a hypothesis comes from, what it says and what the result means substantively are all irrelevant matters. These are substantive matters. A hypothesis can be an informed expectation based on previous research, an indicator of great importance to an organization, an impression from anecdotal experiences or a pure guess. You cannot consult a statistician on where you can find a good hypothesis or what you should hypothesize. You must think what hypothesis to test and why it is so important to test it on your own.

These issues are especially important for those who just learnt the procedures in a standard textbook. For example, many examples used in textbooks usually test the hypothesis that a population parameter such as the mean or the proportion is equal to 0, which is also the default value to be tested in most computer software packages. But why do we care about 0? Why not other values? Either rejecting or retaining the hypothesis, does it really matter for answering our research question?

Here is how the test is done. Suppose we are interested in the proportion of all adults in a country who support a certain candidate for a political office. This will be our population parameter P. What does it look like? If we simply want to estimate its value, we should construct a confidence interval. Suppose, however – and this is very important – that there is a specific number that we are very interested in, say 0.45. Perhaps that was the proportion in the previous year, so we are interested in whether this year's figure will be larger than that. Or, perhaps a politician told us that if the proportion was higher than 0.45, then he could use it as an evidence for passing a bill. In short, we must say why we care about that number.

Our objective is to know how likely that this hypothesis – the proportion of adults supporting the policy is larger than 0.45 – is correct. Again, we have no other choice but to carry out a sample survey. Suppose the proportion calculated from the sample data p is 0.41. We may be a bit frustrated because it is smaller rather than larger than 0.45. Conversely, we do not want to say that this particular result is useless; otherwise, why did we produce it in the first place? In the end, the question is: how shall we use the sample result to evaluate our hypothesis? It is very unlikely that they are exactly the same, but what does their difference tell us? Is the difference so big that it forces us to abandon our hypothesis, or is it the case that our hypothesis is actually right but the sample result happens to be smaller due to sampling variation?

To avoid such difficult questions, it would be very tempting to test the hypothesis that the population parameter is equal to the sample value. For this example, we might want to hypothesize that it is equal to 0.41. That is not acceptable because it is cheating to change the hypothesis when the data point to another hypothesis; we must stick to the original hypothesis and make a judgement no matter what the sample result is. It is 0.45, not 0.41, that is *politically important*. Besides, what is the point of test something that you already know?

Before doing the test, we must clearly record our hypotheses. There are two of them: the null and the alternative. The null hypothesis states that a population parameter is equal to a specific value. The alternative hypothesis can take one of three possible forms: the parameter is not equal to, smaller than or larger than that value. A test for the first form is called a two-way test because it goes in both directions. A test for the other two forms is called a one-way test as it points to a specific direction. Which we choose depends on our research interest. Statisticians, however, suggest that we should avoid a one-way test (van Belle, 2002: 15) or only use it after a two-way test, because a one-way test is a specific situation of the two-way test, and it is hard to justify the one-way test without first getting the confirmation from the two-way test.

What we will test is the null hypothesis, not the alternative. The alternative is there only to show what the statement would be if the null is rejected. For people who encounter test of hypothesis for the first time, this is puzzling because the null hypothesis may not be the one that we are interested in. For the above example, the alternative hypothesis would be that the proportion of adults supporting that policy is larger than or at least not equal to 0.45, but the null hypothesis has to be that the proportion is equal to 0.45.

This is because it is very hard, if not impossible, to directly test the hypothesis of our interest. For a hypothesis to be testable, it must have an exact value and a probability distribution to allow the calculation of a probability. The alternative does not satisfy these requirements. This also shows the idea of *proof by contradiction*: it is much easier to show evidence contradictory to no effect than to the presence of an effect.

The next question is: what can we say about P based on our sample estimate p? Here, we must be very clear about the logic because this is where confusions arise and many mistaken statements are made. Although the whole procedure is called 'test of hypothesis', we cannot decide on whether the null hypothesis is right or wrong based on the result from a sample, because the sample is only part of the population and the results may change if we draw another sample. It would be sensible, however, if we reverse the direction of the inference. That is, we move from the population to the sample data, saying: suppose the null hypothesis is right, what result should we expect from a sample? Such a change of inferential direction is very important because it will affect what we can say later on.

Essentially, we are trying to compare the sample result with the value held by the null hypothesis based on the probability distribution supported by the null hypothesis. The statistic that we use for comparing the two values is called 'the test statistic', which is usually the difference between the two values standardized by the sample error:

$$\text{Test statistic} = \frac{\text{Sample value} - \text{hypothesized value}}{\text{Standard error}} \tag{5.9}$$

For testing a hypothesis about a proportion, the test statistic will be:

$$z = \frac{P - \pi}{\sqrt{\frac{P(1-P)}{n}}} \tag{5.10}$$

If the null hypothesis is about a mean, then the test statistic will be:[14]

$$z = \frac{\overline{X} - \mu}{se} \tag{5.11}$$

The value of the test statistic can then be used for finding out the probability that the sample values should be at and beyond the magnitude of the observed sample value. Such probability is the *p*-value in hypothesis testing. This can be done because we assume that the test statistic follows that particular distribution, and the distribution can show the probability.

The logic is that, as the *p*-value is the probability of observing the sample estimate when the null hypothesis is right, if the *p*-value is very small, then the result

---

[14]Originally, this should be a *t* test (replacing the *z* with *t*) as the distribution of the test statistic is not exactly a normal distribution. However, the two distributions are almost the same when the sample size *n* is large (more than 100). As this is normally the case for social sciences, there is no need to always distinguish between the two.

undermines the credibility of the null hypothesis, because the observed sample result is far too different from the result when the null hypothesis is correct. How small is small? Here is where an arbitrary threshold comes in, which is called 'the significance level', usually set at 0.01, 0.05 or 0.1. It must be set up before the test starts; otherwise, the whole point of testing is lost.

Some people find this probabilistic interpretation not only cumbersome but hard to keep in mind, even when they accept it as the right interpretation. The problem is that it is much easier to think in deterministic terms, which is why words such as 'accept' and 'reject' are so popularly used. That is, if the p-value is smaller than the significance level, the null hypothesis is rejected; if it is larger, accepted. Even lecturers teaching statistics use these words so that their students can easily remember them and use them in homework assignments and exams. Those statements tend to make a firm, deterministic and final judgement on whether the null hypothesis is true – we reject it because it is false or we accept it because it is true.

The fact is, we can never know whether it is true or false based on the sample result. When the p-value is smaller than the significance level, all we can say is the following: the probability that we would observe the sample result given the null hypothesis is true is smaller than the probability that we set up before the test. In this sense, it should become clear that what we can learn from hypothesis testing is very limited.

When conducting statistical inference, we can either construct a confidence interval or test a hypothesis. The reason for making a particular choice is straightforward: when we have no idea of the magnitude of the population parameter and simply want to estimate it, a confidence interval will help. When we do have an idea of its magnitude and want to know how likely the sample data would support us to use this value as an estimate of the population parameter, we will test that idea.

Are they equally important for social research? The answer from David Knoke and his colleagues is no:

> Although hypothesis testing has a long tradition in the social sciences, we strongly believe that *estimation is much more useful and important than hypothesis testing*, because virtually any statistical hypothesis can be rejected by simply choosing a large enough sample size. (2002: 100, emphasis original)

I think there are two other reasons for urging more frequent use of confidence interval than hypothesis testing. First of all, social researchers should concern themselves more with the precision of their measurements of social phenomena, which are of enormous importance for the development of social theories and social policies. It is very hard for social sciences to earn any respect without being able to provide such reliable measurements.

Second, the hypotheses tested in social science publications are overwhelmingly too simple to be really sensible or useful, and there has been too much emphasis on the statistical significance of such tests. For example, most hypotheses state that the interested value is 0, and it is rare that a more informed and exact value is tested.

Unless the value 0 is indeed very important in a particular context or has a strong theoretical bearing, it does not matter very much whether the hypothesis is rejected or not: if it is very unlikely to be 0, then what is it? When we test the hypothesis that the coefficient of a variable in a statistical model is 0, even if the results show that very unlikely it is 0, does that mean we should take it seriously in practice? Or, if the chance that it is 0 is larger than the predetermined 0.05, shall we throw away that variable? All these difficult questions indicate the weak connection between statistical analysis and theory in social research.

SIX

Studying the Relationship between Two Variables

The relationship of two variables, say X and Y, involves several aspects. First, *direction*, i.e. whether one variable comes at least analytically a priori – as a predictor or a cause – to the other. If we do not have any knowledge or theory about such direction, then we must treat the relationship as symmetrical; accordingly, our analysis focuses on the association (or correlation) only.[1] If we do have an interest in the direction, then we can use regression models. This explains why there are two parts in this chapter.

The correlation of two variables can be studied with regard to its *presence* (whether there is a relationship), *strength* (how strong the relationship is) and *sign* (whether the relationship is positive or negative). Not all statistics can inform us about all three aspects. Sometimes, a statistic can only be used as a piece of supporting evidence for the presence of the association. The results can only tell us the probability that the observed association is purely a consequence of chance, and nothing more.

Regression can *never suggest or confirm* the causal relationship of the two variables; it is *only a mathematical representation* of our theory about such causal connection.

---

[1]Here, we use the words 'correlation', 'association', 'connection' or 'link' interchangeably.

Different methods should be applied with respect to the level of measurement of the variables. When both variables are continuous, it is appropriate to employ simple linear regression. When the response variable (the target of explanation) is continuous while the explanatory variable (the predictor or the believed cause) is categorical, we use analysis of variance (ANOVA). When the response variable is categorical, a logistic regression model is the most useful, regardless of the explanatory variable's level of measurement.

PART 1 ASSOCIATIONAL ANALYSIS

Two Continuous Variables

By 'the association of two continuous variables' we refer to the regularity (or irregularity) with regard to the paired values of the two variables: when one variable's value goes in a particular direction, does the other go in the same direction, the opposite direction or no direction at all? If there is no regularity at all, then we cannot say anything about the change of one variable's values based on that of the other. If there is regularity, it will come in different shapes: values of both variables go in the same direction; values of one variable go up while those of the other come down; the differences of one variable's values get larger and larger with the increase of another variable's values and so forth.

The most efficient way of examining the situation is to produce a scatter plot. A dot in the plot represents a case carrying the respective values from the two variables. By mapping all the cases on a same space we can easily see whether a certain kind of regularity emerges (see the examples below).

The numerical method for analysing such regularity is the correlation coefficient (usually presented by r), which takes a value in the range of -1 to $+1$:

- If it is -1, then the two variables have a perfect negative relationship; that is, when one variable increases, the other decreases, and we can know exactly what one variable's value will be if we know the value of the other variable.
- We have the opposite situation if r equals $+1$, the positive one-to-one corresponding relationship.
- If it is 0, then the two variables have no relations at all – we cannot make a reasonable guess of what value one variable will take given the value of the other variable, no matter in which direction.

When analysing real data, the r is usually a decimal number between 0 and -1 or between 0 and $+1$. The sign indicates the direction of the relationship while the absolute value shows the strength of the relationship.

Graphically, the relationship between two variables can be presented with a scatter plot, a two-dimensional space with each variable being one dimension. The scatter plots in Figure 6.1 show the connection between the value of r and the shape of the relationship (Moore and MaCabe, 2006: 126).

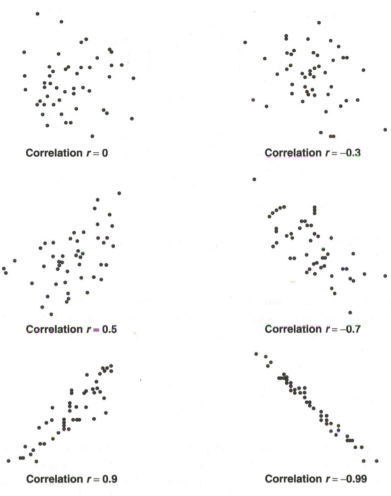

Figure 6.1   Relationship between *r* and scatter plot

Source: Introduction to the Practice of Statistics, Fifth Edition © 2005 W.H. Freeman and Company.

How does the *r* work in measuring the relationship of two continuous variables? The key here is to capture the movement of one variable's values given the movement of the other variable's values. An effective way of showing the idea of correlation is to break the two-dimensional space into four sections with the two reference lines $Y = \bar{Y}$ and $X = \bar{X}$, as shown in Figure 6.2 (Chatterjee et al., 2000: 22).

With this graph, we can examine the relationship between two continuous variables by looking at which sections the cases are located in: if most of them are in (1) and (3), then we shall see a positive relationship like the scatter plots with $r = 0.3$, 0.5 or 0.9 in Figure 6.1; if most of them are in (2) and (4) like the scatter plots with $r = -0.3$, -0.7 or -0.99 in Figure 6.1, then there will be a negative relationship; and if they are distributed about evenly across all four sections, then there will be no relationship, shown in the scatter plot with $r = 0$ in Figure 6.1.

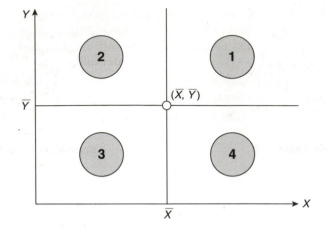

Figure 6.2   Correlation in four sections of a two-dimensional space

Note the reference point $(\overline{X}, \overline{Y})$ of the two means. In effect, the correlation of the two variables is measured by how the values move away from the means. This is exactly the idea of the covariance, a first step of producing the correlation coefficient:

$$Cov(Y,X) = \frac{\sum\limits_{i=1}^{n}(y_i - \overline{y})(x_i - \overline{x})}{n - 1} \tag{6.1}$$

It says that the covariance of X and Y is the sum of the products of the distances between values of Y and its mean and the distances between values of X and its mean, virtually standardized by the sample size. The mean therefore serves as a reference of their movements. The closer one variable follows the other, the stronger the correlation. The products of the two distances can represent the relationship because the sign of the products indicates which sections of the graph in Figure 6.2 the cases are located, thus suggesting the sign of the correlation. We need to neutralize the effect of the sample size as values in larger samples tend to be more varied than those in smaller ones.

For measuring the relationship between two continuous variables, the correlation coefficient is preferred to the covariance because it is not sensitive to the unit of measurement:

$$Cor(Y,X) = \frac{1}{n - 1}\sum_{i=1}^{n}\left(\frac{y_i - \overline{y}}{s_y}\right)\left(\frac{x_i - \overline{x}}{s_x}\right) \tag{6.2}$$

in which s_y and s_x are the standard deviation of Y and X, respectively. For example, the value of covariance will be different if we change the units of the two variables from year to month or from the US dollar to the British pound. Rarely are we actually interested in these units; it is the relationship that we are genuinely interested in. To get rid of the effect of different units, the covariance is standardized by the product of the two variables' standard deviations; therefore, the units in the numerator and the denominator cancel out.

Keep the following points in mind when using the correlation coefficient. First, it represents only a *linear* relationship, i.e. a relationship that can be represented with a *straight* line in a scatter plot. There are many situations in which the two variables are tightly related to each other but the relationship cannot be represented with a straight line, such as a curve line, a cycle or any other shape. In other words, while a correlation coefficient close to −1 or +1 indicates a strong association, two strongly associated variables may have a correlation coefficient close to 0 *if they are related in a nonlinear manner*. Put in another way: a coefficient close to 0 does not necessarily mean that the two variables are not correlated at all; they may not be correlated, or they may be correlated in a way different from a straight line.

Second, like the mean, the r is sensitive to extreme values as well. It is always wise to examine the distribution of each variable and the scatter plot before producing and interpreting the correlation coefficient.

Third, the magnitude and the statistical significance of the correlation coefficient (actually, all sample statistics) are two different things, and one does not necessarily have anything to do with the other. This means that a large r (close to either −1 or +1) may or may not be statistically significant; that is, the probability that the coefficient *in the population* equals 0 may remain higher than we expect even if the coefficient calculated *from a sample* is quite large. Conversely, a small sample coefficient may be statistically significant; that is, even if the sample coefficient is close to 0, we may not have enough evidence for rejecting the hypothesis that the population coefficient is 0. Therefore, 'it should also be borne firmly in mind that rejection of the null hypothesis simply tells us that the population value is not zero, and tells us nothing about either its actual value or its practical importance' (Krzanowski, 2007: 167).

Two Nominal Variables

Method 1: The Chi-square Test

Before discussing the details of this method, it is necessary to know the basic components of a table.[2] We use r to refer to the number of rows and c the number of columns, and it is a convention to let r go before c. For example, a 2 × 2 table has two rows, two columns and four cells. When the values of the same row or the same column are added up, we have the row or column totals (or 'marginal totals'). Further, the sum of

---

[2]A commonly used term is 'contingency table', but note that not all tables are contingency tables. In a contingency table, every case belongs to one and only one cell and all cell counts must add up to the total number of cases. Not all tables satisfy this requirement.

all row or column totals is the grand total. Put together, for a 2 × 2 table, we have the following notations (see Table 6.1).

Table 6.1   A generic 2 × 2 table

		Variable 2		
		Category 1	Category 2	Row total O_{1+}
Variable 1	Category 1	O_{11}	O_{12}	O_{1+}
	Category 2	O_{21}	O_{22}	O_{2+}
Column total O_{+j}		O_{+1}	O_{+2}	Grand total O_{++}

We use the letter O to indicate that the numbers are *observed* frequencies, i.e. the number of cases with those particular categories, as opposed to *expected* frequencies to be discussed below. There are two subscripts for each frequency: the first one indicates the number of row and the second the number of column. For example, O_{21} is the observed frequency in the cell at the intersection of the second row and the first column. For row marginal totals (O_{1+} and O_{2+}), the first subscript remains the same while the + sign indicates the sum of the frequencies across columns in the same row. The reverse is true for the column marginal totals. Subscripts of the grand total are ++ as it adds up the frequencies across both rows and columns. These notations can be extended to a table with more rows and columns.[3]

How shall we analyse the relationship between the two variables in such table? Or, what numerical evidence shall lead us to conclude that there is (or is not) a relationship between the two variables? One important strategy of statistical reasoning is to set up a threshold against which the observed data will be analysed, with the threshold representing a hypothesis, a reference point or a theory. By comparing and measuring the difference between the data and the threshold, we can conclude whether the data support the hypothesis.

What is that threshold? If we are to use the data to show any relationship of the two variables, then the threshold should be no relationship so that how far away the data are from such 'null situation' will indicate the chance of relationship. But what should the null situation (no relationship) look like?

Let us take a concrete example. Suppose we are interested in the relationship between gender and smoking. Assume smoking has two categories, 'smoking' and 'non-smoking', we shall have a 2 × 2 table. Suppose that there are 100 respondents, how would we put them in a table if there is no relationship between gender and smoking? The answer is, 100/4 = 25 in each cell.[4]

Why do the same frequencies indicate no relationship? The logic is that if there is a relationship, then it must make a difference; as there is no difference across the categories, there must be no relationship.

Another way of deriving the 25 is to use the marginal totals: there are 50 females and 50 males, and there are 50 smokers and 50 non-smokers (evenly distributed

---

[3]The rows and columns are also referred to as the dimensions of a table. Thus, a table with three or more rows and columns is usually called 'a higher dimension table'.
[4]Remember that the 4 is the product of r and c (the number of rows and columns, respectively).

because of no relationship). For the cell of female smokers, the frequency would be $(50 \times 50)/100$, i.e. 25. By the same logic, all other cells have the same number. It is called 'the expected frequency' under the assumption of no relationship.

The idea of the chi-square test is to measure the distance between the expected frequencies and the actually observed frequencies. The distance will then be taken for evaluating the probability of an existing relationship:

$$\chi^2 = \sum_{i=1}^{r} \sum_{j=1}^{c} \frac{(E_{ij} - O_{ij})^2}{E_{ij}} \qquad (6.3)$$

In (6.3), the numerator – the difference between the expected frequency E_{ij} and the observed frequency O_{ij} – reflects such idea.[5] We have to square the distance up so that negative and positive distances will not cancel each other out when we add them up. We also need to standardize the distance by the expected frequency as the distances may vary according to the size of the expected frequency, which is a mathematical rather than conceptual consideration.

A subtle and easily overlooked feature of the chi-square statistic is that it depends on not only the expected and the observed frequencies but also the size of the contingency table, i.e. the number of rows and columns (represented by i and j, respectively). To see its effect, compare the above 2×2 table with a 3×3 table. The number of rows and columns has increased from 2 to 3, but the total number of cells has increased more dramatically from 4 to 9, more than doubled! If the grand total remains 100, then the expected frequency in the 3×3 table would be a bit more than 11 (100/9), less than half of the 25 in the 2×2 table. Statisticians use 'the degrees of freedom' (*df*), here equal to $(r-1)(c-1)$, to reflect such effect. The 1 is taken away because the frequency of the last cell in a row or a column can be determined by subtracting the sum of all other frequencies from the row (or the column) total.

Imagine what would happen if r and c get bigger and bigger. The total number of cells will increase multiplicatively! For example, a 10×10 table will have 100 cells. For a given grand total, which is usually the sample size, the data will look increasingly sparse – some cells have very few cases or even no cases at all. For those cells, the chi-square is not so effective anymore since there is not much information for it to capture. In addition, as the expected frequency is the denominator, it would be meaningless when it turns out to be 0 (no cases at all). This is why a condition is usually imposed on the use of the chi-square test: if more than 5% of the expected frequencies are smaller than 5, then those sparse categories need to be combined together to generate larger frequencies.

How large does the sum of the distances between the expected and the observed frequencies have to be to show a relationship between the two nominal variables? We obtain the probability of no relationship, or the *p*-value, by comparing the chi-square value that we calculated from the data with a threshold based

---

[5]The two big sigma signs mean adding up all the squares of the distances divided by the expected frequency.

on the theoretical chi-square distribution. Given the distance between the two frequencies, a corresponding p-value shows the probability that the relationship of the two variables is by chance (that is, no genuine relationship).

Note that, neither the chi-square value nor its p-value *directly* measures the *strength* of the relationship, as some have claimed.[6] Although a large chi-square value or a corresponding very small p-value (less than 0.05 in common practice) will lead to evidence of stronger relationship, it is *not a direct measurement of the relationship's strength by itself*. Rather, it is a measurement of *the strength of the evidence* against the null hypothesis of no relationship. In other words, it provides the evidence for *the presence, not the strength*, of the two variable's relationship. This is a major drawback of the chi-square test, which does not provide a direct indication of how strong the relationship is.

Another important limitation is that it does not tell us where the relationship exists when the probability of non-relationship is below the predetermined threshold (or significance level). This is the situation especially for relatively larger tables, in which some cells may provide most of the differences between the observed and the expected values while others contribute very little. As an *overall* measurement, the chi-square value does not reveal the uneven distribution of influence among the cells. Therefore, we should not stop analysing the table even when the relationship is statistically significant. Further examination of the table is needed in order to find out which cells are the major sources of evidence, and these cells will give us a better idea of where the relationship comes from.

Method 2: The Odds Ratio

Statisticians have created several indicators of the strength of the two nominal variables' relationship, such as *Yule's* Q and *Phi*. However, I believe we should concentrate our discussion on another statistic: the odds ratio.[7] Two reasons follow. First, *Yule's* Q and *Phi* do not have any particular advantage over the odds ratio. Second, the odds ratio is applicable to larger tables and constitutes a foundation for statistical models on categorical response variables, including the logistic regression and log-linear models.

Let us take the example of the relationship between identity and ethnicity in Britain. In *Living in Britain*, a report produced by the UK's Office of National Statistics (Walker et al., 2002: 24) based on the 2001 General Household Survey, we can find the percentages of people over 16-years-old who identify themselves as British or otherwise by their ethnicity (to facilitate the following discussion I have calculated the absolute numbers as well (see Figure 6.2)).

---

[6]For a most recent example, Krzanowski claims that 'Any departure from independence is then deemed to indicate association, and the greater the departure the stronger is this association' (2007: 169).
[7]Readers who would like to learn *Yule's* Q and *Phi* can consult, for example, Chapter 5 of Knoke et al. (2002).

Table 6.2 British identity and ethnicity

	White	Ethnic minority	Row total
British only	4,437 (29%)	602 (51%)	5,039
Others	10,862 (71%)	579 (49%)	11,441
Column total	15,299	1,181	16,480

Is there any relationship between British identify and ethnicity? To see the benefit of using an odds ratio, let us study the relationship by, first, carrying out a chi-square statistic, which is 249.34 with $(2–1) * (2–1) = 1$ degrees of freedom. The corresponding p-value is smaller than 0.001, much smaller than the usual threshold of 0.05, indicating an extremely low probability of no relationship.

In generic terms, the odds of having an attribute are defined as follows:

$$\text{Odds} = \frac{\text{Probability of having the attribute}}{\text{Probability of not having the attribute}} \tag{6.4}$$

In our example, the attribute of interest is the British identity, and the probability is measured by the proportion of people who have identified themselves as British only. Here, we have two groups, white and non-white; therefore, we have two odds, one for each ethnic group:

$$Odds_W = \frac{0.29}{0.71} = 0.41$$

$$Odds_{EM} = \frac{0.51}{0.49} = 1.04$$

For the whites, the probability of identifying themselves as British only is 41% of the probability of not doing so. For non-whites, that increases to 104%. These numbers provide us with a sense of the connection between the two attributes, but we are still short of an exact measurement of the strength of their relationship, because we are still looking at the probabilities separately for each ethnic group. The idea of the odds ratio, usually represented with the Greek letter θ (theta), is to use the ratio of the two odds as a way of connecting the two variables together:

$$\theta = \frac{Odds1}{Odds2} \tag{6.5}$$

For our example, $\theta = 0.41/1.04 = 0.39$, which means that the odds of identifying as British only *by the whites* is only 39% of the odds by non-whites. By measuring the relative size of the odds, the odds ratio offers us a single indicator of the strength of the two variables' relationship.

Does 0.39 suggest a strong relationship? To answer, we need to have an idea of the range of values that an odds ratio can take. Because all the numbers needed for calculating an odds ratio are positive proportions, an odds ratio is always positive. Therefore, we cannot tell the direction of the relationship based on the sign of an odds ratio, as we can with a correlation coefficient. Furthermore, as a ratio, an odds ratio can never be exactly 0 for representing no relationship. Rather, it is the number 1 that indicates no relationship.

To see that, use Table 6.1 again:

$$Odds1 = \frac{O_{11}}{O_{21}}$$

$$Odds2 = \frac{O_{12}}{O_{22}}$$

Therefore,

$$\theta = \frac{O_{11}/O_{21}}{O_{12}/O_{22}} = \frac{O_{11}O_{22}}{O_{12}O_{21}}$$

When all the four frequencies are the same, θ will equal to 1. But recall from the previous discussion that if the frequencies are the same, then there is no evidence of any relationship. This is why the reference point of no relationship is 1, and the further away it is from 1 – in the direction of either approaching 0 or approaching the positive infinity – the stronger the relationship will be. Which way it moves from 1 depends on how the variable categories are arranged in the table. For example, if we swap the positions of 'British only' and 'Others' while still keep the categories of ethnicity, then the odds will be:

$$Odds_W = \frac{0.71}{0.29} = 2.45$$

$$Odds_{EM} = \frac{0.49}{0.51} = 0.96$$

And the odds ratio will change to $\theta = 2.45/0.96 = 2.56$, which is exactly the inverse of the previous odds ratio 0.39, because we have reversed the positions of the categories. Our interpretation needs to be reversed too: the odds of non-whites identifying themselves as British only are about two and half times the odds of whites doing the same.

As we did for correlation coefficient, we can also test the hypothesis of no relationship on the odds ratio. There are two differences though. First, the null hypothesis is that the odds ratio in the population is 1 rather than 0. More importantly, the odds ratio does not follow a normal distribution, so we cannot use the formula for calculating the standard deviation for the normal distribution. Statisticians have created a special way of inferring for the odds ratio. There is no need to go into the details here, however, as computer packages will automatically report relevant statistics.

Two Ordinal Variables

The statistics for measuring the strength of the association between two ordinal variables must capture the ranking order of the values. The idea is to compare a pair of cases with regard to their values for the two variables and see whether their values point to the same direction. If they do, then these cases are called 'concordant pairs'. The more such cases there are, the more positively correlated the two variables are. Conversely, if there are many cases whose values point in the opposite directions – called 'disconcordant pairs', then the two variables are negatively correlated. If the number of cases moving in the same direction is about the same as the number of cases moving in the opposite directions, then the two variables are not really correlated.

Suppose we have two ordinal variables, X and Y, each having three ordered categories, 1, 2 and 3, representing values from the lowest to the highest. We can then organize the information in a 3×3 table (see Table 6.3).

Table 6.3   A generic 3×3 table of two ordinal variables

		Y		
		1	2	3
X	1	a	b	c
	2	d	e	f
	3	g	h	i

The letters (from a to i) in the table represent the observed number of cases. How many concordant and disconcordant pairs are there, respectively? The cases in any particular cell have the same value on X or Y, for example, there are d number of cases that carries the same value of 2 on X and the same value of 1 on Y, so any pair of cases from that cell are neither concordant nor disconcordant. To find a pair of either concordant or disconcordant pair, we have to choose two cases from two difference cells, respectively.

Let us focus on concordant pairs first. As for these pairs one case's values are higher than those of the other on both X and Y, we will not find them in cells in the same row or column because they have the same value either on X or Y. Therefore, starting with cell a, we know that only cases in cells e, f, h and i can form concordant pairs with those in cell a.

Moving on to cell b, it is clear that only the cases in cells f and i will form concordant pairs with those in b. Cases in a, c, e and h have the same value with those in b either on X (a and c) or Y (e and h). Cases in d and g do not form concordant pairs with those in b because they have higher values on X but lower values on Y. We cannot find any pairs for cases in c, f, g, h and i because no other cells have cases with higher values.

Following the same logic, we have the total number of concordant pairs as follows: $a(e + f + h + i) + b(f + i) + d(h + i) + e * i$. Moving in the opposite direction, we can find the total number of disconcordant pairs: $c(d + e + g + h) + b(d + g) + f(g + h) + e * g$.

It is clear that the total number of either type of pairs depends not only on the frequencies but also the number of rows and columns.

Method 1: Gamma

The idea of *Gamma* is to examine how many more pairs of concordant pairs than disconcordant pairs of all these pairs:

$$G = \frac{n_c - n_d}{n_c + n_d} \tag{6.6}$$

where n_c is the total number of concordant pairs and n_d is the total number of disconcordant pairs.[8]

Similar to the correlation coefficient, this statistic has the range of −1 to +1. When $n_d = 0$ (there are no disconcordant pairs), $G = n_c/n_c = 1$; that is, all pairs are concordant or have values moving in the same direction, so the association is perfectly positive. In the opposite situation, when $n_c = 0$ (there are no concordant pairs), $G = -n_d/n_d = -1$, the association is perfectly negative. When $n_c = n_d$, we have half of the pairs concordant and the other half disconcordant, indicating the lack of overall direction, hence $G = 0$.

Method 2: Tau c

This statistic was invented by Sir Maurice George Kendall (1907–1983), thus usually known as *Kendall's tau*. Actually, there are three of them, *a*, *b* and *c*, all for measuring the association of two ordinal variables. *Tau a* does not adjust for the number of tied pairs (pairs that are neither concordant nor disconcordant), *tau b* does this adjustment but for a square table (there are same number of rows and columns), and *tau c* is the most flexible, adjusting the number of tied pairs and suitable for rectangle tables, which is why it is the most popular:

$$\tau_c = (n_c - n_d)\frac{2m}{n^2(m-1)} \tag{6.7}$$

where m = the smaller of r (rows) or c (columns) and n is the sample size.

The first part of the right-hand side of the equation clearly suggests that *tau c* is also based on the difference between the number of concordant pairs. But why $\frac{2m}{n^2(m-1)}$? Like *Gamma*, we would expect a denominator so that we can see the relative size of $(n_c - n_d)$, but the current denominator $n^2(m-1)$ is puzzling. The answers is that the denominator has been transformed. Originally, it was $\binom{n}{2} = \frac{n(n-1)}{2}$, which is the total number of all possible pairs of cases.[9] So,

---

[8]We can exchange the positions of these two numbers, but then the meaning of Gamma will be reversed.

[9]This comes from the following derivation: $\binom{n}{2} = \frac{n!}{(n-2)!2!} = \frac{n(n-1)(n-2)!}{(n-2)!2!} = \frac{n(n-1)}{2}$.

$\frac{(n_c - n_d)}{\frac{n(n-1)}{2}}$ is the proportion of the difference between concordant and disconcordant pairs out of all pairs of cases. The two will flip over to join the numerator. We should retain $n(n-1)$, but as most of the times n is quite large, so it is all right to replace $n(n-1)$ with n^2. Now we have $(n_c - n_d)\frac{2}{n^2}$. Finally, $\frac{m}{(m-1)}$ is used to adjust

the effect of the table's size. It is more liberal to use the smaller instead of the larger out of the row and the column numbers because $\frac{m}{(m-1)}$ will be larger.

Like *Gamma*, the value of *tau c* ranges from −1 to +1. It is important to note, however, that because *tau c* uses all possible pairs as the denominator, which is almost always larger than the denominator of *Gamma*, $n_c + n_d$, the absolute value of *tau c* is always smaller than *Gamma* for a particular table. It is therefore inappropriate to make any direct comparison between *tau c* and *Gamma* when analysing two ordinal variables, even more inappropriate to choose a particular statistics purposefully in order to show a stronger or weaker association.

To illustrate, take the example of the relationship between social life and positive feeling about life, two variables from Round 3 of the European Social Survey (2006). 'Social life' is measured by the frequency of socially meeting with friends, relatives, or colleagues, and it has seven ordered values: 'never', 'less than once a month', 'once a month', 'several times a month', 'once a week', 'several times a week' and 'everyday'. For feeling about life, respondents were asked to rate their agreement with the statement 'I feel what I do in life is valuable and worthwhile' by choosing one of the following ordered categories: 'agree strongly', 'agree', 'neither agree nor disagree', 'disagree' or 'strongly disagree'.

Measuring the strength of this relationship, *Tau c* is −0.054, whose absolute value is smaller than the *Gamma* value of −0.093. Substantively, it suggests that people more frequently being social with others are more likely to feel positive about their life, although the relationship seems to be quite weak.

PART 2 REGRESSION ANALYSIS

We now consider the situation in which the relationship between two variables has a direction. Such directional relationship is more appealing as it denotes a sense of explaining power. Keep in mind, however, that that is a theoretical matter and the statistical models discussed below can only represent, or perhaps support, but cannot prove the directed relationship.

Simple Linear Regression

Now, let us take a closer look at the simple linear regression model:

$$Y = \beta_0 + \beta_1 X + \varepsilon \tag{6.9}$$

This equation is for the population and you can tell from the use of Greek letters; if it is for sample data, the custom is to use English letters a and b to replace β_0 and β_1, respectively. In this equation, the effect of X is directly represented by its coefficient, β_1 which can be interpreted as the change of Y given one unit change of X. β_0 is the baseline value (or the constant), the value of Y when $X = 0$. If $\beta_0 = 0$, then the line goes through the point where both X and Y are 0, and a regression model with $\beta_0 = 0$ is called 'regression through the origin' as it goes through the origin $(0, 0)$. Because our main interest lies in the effect of X on Y, we are much more interested in the value of β_1 than in β_0.

The last term ε (epsilon) is very important because it embodies the underlying idea and the assumptions of this statistical model, although it is not directly shown in a model on sample data. Without the error term, the model becomes $Y = \beta_0 + \beta_1 X$, which says that we can make a 100% accurate prediction of Y as long as we know the values of all three terms on the right-hand side. If that is true, then all the points in a scatter plot will fall onto the straight line that corresponds to that equation. Unfortunately, data from probability surveys are almost never so clean and tidy. We would be very satisfied if we can see any general pattern. In reality, we cannot predict the exact value of Y based on X. There are always discrepancies between our predictions and the actual values of Y, and this is why ε is needed and referred to as 'the error term'. To a large extent, the whole business of regression analysis is about *minimizing the error terms without paying the unbearable cost of systematically misrepresenting the pattern in the data.*

Before learning how the above objective is achieved, we need to understand some basic terms. Every word in 'simple linear regression' has a specific meaning. It is 'simple' because there is only one explanatory variable. Next, 'linear' means that the parameters (in this case, β_0 and β_1) come into the equation 'linearly', i.e. they are not involved in any expression for curved lines, such as the power, exponential or log functions. For example, $Y = \beta_0 + (\log\beta_1)X + \varepsilon$ is not a linear model because β_1 is in a logarithm function. Such 'nonlinear models' are rarely used in the social sciences. But the model will remain linear even when the explanatory variable is in a curve linear function. That is, $Y = \beta_0 + \beta_1 \log X + \varepsilon$, is a linear model because the parameters are not in the log function. Models like this remain linear as we can replace the nonlinear part with another explanatory variable. For this example, by defining $X_2 = \log X$, we have $Y = \beta_0 + \beta_1 X_2 + \varepsilon$, which is still a linear model. In contrast, for the model $Y = \beta_0 + (\log \beta_1)X + \varepsilon$, replacing X cannot make the model linear since the nonlinear function of the parameter β_1 is always there.

The meaning of 'regression' is rather complicated, although many people know the term 'regression toward the mediocrity', coined by Francis Galton in the late 1880s. Originally, it was referred to the movement of the response variable's extreme values toward the mean after taking into account of the explanatory variable. Later, its meaning was generalized to the following question: if we want to find a straight line that can capture the relationship of two variables in a scatter plot, as there is more than one line that can do this, which one would be 'the best'? A reasonable criterion would be the difference between the predicted and the observed values. The smaller the difference, the better the performance of a model. This is the idea of 'the least square method', which aims to find the values of the regression coefficients (or the parameters) that will generate the smallest differences between the predicted values and the observed values of the response variable. How to achieve that is a purely mathematical matter, which we shall not go into here.

The above logic works only when the linearity assumption can hold, that is, it is reasonable to represent the relationship with a *straight* line. If this is not the case, then it is misleading to construct a simple linear regression model. Anscombe (1973) provided the most forceful illustration of this point. Although using some hypothetical data, he showed that the same regression line could represent very different relationships (Figure 6.3).

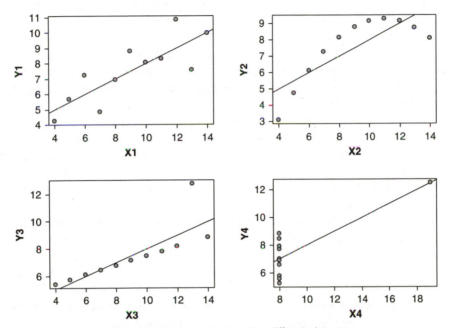

Figure 6.3   Anscombe's Quartet: Same regression line, different datasets

It cannot be clearer that *had we not checked the scatter plot and only produced the regression model, we could have been seriously mistaken.* The message to take home: always check the plot when using a linear regression model.

Once the estimated values of the coefficients are obtained, two more tasks remain making inference about the coefficients and checking the assumptions held by the model. We shall have more discussions on the second issue for multiple regression models. For simple linear regression, the main inference is to test the null hypothesis that the coefficient of the explanatory variable β_1 is 0. The routine is that if the *p*-value of the test score is below 0.05, we say that the coefficient is statistically significant; otherwise, it is not.

As pointed out before, what has been tested is an extremely modest claim, i.e. whether the explanatory variable has any effect *at all*. Shall we take a variable seriously as long as its effect is very unlikely to be 0? There is no universal answer to this question as it depends on the nature of the variable and our research question. It would be more useful if social researchers set up the value of the interested coefficient based on literature review or theories. However, this is rarely done because researchers do not have such a value in mind, or because they cannot agree on a particular value.

ANOVA

When the explanatory variable is categorical, it does not make sense to talk about one unit change of a categorical variable. We may say that the explanatory variable's coefficient indicates the change of the response variable when the explanatory variable changes from one category to another. The trouble with this interpretation is that very likely the response variable has many different values for a particular category, so it is very unclear what we mean by 'the change of the response variable'. What we can do is to compare *the means* of the response variable across all the categories.

Take the popular example of income (the response) and gender (the explanatory). Incomes among men or women are very different, so we cannot determine the change of income by the change of gender. Instead, it is meaningful to compare the change of *the means* of income across the two gender groups. If the means differ significantly (in statistical terms), then we have some evidence for the effect of the categorical explanatory variable.

This brings us to the central question about analysis of variance (ANOVA): to what extent can we contribute the difference of the means to the categories rather than to the difference within each category? In other words, both the difference within each group and the difference between the groups are responsible for the differences among the cases, how can we determine that it is the latter rather than the former that is at work? An exploratory and graphical method is to create box plots side by side, one for each category. Using the Round 3 data from the European Social Survey, I created a box plot for comparing the number of hours chosen to work between males and females in the UK (Figure 6.4).

These plots show that on average, men tend to choose longer hours of work, but the variation among them is much larger than that among women. However, they cannot tell us how probable that the difference between the two groups is due to chance rather than the categorical attributes.

The formal methods are numerical. If the explanatory variable has only two categories, then we can test the null hypothesis that the means of the two categories are the same. A major limitation of such test is that it does not take into account of the difference within each category, as such difference is concealed by the means. In addition, the test has to be on a pair of means. When the number of categories is three or more, it is impossible to carry out several tests simultaneously. The *F*-test in ANOVA can go beyond these limitations.

The idea of the *F*-test is to use the ratio of 'the between group difference' to 'the within group difference' as the basis for either rejecting or retaining the null

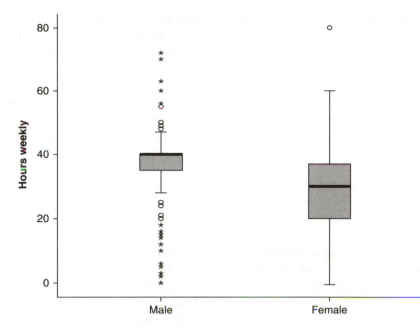

Figure 6.4 Difference between males and females in terms of the number of hours chosen to work, UK, 2006

hypothesis that it is chance rather than group membership that is responsible for the differences between the group means. As usual, we set up a threshold (the significance level, usually 0.05) and then calculate the test statistic from a particular set of data, which we shall explain below. Next, we put our sample statistic onto the theoretical distribution of the statistic to find out the probability of pure chance (the *p*-value). Finally, we make our decision by comparing the *p*-value and the significance level. Now let us examine the ANOVA table (Table 6.4).

Table 6.4 Components of the *F*-test

Source	Sum of squares (SS)	df	Mean sum of squares (MS = SS/df)	F
Between group	$SS_B = \sum_{j=1}^{J} n_j (\overline{Y}_j - \overline{Y})^2$	$J-1$	$MS_B = \sum_{j=1}^{J} n_j (\overline{Y}_j - \overline{Y})^2 / (J-1)$	MS_B / MS_W
Within group	$SS_W = \sum_{j=1}^{J} \sum_{i=1}^{n_j} (Y_{ij} - \overline{Y}_j)^2$	$N-J$	$MS_W = \sum_{j=1}^{J} \sum_{i=1}^{n_j} (Y_{ij} - \overline{Y}_j)^2 / (N-J)$	
Total	$SS_T = \sum_{j=1}^{J} \sum_{i=1}^{n_j} (Y_{ij} - \overline{Y})^2$	$N-1$		

Three numbers are involved: each case's score on the response variable, Y_{ij} (the subscripts indicate the *i*th case in the *j*th group), the mean of each group, $\overline{Y}_j$, and the grand mean, $\overline{Y}$. Our plan is to break up the total amount of difference between the cases, represented by SS_T, into two parts, one for between groups (SS_B) and the other for within groups (SS_W); that is, $SS_T = SS_B + SS_W$.

Starting with SS_B, as we did for the standard deviation and the variance, we measure the differences to a common reference point, i.e. the grand mean.[10] Similarly, for each group, we calculate the difference between each score and the group mean (and square them up), and add them up across the groups. The ratio SS_B/SS_W represents the between group differences relative to those within groups. However, SS_B is clearly influenced by the number of groups (J) and SS_W by the sample size (N). Therefore, we standardize the square of differences by the degrees of freedom, respectively to each statistic, giving us the mean sums of squares.

Finally, the F score is the ratio of the between group differences to the within group differences, refined by their respective degrees of freedom. Now it should be clear that the larger the F, the more the between group differences outweigh the within group differences, offering stronger evidence for the effect of group memberships, so the p-value will be smaller.

People can be grouped into different ethnic groups, regions, educational levels and so on, all of which may contribute to the differences of income among them, but we have only looked at gender. Similar to simple linear regression, where we use only one explanatory variable, the ANOVA we have learnt involves only one-way of grouping; hence the term 'one-way ANOVA'. When two or more categorical variables are included for studying a continuous response variable, our analysis will be multi-way or multiple analyses of variance. The basic logic, however, will remain the same.

Keep the following two important points in mind. First, the F-test is about comparing means; therefore, it is essential to check whether the response variable is about normally distributed for the whole sample *and for each group* as well. Second, like the chi-square, the F score is a summary statistic – look at how many sums it has done. As a result, we have to pay the price of losing all local information for the sake of obtaining an overall statistic. When we have many groups, the researcher should check out where the main differences lie after testing the null hypothesis of no group effect.

Simple Logistic Regression

The situation for simple logistic regression is the opposite to ANOVA: now the response variable Y is categorical and the explanatory variable X is metrical. This type of models are very useful for social research as most of the target phenomena are categorical variables, such as whether a crime was committed.

Initially, we can still use the model $Y = \beta_0 + \beta_1 X + \varepsilon$. But as X is metrical whilst Y is categorical, this model has one major difficulty: each X corresponds to predicted value of Y but Y has only a very limited number of observed values. For example, we want to know whether income can somehow predict whether people

---

[10]Again, the differences are squared up to avoid cancellation of negative and positive numbers, and the differences are weighted by the number of cases in each group, n_{ij}.

go to vote or not. Income as the predictor can take millions of values while there are only two possibilities for the response, yes or no. People earning very different incomes may do the same thing (vote or not vote), so we might produce many values about people's voting behaviour with our knowledge of people's income. Most of these produced values, however, do not make sense because there are only two sensible voting behaviours.

It is clear that some transformation has to be done. If we insist on having only two values for the response variable 'voting', then one strategy is to group all the values of the explanatory variable 'income' into two bands, say '$50,000 and under' and 'above $50,000'. Although the response variable will have only two possible predicted values now, the results still may not make sense because the two values may not be 1 or 0. That is, it will not be as clear as that people with income under $50K will not vote while those with an income above $50K will, because it is very unlikely that the right-hand side of the equation will happen to be exactly 0 or 1.

It is more sensible to move in the opposite direction, that is, to transform the response variable so that it will allow the explanatory variable to keep its metrical nature. In the meantime, the transformation should not obscure the interpretation of the coefficients. It is the statistician's job to strike a balance between these two demands, and they have proposed the following model:

$$\ln\left(\frac{\pi}{1-\pi}\right) = \beta_0 + \beta_1 X \tag{6.10}$$

Here, π is *the probability* of having a particular attribute (such as voting). Previously in this chapter we learnt that $\frac{\pi}{1-\pi}$ is the odds of having an attribute. Therefore, the right-hand side is the natural logarithm of the odds. This transformation satisfies the first demand of reflecting the continuous nature of the predictor, because $\ln\left(\frac{\pi}{1-\pi}\right)$ can take any value from the negative infinity to the positive infinity.

Moreover, this transformation reflects the curve-linear relationship between π and X. When solving for π, the above logistic regression model can be written as:

$$\pi = \frac{e^{\beta_0 + \beta_1 X}}{1 + e^{\beta_0 + \beta_1 X}} \tag{6.11}$$

where e is the base of natural logarithm (about 2.72). If we map out π and X in a graph, we will see the curve-linearity of their relationship. Similar to the simple linear regression, where the direction of relationship changes according to the sign of correlation or regression coefficient, there will be two curves, one is S-shaped when β_1 is positive and the other the mirror-image of the S-shape when is β_1 negative.[11]

The S (including the reverse-S) shape can capture the relationship between a continuous attribute and the probability of having a categorical attribute. For

---

[11]The Academic Technology Services at UCLA has produced an illustration at the following website of how the logistic regression curve changes with different values of the model's parameters: http://www.ats.ucla.edu/stat/sas/teach/grlog/grlog.htm (accessed 18 January 2009).

example, income and voting: the probability of going to vote stays very low for people of low incomes but increases considerably after a threshold of income and finally eases off for the very rich. *The rate of increase* of the probability is very low for both the very poor and the very rich, because none of them have strong motivation of participating in political elections, although their motivations may be very different. It is for the middle class that income has the most visible effect on getting them to vote. We can also formulate a theory or observe a relationship between a similar but negative relationship between income and the probability of divorce. Empirical research is needed to confirm such theories, of course.

For the second requirement of easy interpretation, the logistic model is not ideal. Following the logic of simple linear regression, we could β_1 interpret as the change of log odds with one unit change of X. Unfortunately, the meaning of log odds is far from clear.

Another option is to rewrite the model with the odds as the subject:

$$\frac{\pi}{1-\pi} = e^{\beta_0 + \beta_1 X} = e^{\beta_0}(e^{\beta_1})^X \tag{6.12}$$

Such transformation allows us to see the effect of one unit change of X on the odds. For example, when X changes from 0 to 1, the odds changes from e^{β_0} (when $X = 0$) to $e^{\beta_0}(e^{\beta_1})$ (when $X = 1$). That is, the odds changes by e^{β_1} *multiplicatively*. This remains unsatisfactory as it is still hard for most people to understand multiplicative effect.

The easiest, and therefore the most popular, interpretation is to use the odds ratio. Suppose X changes from a to b, let us see what the odds ratio will be. When $X = a$, $Odds_a\ e^{\beta_0}(e^{\beta_1})^a$, and when $X = b$, $Odds_b = e^{\beta_0}(e^{\beta_1})^b$. Therefore, the odds ratio is:

$$\frac{Odds_a}{Odds_b} = \frac{e^{\beta_0}(e^{\beta_1})^a}{e^{\beta_0}(e^{\beta_1})^b} = e^{\beta_1(a-b)}$$

This is better because we can relate the change of X to the odds ratio of whether Y has a particular attribute or not. For example, when $\beta_1 = 0$, then the odds ratio equals to 1, which means X has no effect at all.[12] Recall that an odds ratio of 1 indicates no relationship between two variables, the interpretation of the regression coefficient is consistent with the interpretation of odds ratio. For one unit change of X, say from 0 to 1, the odds ratio will be e^{β_1}; therefore, we do not have to interpret β_1 anymore. All we have to say is how many times (or percentages) the first odds (having the attribute, such as having voted or divorced) is of the second odds (not having the attribute, having never voted or divorced) given one unit change of X (for example, £1000 change of income).

---

[12]By algebraic definition, any number to the power of 0 is 1.

SEVEN

Linear Regression Models and Their Generalizations

Often social researchers are interested in the relationships of several variables in a single analysis. In this chapter, I account for the variation of one response variable with the added effects of a set of explanatory variables. Such distinction between the explanatory and the response will apply to all the models that I shall introduce below.[1] We shall start with the multiple linear regression models with one *metrical* response variable and two or more explanatory variables that can be *either metrical or categorical*. The model with all the variables being metrical will be taken as a reference.[2]

Then we generalize the above models in two directions. The first generalization is on the response variable, previously metrical but now categorical. It can be (1) 'binary', with only two possible values, such as yes or no, (2) 'multinominal', having three or more values with no ranking, such as marital status or (3) 'ordinal', having three or more ordered values, such as levels of agreement of a statement. Models dealing with these response variables come under the umbrella term 'logistic regression models'. Another special type of response variable is the count of observations, such as the number of events or observations in a contingency table. We

---

[1] 'Multivariate statistics' are statistical methods that study the relations among a group of variables without making such a distinction. We shall learn some of them in the following chapters.

[2] If all explanatory variables are categorical, which is a multiple version of the ANOVA model we discussed in the previous chapter, the method is referred to as 'multiple analysis of variance' or MANOVA. If only some explanatory variables are continuous, the method is called 'multiple analysis of covariance' or MANCOVA. However, we shall not spend much time on the differences between these models.

shall use 'loglinear models' for study this type of response variables. When the response variable is not metrical, an important implication for statistical analysis is that its distribution is no longer normal; therefore, the previous methods suitable for multiple linear regression models do not apply. The solution is to transform the categorical response variable in order to obtain normality, and we shall learn the exact forms of these transformations and their implications for our interpretation of the models. The second generalization is to incorporate the effects of the grouping relations among the cases into the models, and these models are called 'multilevel' or 'hierarchical' models.

Please remember that our focus here is the underlying logic of these models rather than their mathematical properties or estimation of parameters. This is particularly necessary not merely because the mathematical aspects have been covered by many other excellent books but more importantly because many critical comments have been made on general linear regression models since the early 1980s. A central issue is whether, and if yes, how the ways in which the variables are connected in such models make substantive sense for social research. What exactly is the function of these models for social research? Is it for exploring patterns, predicting and forecasting, testing hypothesis or establishing causal arguments? *All linear regression models should be mostly used as tools for exploring patterns in data, making comparisons between subgroups and making predictions, but not for making causal arguments.* These models may help collecting evidence for testing a causal hypothesis, but such a function is highly limited due to the way the data are produced (observed instead of experimental) and the restrictive conditions under which causal arguments can be made. If these points are accepted, then there should be no need to criticize linear models for not being able to make sensible causal arguments.

The Basic Idea of Multiple Linear Regression Models

Mathematically, the relationship of the explanatory variables with the response can be expressed in several ways. I have found the following formula intuitively the easiest to understand as it reflects the structure of the data matrix:

$$y_i = \beta_0 + \beta_1 x_{i1} + \beta_2 x_{i2} + \ldots + \beta_p x_{ip} + \varepsilon \quad (7.1)$$

Here, i indicates the identification number of each case, as there are n cases (the sample size, $i = 1, 2, \ldots, n$). Each case is measured on the response variable y and p explanatory variables (x_1 to x_p). As our interest is usually in variables rather than cases, so people normally drop the subscript i and use capital letters to represent the variables:

$$Y = \beta_0 + \beta_1 X_1 + \beta_2 X_2 + \ldots + \beta_p X_p + \varepsilon \quad (7.2)$$

Because the Xs are connected together linearly for predicting the value of Y, their effects are *additive* to each other: the model claims that the values of Y is a baseline value (β_0) plus the effect of X_1, plus the effect of X_2, till the effect of X_p. And the relative or unique effect of each X is reflected in the sign and the magnitude of the variable's coefficient, i.e. the βs.

All the effects accounted for by the Xs constitute 'the deterministic part' of the model. There is a probabilistic part as well, i.e. the error term ε (epsilon), which is expected to be very small after the effects of Xs are taken into account; otherwise, there must be something wrong with the model – either some important Xs have been missed out, or the Xs should have been connected in a different way, or the βs have not been properly estimated. These are called 'specification errors'. In addition, the effect contained in ε should have nothing to do with those of Xs; otherwise, we do not know whether it is the Xs or something else that is at work. It is also assumed that ε has a normal distribution with a mean of 0 and a constant variance. Finally, the error term for each case has nothing to do with that of another case, which means that all the cases are independent of each other with regard to the relationship under study.

Analysis of these assumptions should be *an inherent part of the modelling process*, and violations of them indicate that the model has missed out an important feature of the variables' relations. Published studies, however, rarely report whether any assumption was violated and what was done when a violation was found. These issues are important *statistically as well as conceptually*, and we shall go back to some of the conceptual implications of these assumptions in the last section of this chapter.[3]

In (7.1) and (7.2), the regression coefficients refer to the parameters in the population, which we shall estimate with the data. The estimation procedure is purely a mathematical matter, which we can skip here. Usually, English letters will be used for representing the estimated coefficients, thus:

$$\hat{Y} = b_0 + b_1 X_1 + b_2 X_2 + \dots + b_p X_p \tag{7.3}$$

Or we can write it in the data matrix format:

$$\hat{y}_i = b_0 + b_1 x_{i1} + b_2 x_{i2} + \dots + b_p x_{ip} \tag{7.4}$$

The ^ (hat) on top of Y (or y) indicates that this is a value estimated based on the model and the data. That is, once all coefficients are estimated, we can plug in the values of the xs to calculate the $\hat{y}_i$ for each case. Note a major difference between (7.4), (7.3) and (7.2), (7.1): the error term is gone. This is because (7.4) and (7.3) are estimated models; therefore, they are deterministic.

Many students confuse the error term with another seemingly similar term: the residual. Keep in mind that while the error term is part of the model representing the unexplained part of the response variable's variation, the residual is not part of the model. Rather, the residual is defined as the difference between the observed

---

[3] Discussions of the assumptions in linear regression models are covered in most standard texts. Peter Kennedy (2008) explained some other assumptions in his *A Guide to Econometrics*. For a focused introduction to social science students, the reader can consult Berry (1993).

value y_i in the data, and the predicted values y_i that we have calculated based on the model. That is:

Residual = Observed value − Predicted value

If the predicted value is very close to the observed value, then it means the model performs pretty well. Therefore, the residual is usually used to assess the model's performance (see more below). As we would like to find a model that has the smallest overall residuals, modelling is a process of finding the optimal solution, not a one-off hit, because we search among a group of models for the one that is able to generate the smallest overall residuals.

After the computer helps us estimate the regression coefficients, what do they tell us? Recall that for simple linear regression we interpret a coefficient as the change of Y given one unit change of X. With multiple explanatory variables, this interpretation is valid only when the Xs have nothing to do with each other. This is the very meaning of the additive assumption: the effects of Xs are added up together to predict the value of Y. But it is only meaningful to add up the effects *when each effect is unique*; otherwise, you are not actually adding the genuine effect of X_2 but the effect of something else as well if X_2 is a product of another variable. Therefore, the precise meaning of each coefficient is an estimated measurement of the *unique* effect of its corresponding explanatory variable. This is why people usually talk about the effect of an explanatory variable *when other explanatory variables are held constant, controlled or taken into account*.

In reality, it is rare that the explanatory variables are not associated at all. So, how can their effects be disentangled from each other so that each variable's unique effect can be specified? The ideal method is to conduct an experiment, in which the respondents are randomly exposed to different effects and the researcher can manipulate the level of the explanatory variable. The researcher can then single out the effect of a particular explanatory variable by setting the levels of other explanatory variables constant. Being constant, these variables do not change with the interested explanatory variable, so the interested variable's effect could stand out. *Ideally, all explanatory variables are not correlated at all but each of them is highly correlated with the response variable*. An ideal linear regression model can thus be thought of as a perfect team, each member having a unique talent but all the talents are complementary to each other. Figure 7.1 illustrates this ideal situation with three explanatory variables.

In Figure 7.1, the largest circle represents the total variation of the response variable, and each of small circles represents the proportion of each explanatory variable's contribution to accounting for the total variation (the largest circle). This is an ideal because, on the one hand, these explanatory variables have successfully explained 90% of the total variation (only 10% unoccupied by the small circles) and, on the other hand, the small circles do not overlap each other, showing each variable's unique effect.

When the explanatory variables are associated with each other, especially when the associations are strong − statisticians call it 'multicolinearity' − it is very difficult to know the unique effect of a particular variable. But if we do not know the

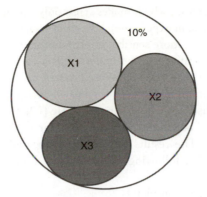

Figure 7.1 Ideal situation for a multiple linear regression model

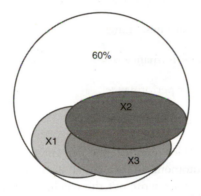

Figure 7.2 Realistic situation for a multiple linear regression model

unique effects, then it is not appropriate to add them up, because there is little to gain in adding one variable when most of its effect has already been represented by another already in the model.[4] In contrast to the above ideal situation, Figure 7.2 shows this more realistic but less satisfactory scenario.

In the social sciences, the percentage of the explained variation is usually quite small – it is very common for the percentage to fall in the range of 20–30%, leaving the majority of the variation unexplained. In contrast, the effects of the three explanatory variables are muddled up together as they are correlated to each other.

Researchers, however, may not want to drop any of the explanatory variables simply because they are highly correlated. After all, there is no rule on how correlated the variables have to be so that one of them should be dropped from the model. Researchers may also want to keep all of them for theoretical or substantive reasons.

Because of this difficulty of manipulating the explanatory variables and disentangling their relations, the above interpretation of regression coefficients, although standard in textbooks and widely used in practice, does not actually make much sense, especially for social science research. Gelman and Hill (2007: 34) call it 'the

---

[4]This is one of the reasons why many academic journals ask authors to report the correlation matrix.

counterfactual interpretation', which makes sense only under very strong conditions (manipulation and control in experiments). As most social sciences studies are observational studies, we need a more sensible interpretation, which they call 'the *predictive* interpretation'. This interpretation understands a coefficient as *the average – or statistically speaking, the expected – difference between two subgroups on the response variable when the two groups have the same value on other explanatory variables.*

To illustrate, let us discuss the following example (Chatterjee et al., 2000: 52–9). A survey was conducted on employees' rating of their supervisor's job performance (Y) in an organization. The results were then aggregated within each of the 30 departments (*n* = 30). The following six explanatory variables were included:

X_1 = Handles employee complaints

X_2 = Does not allow special privileges

X_3 = Opportunity to learn new things

X_4 = Raises based on performance

X_5 = Too critical of poor performance

X_5 = Rate of advancing to better jobs

The values of these variables represent the percentage of positive responses after making the scores dichotomous, so they are all in the range of 0 to 100. It would be a very long equation if we write out the whole model with so many variables and their estimated coefficients, so the usual practice is to produce a table with additional information for further statistical inference (Chatterjee et al., 2000: 63), see Table 7.1.

Table 7.1   Regression output for the supervisor performance example

Variable	Coefficient	s.e.	t-test	p-value
Constant	10.9	11.6	0.93	0.36
X1	0.6	0.2	3.81	0.00
X2	−0.1	0.1	−0.54	0.60
X3	0.3	0.2	1.90	0.07
X4	0.1	0.2	0.37	0.72
X5	0.0	0.1	0.26	0.80
X6	−0.2	0.2	−1.22	0.23
n = 30	$R^2 = 0.73$	R_a^2	$\hat{\sigma}$	df = 23

Notes: In this table, s.e. stands for standard error, *df* is the degrees of freedom, and we shall explain the meaning of R^2 later. I also have reduced the number of decimal points of the coefficients and their standard errors (s.e.) from four to two.

How shall we interpret the meaning of the estimated coefficients? Take 0.6 of *X1* (handling complaints) as an example. The standard or 'counterfactual' interpretation is that the percentage of overall positive rating would increase by 0.6 percent if the percentage of positive rating for handling complaints increases by 1 percent, *with the other five explanatory variables being held constant*. Clearly, this assumes *a hypothetical experiment* in which we can set the employees' ratings on the five variables on a particular level while only letting $X1$ change. Obviously, we cannot do that in a social survey.

Now let us adopt the predictive interpretation suggested by Gelman and Hill. If two departments, say A and B, have the same percentages for variables $X2$ to $X6$ and if A is one percent higher than B on $X1$, then A will be 0.6 percent higher than B on Y. In essence, we are *comparing two subgroups* in terms of the predictive effect of the focused variable on the response variable when they have the same values on other variables. It is clearly more realistic to say that two cases share the same value on an explanatory variable than to say that the variable's value is held constant.

Besides the meaning of regression coefficients is the matter of their size. Not many social researchers are seriously interested in *the exact magnitudes* of the coefficients. Interpreting the magnitude of the coefficients from a substantive concern has not become a widely adopted practice. For the above example, is 0.6 a big increase of the overall rating? While it is arbitrary to define 'big' or 'small', there should be consideration of whether the magnitude is ignorable, considerable or substantial with regard to common sense or a professional standard. Due to the tenuous connection of the coefficients to a substantive context, few published papers discuss the *substantive* meaning of the 95% confidence interval of a coefficient.

Many social researchers are more interested in the statistical inference of each coefficient. The most popular inference is on the hypothesis that each coefficient is 0. If the probability that such hypothesis is true is below a preset significance level, normally 0.05, then we reject the hypothesis and the coefficient is claimed to be statistically significant; otherwise, the null hypothesis is retained and the coefficient is not statistically significant. For a specific model, some coefficients are significant while others not, or they are significant at different levels (the *p*-values are smaller than 0.1 or 0.01).

A difficult question to answer is: what *substantive* significance do these statistical results carry? It is understandable that researchers are concerned with the hypothesis that a particular coefficient equals to 0, because if it is indeed 0, then that variable has no effect on the response variable. There are however two problems with such reasoning. First, it may not be so easy to determine the fate of a null hypothesis. For example, if the *p*-value for a variable's coefficient is 0.07, such as that for $X3$ in the above example, should we reject or retain it? We should reject it if we preset the significance level at 0.05, as it normally is, but we should retain if the significance level is set at 0.1. Does the difference between 0.05 and 0.1 matter for the social researcher? Such question is rarely if ever discussed in the literature.

Another problem is that even if we reject the null hypothesis, how much does its effect have to be for it to be taken seriously from a substantive point of view? Or how small does the effect has to be for it to be discarded? This relates to a central issue throughout this whole book: *what substantive points we can make based on statistical reasoning?* These questions are hard to answer because *there are no substantive criteria; all we have are statistical criteria.* For statistical analyses to be more relevant and useful, social researchers should set up substantive criteria.

Finally, researchers need an indicator of the performance of a multiple linear regression model. The most widely used is the R^2. I have already shown its meaning intuitively with the percentages in Figures 7.1 and 7.2. Statistically, we can interpret its meaning in two different but related ways. The first focuses on the predictions made by the model: what would the predicted values of the response variables look like if the model has performed well? As our model is designed to fit the data, we would say that our model has performed well if the values predicted by it ($\bar{y}_i$) are very close to the values observed in the data (y_i). One step further, if these two groups of values are very close, then they should be highly correlated. R^2 is the square of their correlation coefficient.

The other and more popular approach follows the logic of 'proportional reduction of error' (PRE): a well performing model should reduce a larger proportion of error. The error is measured by the sum of the differences between y_i and $\bar{y}_i$, i.e. $\Sigma(y_i - \bar{y}_i)^2$. Because $\bar{y}_i$ is determined by the model (recall that $\bar{y}_i = b_0 + b_1 x_{i1} + b_2 x_{i2} + \ldots + b_p x_{ip}$), a large $\Sigma(y_i - \bar{y}_i)^2$ will suggest that the model fits the data poorly. The total amount of error is measured by $\Sigma(y_i - \bar{y})^2$. That is, the error will be the largest when we predict only with its mean, which is obviously the crudest estimate. In the end, we define R^2 as the proportion of error reduced thanks to the model:

$$R^2 = 1 - \frac{\sum (y_i - \hat{y}_i)^2}{\sum (y_i - \bar{y})^2}$$

From the opposite perspective, the error reduced by the model can also be interpreted as the contribution of the model. We can also transform this equation into:

$$R^2 = \frac{\sum (\hat{y}_i - \bar{y})^2}{\sum (y_i - \bar{y})^2}$$

whose numerator indicates the improvement made by the model on the crude estimate of $\bar{y}$. As the denominator measures the total variation of y_i, R^2 is commonly interpreted as the proportion of the response variable's total variation explained by the explanatory variables.

Because a better fitting model will have a larger R^2, it is attractive to look for a model that will generate a large R^2. For the above example, the R^2 is 0.73, which is very high in social science studies. There is no widely accepted standard, however, of a decent size. This is another pitfall that students of social research should watch out for. R^2 may be heavily influenced by the number of Xs, the relationship between them and Y, and we must ensure it makes sense to include so many explanatory variables in our model. R^2 will always increase if we add an X that is somehow correlated with Y, and it will not decrease even if X has nothing to do with Y, because the correlation, no matter positive or negative, will be taken up positively by the squared differences. *Do not include more Xs simply for the sake of increasing the value of R^2!* Sometimes, we should even expect a small R^2 if we do not believe those explanatory variables can account for so much of the response variable's variation.

Generalization on the Response Variable – Generalized Linear Models

It is appropriate to use the above 'classical linear regression models' only when some conditions are satisfied. One is that the response variable is measured at the metrical level and it has a normal distribution. This is reasonable because what is predicted by the linear combination of the explanatory variables is *the mean* of the response variable.

Very often, however, the target variables interesting to social researchers are categorical. The distributions of categorical variables are simply not normal. Here are a few examples: whether people vote or not, preferred type of job or ordered levels of support for a policy. They are short of the large number of values whose probabilities could form a distribution close to normality. Even when a variable does have a large or infinite number of values, there is no guarantee that the distribution would be normal. Income is an example, which has enough values for constructing a distribution close to normal, but it is seldom normally distributed in any society. Almost all income distributions are skewed toward the lower end. Finally, variables of counts also defy normal distribution although they have a large number of possible values, such as the number of crimes in a city, the number of transactions between two organizations, frequency of anti-social behaviours and so on.

We need statistical models that can deal with these types of response variables. Since these models are extensions of the classical linear regression model, they are usually called 'generalized linear models'. They remain 'linear' because all the parameters (or coefficients of explanatory variables) are not involved in any nonlinear mathematical operation, such as exponential or logarithm.[5] Linearity can be maintained by transforming the response variable, and we shall learn which transformation is appropriate for which type of variables below. In the end, the transformed response variable can be expressed as a function of linearly connected explanatory variables; consequently, the relationship between the response variable and the explanatory variables is different from that of the classical linear regression model, so our interpretation of the regression coefficients must change correspondingly.[6]

Binary Response Variable: Binary Logistic Regression

We met the simplest version of this model in the previous chapter. By adding more explanatory variables, we have the multiple logistic regression model on a binary response variable:

$$\ln\left(\frac{\pi}{1-\pi}\right) = \beta_0 + \beta_1 X_1 + \beta_2 X_2 + \dots + \beta_p X_p + \varepsilon \tag{7.5}$$

---

[5]Please be reminded that the explanatory variables do *not* have to enter the equation linearly; that is, they can take exponential, logarithm, power or any other nonlinear forms. This does not actually affect the linearity of the model because these nonlinear forms can be replaced with a new variable. For example, we can let $Z = \ln(X)$ and put Z into the equation.
[6]It is also assumed that the parameters do not change from one group of cases to another, which may not hold, but this is a topic we shall discuss in the next section.

Here, the response variable is not the original binary variable, not even the probability (π) that an event happens or a case carries a particular characteristic. The transformed response variable is the natural log of the odds of an event or an attribute. This is 'the logit transformation' that linearizes the nonlinear relationship between π and the Xs. Without it, any X may explain most of the variation of π because π, as a probability, varies in the limited range of (0, 1), leaving very little room of explanation for other explanatory variables.[7]

With a particular set of data, we can estimate the parameters, and the estimated model can be presented as the following:

$$\ln\left(\frac{\hat{\pi}}{1-\hat{\pi}}\right) = b_0 + b_1 X_1 + b_2 X_2 + ... + b_p X_p \tag{7.6}$$

To interpret the coefficients, we have the same three options as we did for simple logistic regression but I suggest we use the odds ratio because many explanatory variables are categorical and the odds ratio is the most effective statistic for describing the association between two categorical variables.[8] That is, we do not interpret b_1 directly; rather, we interpret e^{b_1} as the odds ratio for describing the association between Y and X_1.[9] In addition, we need to follow the predictive approach to take into account the effects of other explanatory variables, of course. For example, e^{b_1} is the odds ratio measuring the direction and the strength of the association between Y and X_1 when the cases have the same values on all other explanatory variables.

Multiple Nominal Response Variable: Multi-nominal Logistic Regression

The response variable becomes 'multiple nominal' when it has three or more categories without ranking order. 'The political party voted for in an election' is an example: respondents are asked to identify one and only one party among three or more options. The new complication is that now the response variable has three or more rather than two categories. A natural solution would be to run a binary logistic regression for each pair of the categories. For example, in the US, we can say the political party variable has four categories: the Democratic, the Conservative, the Independent and Others. We can turn them into three pairs and run a separate binary logic regression model for each of them: Democratic–Others, Conservative–Others and Independent–Others. Note that we are using 'Others' as the reference category. The advantage of this strategy is that it allows the coefficients to be different from one pair to another. Its downside is the inconvenience of running separate models, especially when the number of categories becomes large. Our objective is to achieve the efficiency of modelling all the pairs at the same time while still being able to represent their differences. The solution provided

---

[7]Other possible violations of assumptions (constant and normal distribution of error terms) remain the same as in the simple logistic regression case without the transformation.

[8]Alan Agresti (2007) recommends the use of odds ratios, but Gelman and Hill (2007) still find them obscure.

[9]Most statistics software, such as SPSS, automatically calculate e^{b_1} after b_1 is estimated, so the odds ratios are directly available in the computer output.

by statisticians is to allow the coefficients to remain the same but reflect the differences in the intercept. But if the focal interest is in a particular pair of categories, not actually the response variable in general, it is more desirable to produce a separate model for that pair.

Ordinal Response Variable: Ordinal Logistic Regression

When order is introduced into the categories of the response variable, we can adopt the same strategy of modelling on the pairs. The only difference between ordinal logistic regression and multi-nominal regression is the way the pairs are formed. For a multi-nominal variable, it does not matter which category we choose as the reference. For an ordinal response variable, our model must account for the ranking order among the categories. In social surveys, respondents are frequently asked to report their level of support to a statement on a 5-, 7- or 11-point scale. For example, how much you would agree that 'most people would take advantage of you if they got the chance'. Take the five-point scale as an example (strongly agree = 5, agree = 4, indifferent = 3, disagree = 2, strongly disagree = 1). We can choose either the first or the fifth category as the reference.[10] Suppose we choose strongly disagree as the reference, then we shall have the following four pairs: (1) vs. (2, 3, 4, 5), (1, 2) vs. (3, 4, 5), (1, 2, 3) vs. (4, 5) and (1, 2, 3, 4) vs. (5). Note that we need to collapse all the categories below or above a particular category in constructing the pairs, and it is by doing this we incorporate the ranking order into our model. Therefore, what we are modelling on is the logit (or log odds ratio) of the probability that the response variable takes a value below a particular category. The first pair to be modelled, for example, is:

$$\frac{P(Y \le 1)}{P(Y > 1)}$$

and we model the other three with the same logic. Again, the strategy is to model all the pairs at the same time, assuming constant coefficients for the pairs but allowing different intercepts to represent each of them respectively.

Contingency Table: Loglinear Regression

When all variables of interest are categorical, their limited number of values allows us to organize the data in a contingency table. Because the categories are exhaustive and mutually exclusive, when the total number of cases is given, the number of cases for a particular category is contingent on the numbers of cases for other categories. Loglinear models are more effective than other regression models discussed above for analysing this type of data.

A first important feature of loglinear models is that *the response variable is the cell frequency, not any particular variable per se*. As the cell frequencies are at the

---

[10]We can choose any category in the middle, of course, but that will make our comparisons more difficult to explain and understand.

interactions of variable categories, the target of analysis is the interactive patterns among the variables. The question is not which variables can predict the response variable but *which among the possible interactive relationships of the variables has the highest probability of being responsible for the observed frequencies*. If we have no idea which interaction is responsible for the observed pattern, then we can simply try different models and see which one has the highest chance. Social scientists usually have theory-informed hypotheses, so they can use the results of loglinear models to argue for or against the hypotheses.

Like chi-square tests, loglinear models are also built on comparisons between the observed frequencies with their respective expected frequencies. The expected frequencies are produced under the assumption that there is no interaction at all. Therefore, the bigger the differences between the two frequencies are, the more likely the observed data are results of the interactions of variables.

The effect of each variable is decomposed into the effect of its own (the main effect) and the effect of its interactions with other variables (the interaction effects). A formal connection between these effects should allow us to make predictions of cell frequencies that are satisfactorily close to the observed values. However, similar to the situation that we had for logistic regression models, we cannot put the response variable directly at the left-hand side of the equation because the response is cell frequencies, which are always non-negative (0 or positive) integers and follow a skewed distribution. Statisticians have found that when the response variable follows such 'Poisson' distribution, it can only have a linear relationship with the variables when its natural logarithm is taken. So, for example, if there are three categorical variables, X, Y, Z, and we want to include all the effects (main and interactive) on the observed frequencies F, then we the following full model:

$$\text{in } F_{ijk} = \mu + \lambda_i^X + \lambda_j^Y + \lambda_k^Z + \lambda_{ij}^{XY} + \lambda_{jk}^{YZ} + \lambda_{ki}^{ZX} + \lambda_{ijk}^{XYZ} \tag{7.8}$$

Here, μ is the baseline effect, similar to the intercept in classical regression model. As there are three variables, we use the subscripts (i, j, k) to indicate their position in the contingency table while using the superscripts (X, Y, Z) to indicate which variable's effect a particular λ represents. It is called 'the full model' because it includes all the possible effects; therefore, it can perfectly predict the observed frequency. That, however, is not necessarily desirable as the model simply represents the data (the contingency table) itself. In other words, this model has the lowest level of parsimony. The most parsimonious model, $\ln F_{ijk} = \mu$, however, is the weakest in predicting the observed frequencies.

Our job is to find a model that can strike the best balance between having the smallest number of terms and retaining the power of making good predictions. We explore among the models from in $F_{ijk} = \mu + \lambda_i^X$, adding one term each time, to in $F_{ijk} = \mu + \lambda_i^X + \lambda_j^Y + \lambda_k^Z + \lambda_{ij}^{XY} + \lambda_{jk}^{YZ} + \lambda_{ki}^{ZX}$. This is done from the statistical point of view. A particular effect should by all means be included in the model if you as the researcher think it is substantively important. By good predictions, we mean that the predicted frequencies are close enough to the observed ones, which is usually measured by a chi-square type of statistic X^2 or G^2. Note that here we shall be expecting a small X^2 or G^2, or a large p-value, if we think the model should perform well.

The reader may have noticed that the models introduced in this section differ with regard to the mathematical operation used for transforming the response variable, which in turn is determined by the response variable's distribution. This mathematical operation is called 'the link function' as it shows how the response variable is linked to the explanatory variables.

Generalization on the Case – Multilevel Models

Social scientists are well known for paying attention to contexts: either social, historical or cultural. That the American Sociological Association (ASA) has named its most recent journal *Contexts* well illustrates the point. Nevertheless, while it seems to be a common sense that contexts matter, there are few developed methods that help researchers specify how contexts work. Studies of qualitative nature usually produce descriptions of the studied context with any evidence available to them and then make as many sensible connections as possible to lower level social processes. It is not very clear how the connection between the context and the micro processes is established and evaluated, as there are no widely accepted procedures and benchmarks for making an assessment of the connection.

Researchers using quantitative methods have long tried to make formal analysis of contextual effects. However, their understanding of 'context' is much narrower than that held by qualitative researchers. In statistics, context refers to the characteristics of observation units at a higher level, to which lower level units belong to. For example, the European Social Survey explicitly includes some 'contextual variables' that provide background information at the national level. Statistical models that explicitly model higher level effects are multilevel models.[11]

Dependence among Cases and the Statistical Consequence of Ignoring It

When cases belong to the units of different levels, what matters are not exactly the levels themselves but *the grouping effect* of the same higher level unit. When cases are grouped together, they may be exposed to some common influence from a higher level, and it is this exposure to a higher level effect that demands our attention. As a consequence, observations grouped in a same unit are likely to be more similar than those not in the same unit. Statisticians call such similarity 'dependence', meaning that one observation has something to do with another of the same group.

The dependent structure is reflected in the data matrix. As it is different from the single-level matrix, readers new to multilevel data should pay special attention. Take the following hypothetical example of university students given in Table 7.2.

---

[11] A narrower term is 'hierarchical linear models', which implies a hierarchical structure. Although these types of data and models are quite common, it is possible that some multilevel data may not contain such hierarchical relations. Another term is 'mixed effects models', because, as we shall see later, most multilevel models have both fixed and random effects.

Table 7.2 Data matrix without grouping

Student	Gender	Subject	Hours of study/day	Class of parents	Nature of university	Number of students
0001	M	Science	10	Lower middle	State	12,300
0002	M	Humanity	6	Upper middle	Private	8,800
...	...	...	...	...	...	...
1001	F	Humanity	5	Middle	Private	8,800
1002	M	Business	7	Upper middle	Private	8,800
...	...	...	...	...	...	...
2001	F	Humanity	6	Middle	State	12,300
2002	F	Social science	4	Lower middle	State	12,300

Clearly, this data matrix in Table 7.2 does not attempt to represent the multilevel structure, as students belonging to the same university are not put together. Suppose students 0001, 2001 and 2002 belong to the same university while the other three belong to another, we can reorganize the data as shown in Table 7.3.

Table 7.3 Data matrix with grouping

University	Student	Gender	Subject	Hours of study/day	Class of parents	Nature of university	Number of students
1	0001	M	Science	10	Lower middle	State	12,300
1	2001	F	Humanity	6	Middle	State	12,300
1	2002	F	Social science	4	Lower middle	State	12,300
...	...	...	...	...	...	...	...
12	0002	M	Humanity	6	Upper middle	Private	8,800
12	1001	F	Humanity	5	Middle	Private	8,800
12	1002	M	Business	7	Upper middle	Private	8,800

Now we know which students are grouped together in a higher level unit, who are exposed to the same university characteristics (nature, number of students and so on) that are repeatedly presented for each student of the same university. To avoid such repetition, we can break the above matrix into two, one for students and the other for university, using the university identifier to connect them (see Tables 7.4 and 7.5).

From a technical point of view, there are no important differences between the three formats, and most computer software packages (such as HLM, MLwin) can easily transform one into another. The last one is preferable because it clearly shows how many higher level units there are and how many lower units in each of them.

This is however not the only way in which cases are structured at different levels. Here, each case belongs to one and only one higher level unit, and such structure is called 'nested'. A more complicated situation is that lower level cases belong to two or more higher level units. For example, students may be associated with sports clubs that are organized across different universities, so cases are

Table 7.4　Lower level data matrix

University	Student	Gender	Subject	Hours of study/day	Class of parents
1	0001	M	Science	10	Lower middle
1	2001	F	Humanity	6	Middle
1	2002	F	Social science	4	Lower middle
...	...	...	...	...	...
12	0002	M	Humanity	6	Upper middle
12	1001	F	Humanity	5	Middle
12	1002	M	Business	7	Upper middle

Table 7.5　Higher level data matrix

University	Nature of university	Number of students
1	State	12,300
...	...	...
12	Private	8,800
...	...	...

classified in two or more ways at a higher level. Note that, here each case still belongs to one and only one higher level unit, that is, a single membership of a particular higher level unit. An even more complicated situation is that some cases may belong to two or higher level units of *the same kind*, for example, some students are affiliated to two universities or two sports clubs. That is, they have multiple memberships at a higher level. Researchers need to be aware of these structures in the data, although we will not go into these complexities in this book.

It is important to note that a higher level factor does *not necessarily* exercise any effect on lower level observations. The multilevel structure cannot *by itself* prove the presence of a higher level effect, so we must check whether the dependence assumption holds or not before carrying out any subsequent analysis. If it does not hold, then we can use the models learnt before. But if it does, then we must take the dependence among cases seriously and *explicitly* incorporate that in our statistical analysis. The whole business of multilevel modelling is to deal with the second situation, but showing the grouping effect is a necessary albeit preliminary step. Methods for exploring such effects include plots that show the variations of interested relations across different groups and statistics that indicate strong correlations among cases in the same unit, such as ρ.

The intra-class correlation coefficient (ICC, or ρ) is a statistic for measuring the level of grouping among cases, defined as the percentage of variance accounted for by higher level units. For data with two levels:

$$\rho = \frac{\sigma_{\mu 0}^2}{\sigma_{\mu 0}^2 + \sigma_r^2} \tag{7.9}$$

where $\sigma_{\mu 0}^2$ is the level 2 variance and σ_r^2 is the level 1 variance. Therefore, the larger the value of ρ, the more dependent the cases belonging to the same higher level unit.

Recall that an assumption classical regression models hold is that the error terms are independent from each other. Why? Because if they are dependent on each other, then it is very hard to distinguish the unique effect of one explanatory variable from that of another, as illustrated in Figure 7.3.

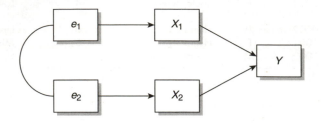

Figure 7.3   Effect of correlated error terms on classical linear regression model

If e_1 and e_2 are correlated, as shown here, then each of them may exert some effect on Y through X_1 or X_2, respectively, therefore confounding the effect of X_1 and X_2. Such dependence is very likely to exist in reality, and one source of such dependence is clustering or grouping. Ignoring the multilevel effects can lead to seriously incorrect substantive conclusions. One consequence is the underestimation of the regression coefficients' standard errors, as is illustrated in Figure 7.4.

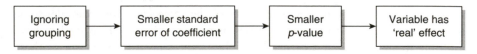

Figure 7.4   Effect of ignoring grouping on statistical significance

Underestimation of variances and standard errors occurs because the variation between groups is not accounted for; when the variation is accounted for, the standard errors will be much larger. Smaller standard errors then lead to smaller p-values, which in the end lead to the substantive conclusion that the explanatory variable has a 'real' but actually inflated effect on the response variable. Clearly, this is a both statistical and substantive problem that has important repercussions.

Advantages of Multilevel Models

Multilevel models incorporate the effects at all levels into a single system of models. There is not just one model for a particular level. Rather, there are two or more models connected to one another. Their first advantage, as I see it, is that they are more realistic while still powerful enough to model the effects at different levels simultaneously. They are realistic because they do not put stringent conditions on the data. The data do not have to be balanced (there are an equal number of cases in each higher level unit or each case has been measured in the same number of occasions). They are powerful because they take higher- and cross-level effects as random variables, and they model both the mean and the variance of these random variables at the same time.

Essentially, multilevel models take the higher level units as a sample from a population rather than fixed group memberships; therefore, the units' characteristics are parameters to be estimated. In single level models, the higher level units are not treated as a sample but as the target of analysis (or the population), and this is why these models can only compare the means across the units while leaving their variances not modelled at all. For the above example, the universities should be taken as a sample of all universities in the US, not the ultimate target groups to be compared. Therefore, it is far from enough simply to compare the universities on any variable's means; the universities' characteristics must be taken as random variables to be modelled.

Basic Ideas of Multilevel Modelling

To construct a multilevel model, we need to consider the following questions:

(1) How many levels are there?
(2) How many predictors are there at each level?
(3) Does the model include random intercept only or both random intercept and coefficients? We need both theory, knowledge of the substantive subject, and data to make the decision.

Table 7.6 illustrates four possible situations when we answer the third question.

Table 7.6   Scenarios of random intercept and coefficients in multilevel modelling

		Coefficients vary at higher level?	
		No	Yes
Intercept varies at higher level?	No	(1) The null model	(4) Not realistic
	Yes	(2) Random intercept models	(3) Random intercept and coefficient models

For the first situation, as there are no explanatory variables (no coefficients), it is often used as a null or starter model. Neither the intercept nor the coefficients vary at the higher level; the model only includes different values for each unit at the lower level (β_{0j}) and the mean at the higher level (γ_{00}). Therefore, it is not different from an ANOVA:

Level 1: $Y_{ij} = \beta_{0j} + e_{ij}$

Level 2: $\beta_{0j} = \gamma_{00} + \mu_{0j}$

Substitute the level 2 model to level 1, we have: $Y_{ij} = \gamma_{00} + \mu_{0j} + e_{ij}$. It is also used for calculating the 'intra-class correlation coefficients' (ICC or ρ as defined before).

The second situation allows the intercept to be random but not the effect of a variable at a higher level. There are two ways of incorporating an effect from a higher level into the intercept. The first takes the group means as the outcomes from a higher level effect:

Level 1: $Y_{ij} = \beta_{0j} + e_{ij}$, same as the null model

Level 2: $\beta_{0j} = \gamma_{00} + \gamma_{01}W_j + \mu_{0j}$, which includes W_j as a higher level variable

Combining them into a single equation, we have $Y_{ij} = \gamma_{00} + \gamma_{01}W_j + \mu_{0j} + e_{ij}$.

The second model includes an explanatory variable whose coefficient varies across levels:

Level 1: $Y_{ij} = \beta_{0j} + \beta_{ij}X_{ij} + e_{ij}$

Level 2: $\beta_{0j} = \gamma_{00} + \mu_{0j}$ and $\beta_{ij} = \gamma_{10}$

Put together:

$$Y_{ij} = \gamma_{00} + \gamma_{10}X_{ij} + \mu_{0j} + e_{ij} \qquad (7.10)$$

For the third situation, we need models that allow both intercepts and variable coefficients to be random. Again, there are two further situations here. In the first model, the intercepts and slopes vary across levels but there are no higher level predictors of those variations:

Level 1: $Y_{ij} = \beta_{0j} + \beta_{ij}X_{ij} + e_{ij}$, same as above.

Level 2: $\beta_{0j} = \gamma_{00} + \mu_{0j}$ and $\beta_{ij} = \gamma_{10} + \mu_{1j}$.

Note the μ_{1j} in the second equation, which represents the additional variability in β_{ij}. Put together:

$$Y_{ij} = \gamma_{00} + \mu_{1j} + (\gamma_{10} + \mu_{1j})X_{ij} + e_{ij} \qquad (7.11)$$

In the second model, intercepts and coefficients are modelled using level 2 predictors:

Level 1: $Y_{ij} = \beta_{0j} + \beta_{1j}X_{ij} + e_{ij}$

Level 2: $\beta_{0j} = \gamma_{00} + \gamma_{01}W_j + \mu_{0j}$ and $\beta_{1j} = \gamma_{10} + \gamma_{11}W_j + \mu_{1j}$

If we substitute the level 2 models into the level 1 model, there will be a cross-level interaction component:

$$
\begin{aligned}
Y_{ij} &= \gamma_{00} + \gamma_{01}W_j + \mu_{0j} + (\gamma_{10} + \gamma_{11}W_j + \mu_{1j})X_{ij} + e_{ij} \\
&= \gamma_{00} + \gamma_{01}W_j + \gamma_{10}X_{ij} + \gamma_{11}W_jX_{ij} + \mu_{0j} + \mu_{1j}X_{ij} + e_{ij}
\end{aligned} \qquad (7.12)
$$

The fourth situation is not realistic at all because it is nearly impossible that the slopes vary while the intercepts do not.

Once the model is constructed, the next task is to estimate the parameters. Researchers need to understand that while the gammas are parameters as they are for the fixed effects, μ_{0j}, μ_{1j} and e_{ij}, are not parameters to be estimated because they represent random effects that are to be determined by further parameters. For these three terms, we assume they are normally distributed with mean 0 and a variance. Obviously, we do not need to estimate their means, but we do need to estimate their variances, which together are called 'the variance components'. The size of these components indicates the variability that has not been counted for by our model. So, all in all, we need to estimate both the fixed effect parameters and the variance components.

To assess how much the model fits the data, we can use the R^2 as we do for ordinary regression models. What new is that we cannot have a single R^2 for the whole model. Rather, we now have an R^2 for each level. If we still follow the logic of a single R^2, then the R^2 may not become larger if we add more explanatory variables to the model, as it will in ordinary regression models. For multilevel models, the R^2s are calculated differently, although we can still interpret it as the proportional reduction of the predictor error. The idea again is to compare two error terms, one from the baseline model (i.e. the model only includes the grand mean), and the other from our preferred model, shown below:

$$R^2 = 1 - \frac{\text{error from preferred model}}{\text{error from the baseline model}} \tag{7.13}$$

If our model fits the data well, the numerator will be small, rendering the R^2 large, indicating better fit. This is the same for all levels.

Some Critical Limitations

After many years of popular use in the social sciences, linear regression models have been under fierce critiques. In this section, I highlight four key issues.

Failure to Study Constant Forces

Let us start with the distinction and the connection of explanatory and response variables. One reason that regression models have been popular among social researchers is that they provide a form for linking the interested phenomenon (the response variable) and some possible factors (explanatory variables) that contribute to the explanation of that phenomenon. This is very attractive because it allows us to firstly select a set of possible factors based on theoretical and substantive considerations and then identify which among these factors have an effect on the response variable based on some predetermined statistical criteria. The results then lend scientific support to the theoretical ideas previously employed for selecting the explanatory variables.

One problem is that a linear regression model does not model on the response variable per se; rather, it is the response variable's *variation* that is to be explained.

This is why in textbooks of mathematical statistics the response variable is written as $E(Y)$, i.e. the expected value of Y, not Y itself, which we can loosely interpret as a general definition of mean.[12] The statistical reason for targeting its variation is that the response variable has very different values when each of the explanatory variables takes a particular value. For example, take the time spent with one's family as the response variable. No matter which explanatory variables we use, once each of them has a particular value, such as gender is female, education is university and religion is Christianity, we shall still witness a certain amount of variation of the response variable among the people with these characteristics.

In Chapter 5 of *Making it Count*, Stanley Lieberson explained why this is a problem: 'Explanation of a variable's variation should not be confused with an explanation of the event or process itself' (1985: 115). Obviously, our objective should be to explain the event or process itself, not simply the variation of a variable. He demonstrated the serious fallacy of studying variation alone by using the example of falling objects and gravity: if we focus on the variables that describe an object's characteristics, such as the object's shape or density, we shall never come to the idea of gravity, because those analyses do not answer the question why the object falls in the first place. Gravity is a *constant* force, which cannot be explained by methods for explaining variations.

A fundamental reason for statistical methods to lose sight of constant forces, I believe, is that statistical methods are inherently comparative. That is, they aim to discover patterns of relations by comparing a large number of cases. They focus their attention on differences, but studying constant forces does not help for such purpose. If we see an overwhelming number of applies falling, some reaching the ground earlier than others, we naturally tend to wonder why some reached the ground faster than others, not why they fell in the first place. In contrast, if we observe only one apple falling or many apples reaching to the ground all at the same time, we may become curious about what force made them fall, not what force made fall at different speeds. *The intention to compare a large number of cases with different values makes statistical methods blind to uniformities and constancies that may be critical for understanding the event or process itself.* Lieberson reminds us not to forget these constant forces. We should try to identify the constant forces that bring about the phenomenon to our interest before explaining any differences across the cases.

Constrained Specification of the Relationship between the Variables

Another problem with linear regression models relates to how the response and the explanatory variables are connected together. For example, they do not allow the response variable to explain *something about its own*; mathematically, we cannot put Y on both sides of the equation, which however is very common in

---

[12]Strictly speaking, the expected value is the sum of the products of each value and its probability. The mathematical definition differs according to whether the variable is continuous or discrete, and its specific form depends on the distribution.

mathematical models. This is why statistical models are special cases of mathematical models. Mathematical models are more powerful because they intend to directly describe a dynamic process, *not simply some attributes* of the process. Clearly, it is more demanding to construct mathematical models, as there is no pre-specified form for linking the variables together, so you must create the form by yourself and justify it with a sensible theory.

In contrast, the way in which the variables are connected in linear regression models is highly limited, even with transformations. We may transform the response variable with logarithm and other operations, but the main structure remains additive. This and the previous problem suggest that statistical methods can be of limited use for the purpose of explaining dynamic processes. Their best use is to compare cases and account for the differences across the cases.

Weak Connection between Theories and Variables

As the constrained forms – linearity, additivity, and so on – cannot represent a great variety of ways in which the parameters are related to each other, we cannot expect linear regression models to be able to effectively represent our theories. A widely held misconception about statistical models is that they are not theories but only *tools* for testing the validity of theories, *assuming that data analysis and theory testing are two separate things*. Social researchers must realize that these models *are* theories. By using these models, the researcher implicitly accepts the underlying assumptions of the models that represent a particular theory. This is why many criticisms have centred on using linear regression models for theoretical purposes.

Perhaps the most forceful criticism comes from Aage Sorenson (1998). He points out that the additive assumption suggests that many researchers understand theories 'as sums of variables': 'The choice of these [independent] variables was said to represent theory, and therefore theory became identified with variables' (1998: 247). As the regression coefficient represents the relatively unique effect of its corresponding independent variable, the variation of the response variable is explained by adding up the effects of these variables, which Soreson jokingly dubs as 'gas station theory' (1998: 248). The root cause of such practice is taking the task of testing a theory as equivalent to identifying the statistical significance of a regression coefficient. Because a variable or a set of variables represent a particular theory, it seems that several theories can be tested simultaneously by comparing the statistical significance of their corresponding coefficients.

A related problem is the use of control variables, which both Lieberson and Sorenson have criticized. I have found Lieberson's comments especially useful (1985: chs 6 and 10). His general point is that because most studies in the social sciences are observational rather than experimental, it is inappropriate to pretend that the effects of the control variables have been controlled in an experimental setting. A counterintuitive implication of this simple observation is that it is only safe to use control variables when their presence does not make a difference on interpreting the effects of the interested independent variables; if their presence does make a difference, then we have to avoid using them *because they have not been actually controlled in the strict experimental sense*. Lieberson is not completely against the use of control variables. What he suggests is to interpret them in a comparative sense (1985: 213–5), which is consistent with the predictive interpretation of regression coefficients that is proposed by Gelman and Hill (2007). The effect of the variable to our interest stands out when the cases have the same value on a control variable. To avoid confusion and misuse, perhaps we should call them 'reference variables' to denote the comparative function of such variables and to avoid the implied experimental setting.

Almost Uniform Effects across the Cases

All problems listed above are about variables. Andrew Abbott (1988, 1992) points out a problem with regard to the cases: once a linear regression model is created, it is assumed that the relations identified in such models hold true for all the cases. In his words, a statistical model can only allow for one story or one narrative.

Overall, Abbott's criticism is fair and correct: users of statistical methods usually come up with only one or very few models for describing the relations among the variables, assuming that they can apply these models for all the cases under study. Statisticians do remind us that we must detect any groups for which the studied relationship may take a different form. For example, the relationship between education and income differs for males and females. Therefore, we need two models, one for each sex group. As we have seen before, such grouping effect has been formally incorporated in multilevel models. The principle applies to more sophisticated methods, such as structural equation modelling, in which researchers can examine whether the same model holds for several groups.

The effort of studying the varying forms of a particular model across different groups, however, soon reaches a limit. The statistical procedure usually cannot handle a large number of groups, and the assumption of constant effect remains intact within each group. Statistical methods are not designed to study the uniqueness of each case. They are tools of summarizing the data. Sooner or later, we have to stop at a certain point and assume that the differences among the cases must be ignored.

EIGHT

Time Matters

Time in Social Research

It is virtually impossible to study anything social without paying attention to time, as social phenomena are always evolving. Nevertheless, data collected that measure temporal change are not easy to come by, and often social scientists have to be reminded to incorporate time into their analysis. All methods introduced in the preceding chapters are for analysing data collected at one particular time point, the so-called 'cross-sectional data'. The best example is a population census. It is required that all data refer to an exact point of time, such as 12 am on 31 December 2000. Ideally, it should be a snapshot of every citizen of the same nation, all standing still at that moment so as to be counted. Cross-sectional sample surveys such as the general social surveys in the US and Europe follow the same idea but in a much smaller scale.

Such data may contain information about time, such as year of birth, time spent on watching television and so forth, which allows us to study some time-related issues. But as all measurements were taken at only one time point, it is impossible to study change over time. Hans-Peter Blossfeld and his colleagues (2007: 5–13) have summarized the limitations of such data as follows:

- Cross-sectional models can only show the net effect of causal variables on stable situations, but stability is very rare in social sciences.
- It is very hard to establish causal relations based on cross-sectional data because they cannot show the direction of causality.
- Cross-sectional data cannot help us discover 'the different strengths of reciprocal effects'.
- There are many potential sources of selective biases, which are 'not only *not observed* but also effectively *unmeasurable*'.

- It is impossible to identify and disentangle 'the time-related selective processes' with cross-sectional data.
- 'Cross-sectional data cannot be used to distinguish age and cohort effects', nor can they identify the effects of historical settings.
- Some time-related factors, for example, multiple clocks, historical eras, and point-in-time events, are simply out of the sight of cross-sectional studies.
- Results from analysis of cross-sectional data cannot tell us how long the studied states have lasted.
- It would be a serious fallacy to generalize results from a particular time point to the whole period of process.
- Explanatory variables in cross-sectional studies could easily overestimate the changes of the response variables because they ignore the effect of the response variable's previous states.

In short, cross-sectional studies suffer from many limitations, so we should observe social phenomena while they are evolving with time – the fundamental idea of longitudinal studies – especially for discovering causal connections among them.

But why do we not give up cross-sectional studies once and for all and invest our valuable money and time in longitudinal ones? The answer is that cross-sectional studies do have their value in some situations. In the first case, it turns out that a snapshot may be good enough. Take the example of census again. After counting the number of people and their basic attributes at 12 am on 31 December 2000, these people will change before we start the next round of counting (usually a decade): some died, others moved to other countries, some got married and babies were born, some lost their jobs while others got a big bonus. When we carry out the next census, what we will be actually observing is the *net* outcome of demographic changes. For example, the total number of people may not change very much but the people we observe in 2010 are not the same group of people in 2000. This is fine unless we do care about who have died, or were born, or immigrated to another country. At least from the government point of view, these changes are not the most important thing to consider. For social researchers, as pointed out in Chapter 1, we can do many things with statistics, and only some of them involve causal analysis based on temporal changes.

This leads to another reason for the survival of cross-sectional studies: if our main research interest is to compare the situations of different groups, then data collected from cross-sectional surveys will serve the purpose well enough. Indeed, statistical methods can offer great help for comparing different groups (Liao, 2002) along many dimensions: gender, race and ethnicity, education, employment and so on. It would be ideal, of course, if we could compare these groups across a period of time as well. Nevertheless, we have to consider the practical issue of cost: is it really worth the time and money to trace these groups over time? It becomes very difficult to do especially when the scope of study is very large. For the social surveys in the US and Europe, most of them remain cross-sectional mainly because it is financially infeasible to repeatedly interview the same group of people every two or three years. The loss of temporality is compensated by a large and diverse sample. Longitudinal designs are more effective in terms of tracing the process of social changes, but they have their own problems, as we shall discover later.

How to analyse time is an even more complicated issue as social scientists follow different methodological paradigms. Andrew Abbott (2001) collected some of his important essays in *Time Matters*, in which he discourages researchers from using statistical methods because they all work under the assumption of linearity, which he considers to be seriously flawed. Historical sociology (too big to give a few references, start, however, with James Mahoney and Dietrich Rueschemeyer [2003]) and biographical studies (Chamberlayne et al., 2000; Roberts, 2001; Moore, 2004) are two other alternatives to statistical methods for studying time.

All these methods concern themselves more with *the order and historical contexts of events* rather than *measuring and modelling the exact effect of time* in social processes. A distinctive feature of statistical methods is that everything related to time has to be measured before they are analysed, such as the timing of events, duration, speed (or rate of change), probability of change of states. These two broad approaches should not be understood as being antipodes – statistical methods could reveal something we could not easily see in a large amount of numeric information, and conversely, the context-oriented approach could provide valuable information for making decisions in specifying statistical models.

The objective of this chapter is to introduce two major statistical methods for analysing time. Each of them has developed into a sub-section in the general discipline of statistics, so in terms of the technical details we are going to scratch only a small part of the surface. Our objective is not to scratch a bigger surface; rather, we aim to learn what methods are out there for analysing time and why they could help us make sense of our data.

For two reasons, we shall start with panel studies, that is, observing approximately the same group of subjects repeatedly at different time points. First, they represent the most rigorous design of studying temporal patterns and effects, and several important longitudinal surveys, including Panel Study of Income Dynamics (PSID) in the US, Socio-Economic Panel in Germany, British Household Panel Study (BHPS), now incorporated in Understanding Society: the UK Household Longitudinal Study (UKHLS), have collected and will continue to collect a huge and valuable amount of data.

The second reason is that the methods for analysing this type of data have the closest affinity with multilevel models that we just learnt in the previous chapter, so it should be easier for the reader to understand some longitudinal models as special cases of multilevel models. Here, each individual is higher level unit and all measurements at different time points are nested within each individual.

Then we move on to a special type of longitudinal data: event histories. While panel studies focus on changes throughout time, event history studies are more interested in the time duration and the probability of experiencing one or more events, such as unemployment, divorce, relapse or recidivism. Common to all these events is *a definite ending point* of the observed process.

What we shall not cover in this chapter is techniques for analysing time series data. Unlike the data collected in social surveys, a time series usually has only one case representing an aggregate entity, such as a market, an industry or a company, which is measured at a large number of time points. Besides the limited number of cases, another requirement responsible for the low popularity of time series analysis in social sciences is that there should be *50 or more* consecutive time points in order to allow for a reliable time series analysis (Warner, 1999: 18; Tabachnick and Fidell, 2001: 837), a condition that most time series in social sciences cannot satisfy. And even if the series is long enough, social scientists use time series only to show a historical trend, not to model the relations among some variables across the time span. For example, social and political scientists with a strong interest in history often encounter such data. Charles Tilly (1972, 1992, 1997), showed the time series of disturbances, protests and military coups in Britain, France and other countries but these time series were presented only as basic background information; most explanatory work was done not by statistically analysing the trend or cycle in the time series but by interpreting historical documents.

This type of data is mostly seen in the fields of finance and economics as financial institutions need to regularly keep good records of an important indicator, for example, the interest rate, the consumer price index (CPI) and the unemployment rate. As the records are usually taken monthly, or at least yearly, the time series can be 50 points long or more. Consequently, most statistical strategies and techniques have been developed to analyse financial and econometric data (Chatfield, 2003; Lutkepohl, 2007). Physical psychologists and medical researchers may also have long time series data if they measure blood pressure, physical movements, utterances of words, on a highly frequent basis.

Regardless of the type of data and the statistical method, there are two general but important points to keep in mind: (1) the interested effects, modelled with coefficients, do not remain constant anymore, and we must use models that can reflect and incorporate the changes over time; and (2) which statistical method we shall use depends on the nature of the process under study, which aspect of the process we really want to know, and how the data were generated for representing the process.

Panel Studies

It helps to start with some design issues before learning the statistical concepts. In a cross-sectional study, data are collected on the cases only once. When researchers do contact *the same* group of subjects again and again with the same set of measurement instruments such as survey questions, we have a panel study. Therefore, a panel study consists of at least two waves. The idea is that the information collected on the same subjects but at different time points would allow the researcher to measure the actual, not simply the net, changes over time. It is often claimed that panel data and longitudinal data in general offer the best evidence for causal analysis, because they demonstrate temporal sequence, a condition for making causal connections. However, such sequence may or may not be an indication of causal relationship. All statistical methods discussed here are treated as tools of exploration, description, and prediction, but not causation.

In designing a panel study, researchers have to answer a few very important questions: When should the first wave start? How long should the gap between two waves be? How many waves should there be or when should we terminate the study? If some subjects disappear or refuse to participate anymore in a particular wave, shall we recruit more to replace them? A problem unique to panel studies is 'attrition'. As the study moves along, a certain proportion of subjects will disappear for a variety of reasons – death, moving house, migration, tiredness and so on, making the number of subjects in later waves become smaller and smaller. To discover the underlying reasons for attrition and how to deal with it are very complicated issues.

The time of the first wave is normally a practical matter, depending on when the researchers are ready for collecting the data. But sometimes there may be a good reason for starting at a particular year, month or day. Targeting a particular cohort – the group of people who happened to be borne in the same year or to experience the same event – is an example. Researchers may be interested in those borne in 2000 as 'the millennium cohort' or those borne during the Second World War.

In addition, we may wish to have a smaller between-wave gap if we can afford in order to gather richer information, but we need to consider whether a particular length of gap has any substantive meaning. This leads to the fundamental question of whether the waves of our study are consistent with the *actual* waves of change in reality, if there are any. As usually we have no convincing knowledge or theory about the actual waves, we would have a better chance of capturing them with more frequent waves. In social research, the gaps between waves are also an effect of the discrete nature of our measurements. Our conclusions will almost exclusively be based on observations made at a few selected time points. It is only in the ideal world of continuous observation that we could stay with our subjects as their shadow all the time in order to know what's going on!

Related to this 'discrete nature' of panel studies is the overall length of time covered: have we observed long enough so that we can observe any *long-term* patterns? If our study does not cover enough waves or last long enough to capture the actual long-term trend, then the data will not be rich enough to show the actual patterns of change and, as a consequence, our conclusions may be seriously flawed.

In real panel studies, the results will almost always show some evidence of change. The question is where the observed changes come from. Note that there is certainly a discrepancy between our data and what the data are meant to measure, and that measurement error may be the source of the observed change. One example is the so-called 'panel-conditioning effect' (Kalton et al., 1989: 249–50): respondents have the capacity of learning about the study from the early waves and thereafter adjust their answers in following ones. So, are the changes observed in later waves genuine or are they results of learning and adaptations? This is a type of measurement errors special to panel studies, and their effect will accumulate over time.

As pointed out before, each respondent can be seen as a higher level unit and his or her responses the lower units. In the previous chapter we learnt that either the 'long' or the 'wide' form could be used to organize multilevel data. However, for longitudinal analysis, Singer and Willett (2003: 20) point out four disadvantages of the wide form. Following their advice, we shall adopt the long form when discussing the statistical methods. Table 8.1 presents a hypothetical example.

Table 8.1   An example of the long form data matrix in a longitudinal study

ID	Wave	Age	Gender	Education	Employment
1	1	20	F	In university	Part-time
1	2	22	F	BA	Unemployed
1	3	24	F	BA	Employed
...	...	...	...	...	...
12	1	22	M	BA	Unemployed
12	2	24	M	MS	Unemployed
12	3	24	M	MS	Part-time
12	4	26	M	PhD student	Part-time
...	...	...	...	...	...
98	1	21	M	High school	Employed
98	2	23	M	High school	Employed
...	...	...	...	...	...
1123	1	24	F	BA	Employed
1123	2	26	F	BA	Unemployed
1123	3	28	F	BA	Employed
1123	4	30	F	BA	Employed
...	...	...	...	...	...

We can see from the changes of age that the survey was conducted every two years. There are four individual respondents in this example, and we can see how many waves each of them participated. Suppose there are total four waves. Respondent no. 1 participated in three waves, no. 12 four waves, no. 98 only two waves, and no. 1123 four waves. This is an example of 'unbalanced data' because the respondents did not participate in an equal number of waves. In the following discussion, we shall assume balanced data because how to deal with unbalanced data is more a practical and technical than a conceptual problem.

The three variables other than 'wave' and 'age' are used to show that some variables are 'time-invariant' (their values do not change with time) such as gender, while others are 'time-variant' (their values do change with time) such as education and employment. Obviously, it is the time-variant variables that will become the target of our analysis.

I should warn the reader that the exploratory methods commonly used for cross-sectional data, such as histograms and scatter plots, usually do not work well for panel data. The first reason is that there are usually too few waves to allow for any reliable identification of changing patterns. Very few longitudinal surveys last for more than a dozen waves. Each individual case's information at different time points constitutes a mini time series, but because there are so few time points it is very hard for us to become certain about the shape of a possible pattern, and this problem is especially astute if the attrition rate is high. In contrast to the small number of time points is the large number of respondents. If we plot the data of thousands of respondents in a scatter plot against wave, you can imagine how messy the plot will be. Although an 'average trajectory' can be fitted, we should avoid using it as we shall commit the 'ecological fallacy' if we infer any individual path of change from the average.

As panel data can be seen as a special case of multilevel data, we can apply the multilevel models introduced in the previous chapter. Suppose there are two levels, we can use a level-1 sub-model for modelling how the response variable varies *within* each individual case (*intra*-individual) and a level-2 sub-model for showing how it varies *between* the cases (*inter*-individual). Our objective is to see whether there are any statistically significant changes across time and individuals. The model becomes more complicated when the response variable is categorical or latent and when time-dependent and time-independent explanatory variables are added into the model. To specify the exact form of the model is the most important as well as the most difficult part of the modelling process.

No matter how complicated the theoretically informed model looks like, as Singer and Willett (2003: 92) recommend, we should always fit the unconditional means model and the unconditional growth model – to be explained soon below – before fitting any other models. The reason is that although our main interest is in the change over time and the variation of change across individual cases, *we must not assume the existence of these variations*. The function of these two models is to establish (or dismiss) these variations – it would be pointless to model changes if there are no changes at all.

Here is the unconditional means model:

$$Y_{ij} = \beta_{0j} + \varepsilon_{ij} \text{ and } \beta_{0j} = \gamma_{00} + \zeta_{0j} \tag{8.1}$$

It is a 'means' model because there is only an intercept in the model, which represents the means. The first equation says that the response variable Y is constant across different time points for individual j. Therefore, if we plot Y against time, then we shall see only flat lines, one for each individual case. Each individual's value can be seen as the mean of Y across all time points; in other words, it is the intra-individual mean. The second equation of the model says that all these intra-individual means share a grand mean, γ_{00}, across all individuals; that is, γ_{00} is the inter-individual mean.

There are deviations from each of the means for each time point or each individual, which are represented by the two error terms ε_{ij} and ζ_{0j}, and we assume that they are normally distributed with mean 0 and its own variance. Note that the purpose of fitting the unconditional means model is not really to estimate the exact magnitude of the means; rather, the value of the model lies in the two error terms because they can tell us whether there is enough variations across time and individuals to be modelled. This translates into a statistical exercise of testing the hypotheses that there is no variation at all, i.e. both ε_{ij} and ζ_{0j} are equal to 0. Although it is very likely that these hypotheses will be rejected, it is worth the trouble to establish the variation. Furthermore, the relative size of each error term's variance can also tell us where most of the variation comes from, across time or across individual cases.

The unconditional growth model moves one step further by including the time variable as the only explanatory variable:

$$\begin{aligned} Y_{ij} &= \beta_{0j} + \beta_{1j} TIME_{ij} + \varepsilon_{ij} \\ \beta_{0j} &= \gamma_{00} + \zeta_{0j} \\ \beta_{1j} &= \gamma_{10} + \zeta_{1j} \end{aligned} \tag{8.2}$$

It is a 'growth' model because it models how Y 'grows' over time, and it is 'unconditional' because *TIME* is the only explanatory variable. The difference between this model and the previous means model is that this model claims that measurements on each individual case do change over time but the rate of change (usually referred to the slope) is constant, and our objective is test whether time is statistically viable with our data. Suppose we want to know how people's level of support to Barack Obama has changed throughout his political campaigns. If both γ_{00} and γ_{10} are statistically significant, then γ_{00} is the level of support at time 0, i.e. the initial stage, the sign of γ_{10} will show us whether the level has gone up or down, and the absolute value of γ_{10} tells us the rate of such change.

Again, deviations from the true values are absorbed in the error terms. Note that we now have three error terms, and their meanings have changed due to the addition of *TIME*. For each individual case j, ε_{ij} indicates the variations around the temporal trajectory across time. The other two error terms, ζ_{0j} and ζ_{1j}, measure the size of variations across individual cases. ζ_{0j} measures the variation with regard to the intercept (or the initial status) β_{0j}, while ζ_{1j} measures the variation about the slope (or rate of change). They are assumed to have a joint normal distribution with means 0, own variance and a covariance. These are all parameters that need to be estimated later on. By examining the statistical significance of these parameters (or testing the hypotheses that they are equal to 0), we can find out the major source of variation. More specifically, estimates of the variances can show whether the variation over time is statistically significant, and the estimate of covariance will show whether the variation of the intercept is correlated with the variation of the slope, i.e. whether the rate of change is somehow dependent on the magnitude of Y at the first time point.

As the target of our models is the change of the response variable over time, we must think very carefully how we define change. Implicit in our interpretation of the coefficients is the notion of *linear* change. That is, we assume that the rate of change remains constant at different time points. It is indeed naïve to automatically accept this assumption. We can check whether it holds by randomly selecting a manageable number of cases, plotting the response variable against time and examining whether a relatively linear pattern exits. However, this is easier said than done. Sometimes, the small number of time points at which the measurements were made is too small to allow a clear pattern to emerge.

In addition, different cases may show different temporal patterns and it may be very hard to see whether a nonlinear pattern is applicable to most of the cases. This is why the linear model is often chosen – it is not because researchers do not want to fit nonlinear models but because it demands much stronger evidence and theory to back up a nonlinear pattern. A linear model is chosen most often due to the lack of alternatives. If there is clear evidence or theory for nonlinearity, researchers of course should adopt a nonlinear model, such as logistic, exponential or inverse quadratic (Singer and Willett, 2003: 232–42).

A related issue is the measurement of change. Given that the linearity assumption does hold, when we interpret a coefficient as the average rate of change of Y given one unit change of a predictor, we use the difference of Y's values measured at two different time points as our measurement of change. Some statisticians (Alison, 1990; Taris, 2000) have pointed out that the differences, usually referred to as 'change scores', can only be used as valid measurement of change under some conditions. For instance, the scores must be reliable to be used for measuring change; if they are not, then the change scores will be even less reliable, especially when they are correlated. The best situation is when they are very reliable but not correlated, and the opposite situation is the worst, i.e. they are very unreliable but highly correlated. A second condition is that the change scores do not depend on the initial score. If they do, then the change scores are not trustworthy anymore because their values depend on the magnitude of the initial score, thereby cannot reflect the true size of change.

There is also an issue for the explanatory variables. A special and tricky question for longitudinal analysis is that some explanatory variables vary with time while others do not. There is no difficulty to deal with time-invariant variables, as their effects are constant throughout time. The complexities lie in those time-varying variables. Without going into the technical details, there are several questions researchers need to consider when planning to add this type of variables into a model. First and foremost, we must be clear about the source of variation of a time-varying explanatory variable, because there are a variety of reasons for the variation. This is an important issue because we must make sure that the variables are temporarily precedent of the response variable. Some are 'natural' outcomes of time, such as age and physical conditions, which change in a certain way no matter how others behave. A more socially relevant example is seniority-based salaries. As these variables are exogenous to the process that we are interested in, there should be no confusion that they are valid predictors of the response variable.

Not all sources of variation are so clear. For example, we may want to explain the likelihood of participation in national election by the level of exposure to media coverage of political events. It is very likely that exposure to media coverage varies with time. The trouble is that it is not necessarily true that people are exposed to media coverage first and then go to vote; the reverse could be true as well – it was for some other reasons that they went to vote, such as peer pressure, which then increased their interest in politics, which in turn made them watch or read more political news. Researchers therefore need to justify the temporal precedence of the time-varying explanatory variables before adding them into the model.

Finally, there are a couple of relatively minor and technical issues. Below is a simple model with only time and another explanatory variable:

$$Y_{ij} = \beta_{0j} + \beta_{1j}TIME_{ij} + \beta_{2j}X_{ij} + \varepsilon_{ij} \qquad (8.3)$$

For this model, we usually assume that and β_{0j} each β_{1j} has its own distribution with mean 0, a variance and a covariance. We make this assumption because we believe they should vary randomly across individual cases. Now, we have another coefficient β_{2j}. In theory, it could have its own probability distribution with 0 as mean and a variance.

However, as this is a multilevel model, more parameters are introduced if we have a new variance. Not only we will have the variance of β_{2j} but we will have two more covariances σ_{20} and σ_{21}. That is, three new parameters need to be estimated because of the addition of one more explanatory variable. It is clear that we will have a large number of parameters – mostly variances and covariances – to estimate if there are many explanatory variables in the model. At some point, the model may not be estimable simply because there are too many parameters. To avoid that, we could stop some coefficients from having random error terms. The question is: Which ones shall be deprived of such treatment? The answer is beyond statistics.

A similar issue is the interaction between *TIME* and time-varying explanatory variables. Model (8.3) only includes the main effect of X; that is, its effect will be the same at all time points. To show that its effect varies across time, we must include an interaction term in the model – after all, that is the very meaning of time-varying variable, that is, its effect depends on the time point, as shown in the following model:

$$Y_{ij} = \beta_{0j} + \beta_{1j}TIME_{ij} + \beta_{2j}X_{ij} + \beta_{3j}TIME_{ij} * X_{ij} + \varepsilon_{ij} \tag{8.4}$$

There could be further complications added to this model. But even for this simple representation, we can easily see that the model could become very complicated if we have several time-varying explanatory variables. In social science publications, models for cross-sectional data usually include 10 or 20 explanatory variables. It is hard to believe that the same could be routinely done for longitudinal data. In the end, the challenge is to find simple but still sensible longitudinal models.

Event History Analysis

Event history analysis is a special case of longitudinal analysis. It is longitudinal because cases are observed and measured repeatedly at different time points. It is special because our main interest is not in the change of a response variable over time but whether and when the cases experience a particular event after we observe them for a certain period of time. For statistical analysis, the history of an event is not represented with narratives that attempt to make sense of temporarily connected events. Here, 'history' refers to the temporal duration of a specific state that has elapsed before an interested event took place. So, we target two main variables: (1) whether the cases have experienced the interested event; (2) how long it takes for them to experience that event.

Event history analysis originates from biological and medical studies, and it is used in engineering as well. This is why you will see some other names in the literature: survival analysis or failure-time analysis. Event, risk and survival are the three key words. Note that the events in medicine and engineering are of a special kind. For medicine, death is the mostly commonly observed event, and those who have not died up to a certain point of time have survived. In engineering, some products passed a certain test while others failed, but again the reference is to a certain point of time – hence 'failure time'. The events under study have two distinctive features: (1) it is *inevitable* that they will happen – sooner or later the patients of a serious disease will die and the products under test will eventually break down if we test them long enough; (2) the events – death or breakdown – are *undesirable*, at least from the cases' point of view, and it is due to such undesirability of the event that the word 'risk' is used.

Not all events social researchers are interested in, however, are necessarily inevitable or undesirable. We may observe a group of unemployed people, some of which may remain unemployed for the rest of their life. Studying friendship among a group of children, we may find that some of them never manage to make a friend till the time our research has to terminate. Some young offenders may not commit any crimes again after release from prison or any rehabilitation programmes. Unlike death or breakdown, social events do not have an internal mechanism that will definitely lead to a particular state. In other words, some patients may never die (Box-Steffensmeier and Jones, 2004: 184–5).

In addition, these events may not be undesirable to those under study: some women may prefer staying at home to taking a low-paid job, some children simply do not want too much peer pressure, and it is desirable for the offenders and the society in general to keep themselves clean. But if the events may not be undesirable, then it could be misleading to still use the word 'risk'. 'Chance' or 'probability' is more neutral and therefore preferable for social research. If 'risk' is retained for the sake of consistency in the literature, we must remember that 'risk' and 'survival' are generic terms.

Now let us take a look at how event history data are collected. In a panel study, we observe the cases at a certain number of time points, and the number of time points is determined by our research objectives and the amount of resources at our disposal. In an event history study, we also have a starting point and an ending point. But there are several important differences between the two. First of all, the starting point of an event history has a special meaning: all cases have not experienced the interested event and therefore they are all subject to the chance of experiencing it ('at risk'). It is possible that some cases have already experienced the event *even before our study started*. Suppose we are observing a group of unemployed people in order to know how long it takes for them to get employed. Some unemployed people may have already found a job before we started our investigation. These people are outside our target of research and usually called 'left-censored' as they are to the left of the timeline of our research (Case A in Figure 8.1).

Second, in a panel study, we usually take measurements on the cases regularly between the starting and the ending points. In event history analysis, we cannot do that because when a case experiences the interested event is out of our control; in other words, we do not know when the event happens to a particular case during the period of our observation. We must record the time between the starting point and the point at which the event happens, *if it indeed happens before the ending point*.

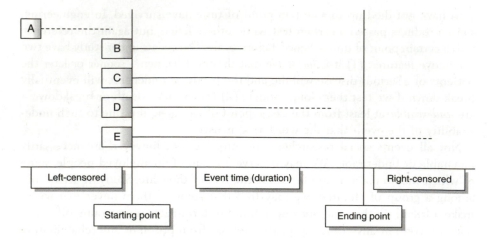

Figure 8.1   Different types of cases in an event history study

Last, at the ending point, we need to record, among those who reach the end point, who has experienced the event and who has not. Those who have not are called 'right-censored' because they move into a situation to the right of our ending point (Case E in Figure 8.1), and we do not know whether they will *never* experience a transition or they will experience it *after the end of our observation*. Others may be censored even before the end of the observation period (Case D). This would pose a serious measurement problem: what value should we record for these cases? We cannot record the event time (from the starting to the ending point) because the case did not experience the event at the ending point. We cannot record 0 because the case did go through the event time. Finally, we cannot dismiss these records either, because they are what we want to study, so our analysis would be biased without them. The only valid record is that the case has been censored, and this is something unique to event history analysis. An advantage of event history models is that we do not have to drop these censored cases; actually, the models can incorporate such cases into the analysis. Similar to missing values, these cases should be censored either randomly or for practical reasons. If they are censored for a reason that is related to our research purpose – systematically censored, then our analysis will be misleading.

Note that the starting point (or the ending point) does not necessarily refer to the real calendar time, although very often this is the case. For example, we may want to take the beginning of the first job as the starting point of a career ('the clock time'). It would be ideal, of course, if they all started at exactly the same time. It is very likely, however, that different people started their first job at different time points: some started in June 2000, others in September 2001 and so on. For these people to be comparable, we would prefer that their starting times are as close as possible. There is no specific requirement, however, as to how close it has to be in order to ensure that no other factor will contaminate the analysis.

The problem is that any gap between starting points may introduce 'the period effect' into the process under study if a particular event, such as 9/11, will shape what we will observe later on. But how should we determine the unit for measuring the event time – should it be minutes, hours, days, weeks, months or years? In principle, the smaller the units, the better as this allows us a higher chance of capturing the exact time of event. Nevertheless, the decision is sometimes influenced by theoretical and practical grounds as well. In order to avoid any confusion over whether the interested event occurs or not to a particular case, an operational and consistent set of criteria must be set up.

Figure 8.1 is only a simple representation of the data collection and measurement processes since it does not take into account a few complicated situations. For example, we may have 'late comers' who join the study after the starting point, and we have to decide how to count the time of duration for these cases. A more complicated situation emerges when the cases could end up in any one of the states that are independent of each other. For the example of employment, a person could become part-time employed, full-time employed or self-employed. Finally, the above figure only shows 'one spell', that is, one complete process from the beginning to the end. Many social phenomena, however, are repeatable and thereby have multiple spells, such as marriage–divorce, unemployment–employment, abstinence–relapse. How to deal with these situations is beyond the scope of this book (see Yamaguchi, 1991; the second half of Singer and Willett, 2003; Box-Steffensmeier and Jones, 2004; Hans-Peter Blossfeld et al., 2007).

Now, let us see what an event-history data set looks like. In social research, time is often measured as a discrete variable. However, for two reasons it is important to remind ourselves that, at least in theory, time is a continuous variable. First, we will lose some information after turning time into a discrete variable. For example, two events took place in the same month may actually have happened in different days. In even history analysis, such cases are labelled as 'tied'. The second reason is that some statistical models are created for continuous variables, although later extensions are made for discrete variables.

If it is acceptable to make time discrete, then we could break the whole observation period – from the starting point to the ending point – into a certain number of time intervals, so in the following data matrix (Table 8.2, the wide form), we could record the number of intervals a case has survived and the interval it was censored if censoring did take place.

The trouble with such matrix is that we cannot learn how things change over time. More importantly, we want to know the change of the probability of experiencing the

Table 8.2   Wide form of event history data

Case	Time of survival	Censored	Time of censoring	...
1		0		
2		1		
3		1		
...				

interested event over the pre-determined time period. To get a sense of what the change looks like, we can find out the proportion of cases that have (or have not) experienced the event, and then plot the proportions against time. That is, we want to have a table like the following, which is referred to as 'the life table' in event history analysis, see Table 8.3.

Table 8.3   A protocol of the life table

Time interval	No. of cases at the starting point	No. of cases left or censored	No. of cases experienced the event	% of cases survived the event	% of cases experienced the event
1					
2					
3					
...					

That is, we count the number of cases at the beginning of each time interval, take away those who left the study (quit or censored) and those who experienced the event during that interval. The result will be the number of cases that survived the event. We then can calculate the proportion of cases that survived or experienced the event.

How can we produce the life table with the original data matrix? The answer is to use 'the long form', because only the long form shows what has happened at each time interval, as shown in Table 8.4.

Table 8.4   Long form of event history data matrix

Case	Time interval	Experienced event?	Censored
1	1	0	0
1	2	0	0
1	3	0	0
1	4	1	0
...	...	...	...
121	1	0	0
121	2	0	0
121	3	0	0
121	4	0	0
121	5	0	0
121	6	0	1
...	...	...	...

For example, Case 1 experienced the event at the fourth time interval and it was not censored; Case 121 did not experience the event up to the sixth interval and was censored perhaps because no observation could be made. Although the data file will indeed be very long with thousands of cases and each case has several intervals, it allows us to easily construct a life table by cross-tabulating time intervals with event and censoring, based on which we can calculate the proportion of survival and experiencing the event, respectively. Eventually, the life table or the graph based on it will show us the distribution of event occurrence over time.

Hazard Function

With the life table, we can introduce two important concepts as the targets of event history analysis. Although people call them 'functions', they are actually two probabilities. The first is the hazard function – hence the letter h. For discrete time, it is defined as the probability of experiencing the event at a particular interval for a particular case:

$$\hat{h}(t_{ij}) = \frac{\text{number of cases having experienced the event}}{\text{total number of cases at the beginning of the time interval}} \tag{8.4}$$

It says that the sample hazard (probability) – this is why it wears a hat – at interval j for case i is the proportion of the cases having experienced the event (or those who 'failed to survive') out of all the cases (usually called 'the risk set') at the beginning of the time interval. As a proportion, its value is always positive and between 0 and 1 (including).

Note that, although each case will have its own hazard function (the 'risk' of experiencing the event), the hazard is not an attribute that the cases carry into the study, nor is it measured during the study. The hazard is calculated based on what has happened to other cases, so it can only be calculated after the study is finished. Later we shall try to model on the hazard, but note that it is different from the response variables we encountered before.

Also, the above definition is *for discrete time only*, because it is only with time intervals, which are always discrete, that we can calculate the hazard. For continuous time, such intervals do not exist unless we artificially construct them. In theory, the probability for a case to experience an event at an 'exact' time point approaches zero. Therefore, we cannot directly define the hazard function for continuous time. What we can do is to apply limit theory and define the hazard as the rate for a specific time point, very similar to the slope of a tangent line of the cumulative probability function of a continuous variable. Without having to learn all the mathematics, the reader needs to keep in mind that for continuous time, we need to use the hazard *rate*, not the hazard probability.

As a rate refers to a specific instant, it is very unlikely that two cases will have exactly the same hazard rate. In contrast, it is very likely that they will have exactly the same probability, as it is more likely that they happen to be in the same time interval. In social research, there is not much need to study continuous time, either because time has not been measured at that level or because our analysis rarely demands that level of accuracy.

A more important reason for focusing on discrete time is that when we make time discrete by grouping its values into intervals, we are following a non-parametric procedure, which means that we do not hold any assumptions about the shape of the variable's distribution. Again, it is very rare in social sciences that we have some compelling justifications for these assumptions. In the end, we had better focus on discrete time and hazard probability. We learn methods for continuous time mainly because they were initially created for time measured at such level, or we would prefer to have a specific model.

Survivor Function

The other important concept for describing event changes over time is the survivor function, the probability that a case will not experience the event or will survive after a certain period of time. It sounds as if it is the very opposite of the hazard function – survival versus failure – but it is not. The reason is that the survivor function does not completely refer to any specific time interval; rather, it shows the probability of survival with regard to *all* previous time intervals. We can obtain a clearer understanding by examining the following definition:

$$\hat{S}(t_{ij}) = \frac{\text{number of cases having survived by the end of time interval } j}{\text{total number of cases in the study}} \tag{8.5}$$

Notice that the denominator is the 'total number of cases in the study', which remains the same throughout, not the total number of cases at the end of time interval j. The numerator, however, will become smaller and smaller over time because less and less cases will survive after experiencing the event. Therefore, unlike the hazard probability, which has no certain direction of change over time, the survivor probability will certainly decrease over time. How fast it decreases and how low it can decrease to depend on each particular situation. If at a certain point it is down to 0.5, then it means that only half of the cases have survived beyond that time point. This point is usually referred to as 'the median life time'. If more than 50% of the cases are still surviving at the last time point of observation, than there is no such median life time for that particular dataset.

But the hazard and the survivor functions do describe two opposite trends. Note that the survivor probability for a particular time interval j is the survivor probability of the previous time interval $(j–1)$ multiplied by the proportion of those who are not subject to experiencing the event at that time interval. We can express the idea with the following equation:

$$\hat{S}(t_j) = \hat{S}(t_{j-1})[1-\hat{h}(t_j)] \tag{8.6}$$

This equation has two very important implications. First, we can estimate the survivor probability not only for the time periods before censoring is applied but also for those after censoring, because we can derive them from previous ones when censoring was not applied yet. But note that the interpretation of these derived probabilities would be a bit different from those observed ones; we derive these probabilities under the assumption that the censoring is made purely due to practical or design reasons and has nothing to do with the actual event itself. Given the assumption holds, the derived survivor probabilities tell us what would have happened to the cases if there were no censoring. The second implication is that when $j = 1$, we have $\hat{S}(t_1) = \hat{S}(t_0)[1-\hat{h}(t_1)]$. But $\hat{S}(t_0) = 1$ because at the very beginning $(j = 0)$ every case is surviving, so $\hat{S}(t_1) = [1-\hat{h}(t_1)]$. Next, $\hat{S}(t_2) = \hat{S}(t_1)[1-\hat{h}(t_2)]$, but as $\hat{S}(t_1) = [1-\hat{h}(t_1)]$, $\hat{S}(t_2) = [1-\hat{h}(t_1)][1-\hat{h}(t_2)]$. In general:

$$\hat{S}(t_j) = [1-\hat{h}(t_j)][1-\hat{h}(t_{j-1})]\dots[1-\hat{h}(t_2)][1-\hat{h}(t_1)] \tag{8.7}$$

Note that there is no longer survivor probability on the right-hand side. This is an excellent example of using algebra to derive an unexpected result: we do not need the survivor probability for the previous time period in order to calculate a particular survivor probability; all we need is the hazard probabilities before that time.

For a particular data set, one should explore the change of the hazard and the survivor probabilities by plotting them against the time periods. This is an important albeit preliminary step for the following statistical modelling process. Just as we check whether the relationship between two continuous variables is linear or not by examining their scatter plot before we run a simple linear regression, exploring the shape of the hazard probability may indicate the specific form of our model.

Modelling Process

To start building a model, we must be clear about what our target is. When building a model for a discrete even history dataset, our target is the hazard probability of experiencing the event, not whether experiencing the event or how long it takes to experience the event. We can answer either the whether or the when question separately, but that is not what we want to model. Our true objective is to answer the two questions at the same time; that is, how the length of time taken to experience the event affects the likelihood of experiencing it. The hazard probability serves this purpose well because it tells us the probability of experiencing the event at a particular time point. By examining its change over time we can have the answer that we really want.

Statistically, we can understand the hazard probability as the probability of taking the value of 1 of the dummy variable whether a case has experienced an event, with 1 as yes and 0 as no. A logistic regression model would naturally come to our mind:

$$\ln\left(\frac{h(t_j)}{1 - h(t_j)}\right) = \alpha_j T_j + \beta_1 X_{1j} + \beta_2 X_{2j} + \dots + \beta_p X_{pj} \tag{8.8}$$

It says that the natural logarithm of the odds of the hazard is a linear function of a time effect plus the effects of some explanatory variables. The time effect is absolutely understandable – the starting point of the hazard is different at each time period because the number of the cases 'at risk' and the total number of cases vary from time to time. However, here we actually do not treat Time as a random variable; rather, it is only an indicator of time period. Therefore, we should actually write it as a series of dummy variables in the model:

$$\ln\left(\frac{h(t_j)}{1 - h(t_j)}\right) = [\alpha_1 T_1 + \alpha_2 T_2 + \dots + \alpha_j T_j] + [\beta_1 X_{1j} + \beta_2 X_{2j} + \dots + \beta_p X_{pj}] \tag{8.9}$$

In this model, unlike the time effect, which by definition will vary over time, the effect of each explanatory variable (the X) remains constant. Because β is the change of the natural log of the odds of the hazard given one unit change of X while other

Xs remain constant, the change of the log odds remain constant over time. This feature of the model is usually referred to as 'the proportional assumption', because β represents the proportion of the log odds of one value of X versus another. Note that, while the effect of an X on the log odds remains constant, its effect on the hazard itself does not, as the relationship between the hazard and the explanatory variables is not linear (logistic).

Please remember that the above model is useful only when time is measured as a discrete variable. When it is continuous, we will have a hazard *rate*, not a hazard probability. Consequently, we can no longer use model (8.9). Neither can we take the hazard rate directly to be the response variable, as its values have a lower bound of 0, although it should never reach 0. Instead, we take its logarithm:

$$\ln h(t_j) = baseline + \beta_1 X_{1j} + \beta_2 X_{2j} + ... + \beta_p X_{pj} \tag{8.10}$$

You must have noticed that the baseline – something similar to the intercept in the classical regression model – is not spelled out. Besides the transformation of the response variable, this is another thing that we have to change for modelling the hazard rate. We cannot use the dummy variables as baselines, as we did for the hazard probability, because the hazard rate is continuous, which cannot be represented with dummy variables – there will be an infinite number of dummy variables, one for each instant. As it is continuous time, we know there must be some kind of a curve. The question is: What does it look like? If we know that, we can represent it mathematically with a function. The trouble is, it is very hard to know.

Statisticians have proposed some functions, such as the Weibull model, the Gompertz model and many log-based models (Box-Steffensmeier and Jones, 2004: ch. 3). These are called 'parametric' models as they reply on assumptions about the distributions of the parameters in those models, which pose two further problems for us. As using any other statistical models, we must ensure no serious violations of these assumptions. Even the assumptions are not violated, what is the theoretical or substantive ground for specifying a particular model? In social sciences it is very rare that we have a strong argument for choosing a particular model. It is very frustrating, but that's the reality: either we do not have a theory at all about a particular social process or we do not know which one of the many proposed theories is actually right. It is for this reason that Box-Steffensmeier and Jones (2004) have repeatedly argued that it is 'a statistical nuisance' to specify time dependence.

The model that they strongly recommend researchers to use is the Cox model. Basically, Sir David Cox's (1972, 1975) solution to the above problem was: leave the baseline function unspecified. As we have used logarithm to transform the hazard probability, all we need to do is to take the natural log of the baseline as well. The model becomes:

$$\ln h(t_j) = \ln h_0(t_j) + [\beta_1 X_{1j} + \beta_2 X_{2j} + ... + \beta_p X_{pj}] \tag{8.11}$$

Taking the anti-log of this equation, we have:

$$h(t_j) = h_0(t_j)e^{\beta_1 X_{1j} + \beta_2 X_{2j} + \ldots + \beta_p X_{pj}} \qquad (8.12)$$

Finally, moving the baseline hazard to the left-hand side, we have:

$$\frac{h(t_j)}{h_0(t_j)} = e^{\beta_1 X_{1j} + \beta_2 X_{2j} + \ldots + \beta_p X_{pj}} \qquad (8.13)$$

This model assumes that the ratio of the two hazards remains the same over time, as the coefficients do not change over time. It is because of the constancy of this ratio that people call the model 'proportional hazards model'. We can make the ratio change over time, of course, if that is a claim we want to make.

The smartest part of the model is that we do not actually lose much by leaving the baseline hazard unspecified, because we do not really need the baseline hazard to estimate and interpret the coefficients. Take the simple situation of having only one explanatory variable that can take two values 0 and 1. When it is equal to 0, the right-hand side of (8.12) becomes $h_0(t_j)$, and when it is 1, the right-hand side is $h_0(t_j)e^{\beta_1}$. The ratio of the two is e^{β_1}, which does not depend on the baseline hazard and time, and that is why the effect is constant. But note that our target has changed: what we really model on is *the ratio* of the two hazards, not the hazard function per se. Fortunately, most researchers do not think that is a big loss at all.

NINE

Statistical Case-oriented Methods

It is true that most statistical methods analyse variables, not cases. There has been an increasing resentment to the use of linear models, dubbed as 'variable-oriented', in the social sciences. The most influential advocate of the 'case-oriented' methods is perhaps Charles Ragin, who has developed 'qualitative comparative analysis' (QCA) for discovering configurations among cases with an ultimate purpose of making causal arguments (Ragin, 1992, 2000, 2008; Byrne and Ragin, 2009; Rihoux and Ragin, 2009).

Valid as it is, the study of cases, however, should not mean that we must abandon variables and all switch to QCA. This and other related methods have their own limitations as well: it is deterministic in causal explanation, it ignores measurement errors in data quality, and it cannot incorporate interaction effects and multiple causes (Lieberson, 1992, 2001, 2004).

After all, we do not have to dismiss variables and statistics in order to study cases. It is hard to imagine that we could study cases properly without using variables and statistics. Variables describe the attributes of the cases under study. If we abandon variables and statistics, we will have to study cases without studying their attributes at all. As quoted in Chapter 3, Daniele Caramani (2009) has made this point extremely clear in his recent book on QCA.

More generally, methods differ not in terms of *whether* they analyse variables or cases but in terms of *how* they analyse variables. The problems with linear models are not really about variables per se, but about how variables should be used and analysed in relation to social theories. If we do not think variables tell us much about causal processes, then we should analyse them for other purposes, such as description and prediction, or use them for analysing causal relations only when the right conditions are satisfied. If we think linear relations among variables do not make any theoretical sense, then we should use nonlinear models or other mathematical operations.

It is misleading to claim that all statistical methods are variable-based. In this chapter we shall learn some multivariate statistical methods for studying grouping structures among cases.[1] Classification is not only an important scientific activity but also has enormous ramifications for our lives (Bowker and Star, 1999). In this sense, biologists and sociologists have the same mission of putting the cases into meaningful taxonomies to facilitate further analysis.

The major limitation of these methods is not that they rely on variables for studying cases but that they are only 'case-*oriented*' without taking *relations* between cases seriously enough. They still try to compare the attributes of different groups of cases. A method that takes a head-on approach to analysing cases is social network analysis (SNA) (Wasserman and Faust, 1994; Scott, 2000; Carrington et al., 2005; Knoke and Yang, 2008). Mathematically, techniques for analysing social networks make use of both algebra as well as statistics, so statistics can find its use even in this genuinely case-oriented method.

Cluster Analysis (CLA)

Cluster analysis can be seen as the reverse process of analysis of variance (ANOVA). In ANOVA, we have categorical explanatory variables and a continuous response variable. The cases are grouped according to the combinations of categories. For example, suppose we have four groups with gender and race: male white, male non-white, female white, female non-white, and we aim to examine whether the groups are significantly different with regard to the interested continuous response variable, such as annual salary.

With cluster analysis, we do not have any information about the respondents' gender and race; all we know is their annual salary. The question is: how many meaningful groups can we classify the cases into? We may happen to find four groups and conclude that they are exactly the same as those in the above ANOVA analysis, but we had no idea what the groups were at the beginning. In this section, we assume that all the variables for predicting group membership are continuous; if they are categorical, then we need correspondence analysis, which we shall learn about later.

More generally, cluster analysis is a method for answering the following question: can we partition the cases into a few groups with regard to a set of selected variables? It is mostly a tool of exploration – we try to find out how many clusters there are and what they mean. We can reformulate our question in a confirmatory mode: if we think there are a certain number of clusters among the cases, can we confirm whether we are right or not by doing a cluster analysis? Unfortunately, the inferential procedures for confirmatory cluster analysis have been barely established.

Why do we want to find groups? The answer is a practical one: because we want to do something to them. The cases of interest to us are all different from each other

---

[1]Due to the limited space I have omitted latent class analysis.

in a certain number of aspects or dimensions. For example, people are different from one another in terms of gender, sexuality, age, race and so forth, and products are different with regard to price, cost, brand and so on. The situation is that we have a policy or a sales strategy but it would be too costly as well as unnecessary for the policy to target each particular individual.

Cluster analysis is a tool for helping us reduce the individuals into groups so that we deal with only a small and thus manageable number of targets. It does this by comparing the cases in terms of their values of the selected variables to our concern. If some cases are similar enough among themselves but are different enough from others, then they form a cluster. Cluster analysis is about measuring the similarities (or the opposite, differences) and making decisions on establishing the clusters. The identification of these clusters will provide the basis for future actions, such as marketing campaigns, poverty relief programmes and enforcement of a personnel policy.

Here is a very important but difficult question: *How do we know we have found the groups?* On the one hand, given that to a certain extent the cases are always similar, we can *always* group some of them together when an indicator of their similarity reaches a specific value. On the other hand, if the grouping process is so arbitrary – it seems there are many groupings out there and all we have to do is pick up 'the natural grouping'. If that is true, then we are not *finding* groups but *imposing* a 'correct' grouping structure on the cases. The line between 'finding' and 'imposing' is very fine. As we shall see below, in almost every step of cluster analysis there is a demand of the researcher's decision, but unfortunately there is not much statistical support for the decision-making.

Given the subjectivity of cluster analysis, I would suggest that researchers keep the following points in mind: (1) take the results of cluster analysis as tentative findings rather than as basis of final conclusions; (2) employ as much theoretical and substantive support as possible when carrying out the analysis and interpreting the results. In general, a cluster analysis involves the following steps:

(1) Choose the variables on which cases will be compared in respect to their similarities (or distances).
(2) Decide on the rules for how cases should be grouped together based on their similarities.
(3) Decide how similarities or dissimilarities between cases should be measured.
(4) Decide on the rules for determining the number of clusters.
(5) Produce a meaningful clustering structure of cases.
(6) Interpret and profile the clusters.

These are not rigid steps. In real analysis we need to go back and forth with trials and errors.

The first question is not a statistical one, as its answer depends on the substantive nature and objectives of the study and the available variables. Statistics cannot resolve the dispute if different researchers choose different sets of variables (usually called 'the clustering variates').

The statistical work starts from measuring the similarity between two cases or intermediary clusters (the clusters formed before all possible clusters have been formed and studied). Although technical details may vary, the principle is to maximize the within-cluster similarities or the between-cluster dissimilarities. Here, we must make decisions on two related issues: our overall approach and the specific measures of distance.

For overall strategy, we can follow either of the following two approaches. The first is non-hierarchical: starting with a certain number of cases, called 'cluster seeds', which have no hierarchical relationships among them. Then we 'grow' the clusters by attaching cases that are close to each of the seeds and eventually bringing every case to a particular cluster. How the seeds should be selected is a key issue, but there are no hard and fast rules. You can select the seeds randomly with a computer program, but you must specify the maximum number of clusters. Again, there is no general guideline for choosing the right number.

Or you can select the cluster seeds on your own. Besides, you must also decide how far away other cases are from the selected seeds so that you can say 'these cases belong to a same cluster as they are similar enough'. After this 'threshold of similarity' is determined, the seeds can be selected in at least two ways. The first is sequential: you can select one seed initially and then bring all the cases within the similarity threshold you have specified into a cluster. Then you do the same for another seed until all cases are assigned a cluster. The second allocation method is parallel: you select several seeds at the same time and proceed to form several clusters simultaneously. A potential problem is that, because the distance is preset, some cases will be requested to belong to more than one cluster or they are not assigned to any cluster. In these situations, adjustments can be made: cases previously assigned to a cluster can be reassigned to another in later analysis. Clearly, selecting the seeds is a highly arbitrary matter and all the following analysis depends on such arbitrary decision.

Most clustering methods widely used now are hierarchical: cases join a cluster in a sequence of ordered steps. This can be done in two opposite directions. First, we can proceed by treating each case as a separate cluster, then gradually joining the nearest cases together into a same cluster according to their similarities, and in the end putting all cases into one cluster. Understandably, this is 'the amalgamate method'.

Second, the reverse is 'the divisive method', by which we start with only one cluster including all the cases, gradually break it down into different clusters, again according to their similarities, and in the end break them into single-case clusters. As this is only a matter of direction, the two methods should generate very similar if not exactly the same results, although most computer packages use the amalgamate method.

Which one should we use, hierarchical or non-hierarchical? It is often recommended that researchers use both methods to reach better supported identification of clusters. That is, use hierarchical methods to identify an initial set of clusters, select a seed in each cluster, and run non-hierarchical procedures with the selected seeds to see if approximately the same clusters are identified.

After a clustering approach is decided, we need to set up a rule for how clusters should be established. Intuitively, the most straightforward rule is 'the nearest-neighbour method'. If we follow the amalgamate approach, we shall measure the distance between any two of them, and the two with the shortest distance come into one cluster. When there are two or more cases in each of the two clusters, the distance between the two clusters is determined by the shortest distance between any case of one cluster to any case in the other. This method is extremely local as it searches for the immediate next neighbour, easily producing a chain-like connection among cases. An obvious problem is that two cases of the same cluster may consequently be more dissimilar than two cases of two different clusters. To overcome that problem, 'the farthest-neighbour method' was invented, which measures the maximum distance between two clusters, splitting the cases into clusters step by step based on such distance. Clearly, both methods are sensitive to extreme values, one to the smallest distance and the other the largest distance.

To go beyond the limitations of both methods, we can use the average distance between the cases of any two clusters. A similar method is to use the distance between cluster centriods – the mean values of all cases on the variables used. As the clusters are evolving from one step to the next, the average or the mean will have to be calculated every time. Finally, there is Ward's method, which measures the distance between clusters with the sum of squares summed over all variables. These methods tend to produce similar results if there are no extreme values or outliers.

Now we turn to the question of measuring the distance between cases and clusters. Intuitively, the most straightforward way is to measure the length of the straight line between two cases:

$$\delta_{ij} = \sqrt{\sum_{k=1}^{p} (x_{ik} - x_{jk})^2} \qquad (9.1)$$

Here, δ_{ij} (delta) is the Euclidean distance between case i and case j; x_{ik} is the value of case i for variable k, and x_{jk} is the value of case j for variable k; p is the number of variables. In short, we compare the two cases by calculating the differences of their values of the selected variables; all the rest are simply mathematical operations. As the distance is more likely to become larger when we have a larger number of variables, we can standardize it with p:

$$\delta_{ij} = \sqrt{\frac{\sum_{k=1}^{p} (x_{ik} - x_{jk})^2}{p-1}} \qquad (9.2)$$

Researchers need to consider two issues related to the variables used. The first pertains to their variability due to units of measurement. If the same unit is used, such as the Likert scale, then this is not a problem. It is very likely, however, that different variables are measured with different units – year, dollar, a five-point scale, an 11-point scale, etc. As a result, distances between cases may become much larger simply because the variables were measured on a more variable scale. If that is the case – researches need to check this – then we can neutralize that effect by using a standardized score, such as the z-score.

The other issue is that the above definition implies that the p variables carry the same amount of weight or importance. That may not be the case if some of the variables are highly correlated to each other ('multicollinearity'), or if we would like to assign different weight to each variable for a theoretical or substantive reason. To incorporate the weight of each variable (W_k),[2] we have:

$$\delta_{ij} = \sqrt{\frac{\sum_{k=1}^{p} w_k (x_{ik} - x_{jk})^2}{p-1}} \tag{9.3}$$

Although the Euclidean measure is perhaps the most widely used, there are some other measures, including the city-block measure, which sums up the absolute values of the differences, the Chebychev measure, which uses the greatest distance across all variables used, and the Mahalanobis measure, which adjusts correlation and weight among the used variables. Their availability has increased the subjectivity of cluster analysis and made researchers obliged to justify their choices.

Once measured, the distances are usually represented graphically with a dendrogram (Figure 9.1),[3] with one dimension showing the case number and the other indicating the distance. The function of such graph is to visualize the distances among the cases and, more importantly, their changes, so that we can see when we have to tolerate a larger distance (or dissimilarity) if we want to put those cases together into a cluster. Figure 9.1 was created based on a sample of 32 cases that I randomly selected from the British part of European Social Survey (Round 3), and the distance is measured based on people's answers to three questions about social trust.[4]

It is clear that we should end up with a three-cluster solution, with cluster 2 having four cases and cluster 3 having only one. The length of the lines indicates the distance or dissimilarity between cases. As there are three long lines at the lower part of the graph, which indicate that the distances between the three groups are much larger than those within each group. In general, we choose the previous number of clusters when we see a large jump of distance. To know who are in each cluster, we need to study how they differ from each other on any aspect of interest to us.

Obviously, it is unfeasible to apply this method when the number of cases is very large. It will be very hard to read out any pattern in the dendrogram with thousands of cases. This is why I selected only 2% of the cases in the original data set.

It may also become difficult for the researcher to determine the number of clusters as more than one solution seems to be sensible. In that case, the researcher

---

[2] The weight can be assigned to each variable based on substantive knowledge, theories or a statistical indicator, such as the decomposition of variance.
[3] A dendrogram can be presented either horizontally or vertically. Figure 9.1 is horizontal, which is clearer when there are a relatively large number of cases. A similar graphing device is the icicle plot, which normally compares cases in terms of their similarity rather than the distance between them.
[4] The three questions use the same format of an 11-point scale, so there is no need to use weights. They ask whether people think 'Most people can be trusted or you can't be too careful', 'Most people try to take advantage of you, or try to be fair' and 'Most of the time people helpful or mostly looking out for themselves'.

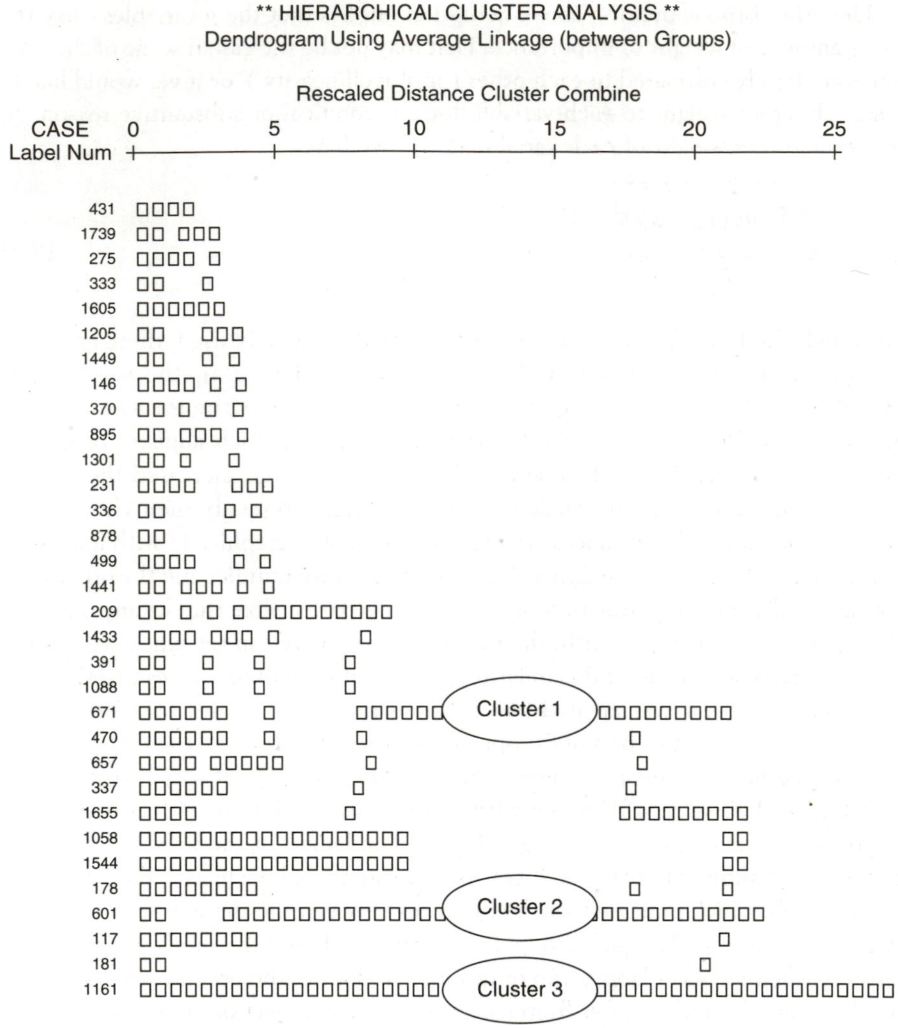

** HIERARCHICAL CLUSTER ANALYSIS **
Dendrogram Using Average Linkage (between Groups)

Rescaled Distance Cluster Combine

CASE Label Num	0	5	10	15	20	25

```
431
1739
275
333
1605
1205
1449
146
370
895
1301
231
336
878
499
1441
209
1433
391
1088
671                                      Cluster 1
470
657
337
1655
1058
1544
178
601                                      Cluster 2
117
181
1161                                     Cluster 3
```

Figure 9.1   An illustrated dendrogram on social trust

must consider whether any one of them makes better sense than others. If none turns out to be better, then two or three solutions may be retained for further investigation and confirmation. The whole process involves profiling the clusters, i.e. identifying the distinctive features of each cluster from different perspectives.

To cope with a large sample, 'the two-step method' has been developed. Its basic idea is very simple: in the first step, a hierarchical method is used to create a number of 'intermediary clusters', and in the second step these intermediary clusters are further clustered; therefore, the total amount of computing will be reduced substantially. The procedure can reach an optimal number of clusters and provide information about the attributes of each cluster so that the researcher could examine whether the clusters are different enough with regard to the interested dimensions. Or, the researcher could set the number of clusters if she has an idea about this number. I find it a good idea to randomly select several small samples and see whether you come up with a relatively stable number of clusters with hierarchical clustering. Once we obtain that number, we can employ the two-step procedure on the whole sample.

The number of clusters and their characteristics constitute the profile of the clusters. After such profile is derived from statistical outputs, there remains a question about its representativeness as it is obtained based on a sample of the population. Unlike many other statistical methods, there are no statistical procedures for assessing the representativeness of the sample profile. The only solution seems to lie in the sampling stage, i.e. to ensure as much as possible that the sample resembles the structure in the population. A related issue is the presence of outliers that may form a cluster of their own. The researcher should check the data for outliers before conducting cluster analysis. If a few outliers are found, they should be treated separately so that they will not contaminate the clustering of the other cases.

To a certain extent, we can validate our conclusions in a couple of ways. The first is to split the sample randomly into at least two samples and see whether we obtain approximately the same profiles. This is only sensible when the sample size is quite large. Another method of validation is to make predictions based on the obtained profile. Obviously, this should be done on a variable that was not included in the clustering variate.

Discriminant Analysis (DA)

The first difference between cluster analysis and discriminant analysis is that in discriminanat analysis *we have already known the groups and which cases are in each of them*. What we want to know is which specific linear relationship of the selected explanatory variables can best predict each case's group membership. While group memberships are the results to be obtained in cluster analysis, they are the targets to be predicted in discriminant analysis. Again, 'group' should be understood as a generic term; that is, groups do not have to be 'natural' such as groups of children in a school but can be classified by the researcher, such as whether the children have experienced any parental transition.

The reader may have recognized that this is a problem that can be dealt with by a logistic regression model: the response variable, group membership, is categorical. Indeed, the two methods – logistic regression and discriminant analysis – serve the same function of predicting group membership, although they do so in relatively different ways. The major difference, at least in my view, is that the logistic approach is much more straightforward and structured than the discriminant one. In effect, a logistic regression model predicts the probability that a case belongs to a particular group based on a linear function of selected explanatory variables, which can be either continuous or categorical. Here, 'a particular group' is simply a value of the categorical response variable, such as voting in the last national election. The target of the model can be expressed as the probability of belonging to a group:

$$\hat{\pi} = \frac{e^{\alpha + \beta_{i1} X_1 + \beta_{i2} X_2 + \ldots + \beta_{ip} X_p}}{1 + e^{\alpha + \beta_{i1} X_1 + \beta_{i2} X_2 + \ldots + \beta_{ip} X_p}} \qquad (9.4)$$

After estimating the coefficients, we can calculate the predicted probability of each membership, based on that we can classify cases into groups. We need to set up a rule beforehand, of course; for example, if the probability is beyond 0.50, then we put that case in the group. This process is relatively straightforward and structured because the explanatory variables entered into the model and how they are entered are pretty much determined by researchers based on their theoretical or substantial knowledge.

In discriminant analysis, the process of predicting group membership is rather *open and indirect*. It is open because it spends more effort on searching for the most powerful predictors and their relations. In theory, researchers can put the selected variables all at once into the analysis – 'the direct method' – but then they would lose the true benefit of conducting discriminant analysis. If cluster analysis is about searching for the most sensible groupings, then discriminant analysis is about searching for the most powerful function of classifying cases so that cases in different classifications are most distinctive from each other. It is indirect as well because it does not directly model on the probability of membership; rather, it requires more preparatory work, which we shall learn below, before classifications are made. Finally, discriminant analysis is more interested in the substantive meaning of the linear combination of the effective predictors, as it attempts to suggest an expected dimension along which the groups differ. In logistic regression analysis, each variable is treated separately and the linear connection does not mean anything.

Now let us go through the steps of statistical analysis. The first thing researchers need to keep in mind is that they should split the whole data set into two parts before carrying out the analysis. *Do not analyse the whole data set straightaway!* The analysis should be done on one part only, usually referred to as 'the analysis sample'. Once the analysis is complete, we shall test the effectiveness of the obtained classification procedures on the other part of the sample, or 'the holdout sample'. The split should be done randomly, and the size of each subsample does not matter very much if the overall sample is very large.

The next step is to select the candidate variables to be used to classify cases. As in some other procedures, this is not really a statistical decision. They are 'candidates' because we shall explore and examine which are the most effective and may drop those ineffective or redundant ones. The only statistical work here is to check whether the assumptions about these variables hold, including normality, linearity, multicollinearity and equal dispersion. Violation of normality is not really a problem, especially for a large sample and for predicting group membership. Linearity is rarely a problem either because there are very few clear nonlinear curves to be found in social science data. Careful attention should be paid to multi-collinearity – if two or more variables are highly correlated to each other, then not all of them shall enter the analysis. Equal dispersion means that the selected variables should have about the same variance–covariance matrices for each group on the response variable. If the groups have very different dispersion matrices, the cases are more likely to be classified into a group with a larger dispersion because that group can cover a wider range of values. The test statistic for this assumption is usually Box's M. Our analysis can proceed if it is not significant. But if it is significant, then the matrices are highly unlikely to be the same, so some transformations are needed in order to make it insignificant.

After the variables are selected, we need to carry out some preliminary tests to see whether the cases are indeed differentiated on each of these variables. As these are continuous and normally distributed (or roughly so), we compare the means of each variable across the groups. For example, suppose there are three groups on the response variable: voting for Barack Obama, voting for John McCain or voting for a third candidate, and one of the explanatory variables is years of schooling. We need to test the hypothesis that group means of schooling are the same. This can be done by several tests: Wilks' Lambda, the F-test or Mahalanobis D^2. They will lead to the same conclusion in terms of statistical significance, but Mahalanobis D^2 has been claimed to be the most versatile statistically.

In the end, we aim to obtain a function that can be generally expressed as the following:

$$D_{pi} = \alpha + W_1X_{1i} + W_2X_{2i} + \ldots + W_pX_{pi} \tag{9.5}$$

This is the discriminant variate (or function) that will generate the scores used to discriminate the cases. The index p indicates the number of selected variables and i the number of case. Clearly, the function is in the same form as a classical regression model – the target variable, here D_{pi}, is a product of a series of explanatory variables linearly connected together and weighted by a corresponding coefficient. The major difference is that D_{pi} is not a variable in the data set or any transformation of it, as the response variable in regression models. This is why discriminant analysis is an indirect way of classifying cases – we do not model on the group membership variable directly; rather, we create a score for each case based the linear combination of several explanatory variables as a first step and then use the score to classify the case's group membership.

In addition, we may have more than one variate (function). The number of functions is determined by the number of groups on the response variable as well as the number of explanatory variables. If there are two groups – it cannot be one – we need one function. If there are three, we need two: one for differentiating group 1 from groups 2 and 3, and the other for differentiating group 2 from group 3. In general, we need $(g - 1)$ number of functions, with g being the number of groups. If there are three groups but we have only one explanatory variable, we can only have one function, not two. But if there are three groups as well as three explanatory variables, then we can still have two functions. In short, it is *the smaller number* among $(g - 1)$ and p that determines the number of functions that can be used. This is why discriminant analysis is an open process: we can try different functions and search for the most effective in predicting group membership.

That process involves intensive mathematical computing, but there is no need for us to learn the details. We must understand the basic ideas. As pointed out before, variables can enter a function in three different ways: at the same time, in an order decided by the researcher or in an interactive sequence based on statistical criteria. Because we are searching for the most discriminating function, we would prefer the last option. Each explanatory variable should make a unique contribution; if its effect is redundant with another, then one of them will drop out. For the discriminant functions, if there are two or more, they also should make independent contributions. That is, the second function's effect should be measured only after the first one's has been removed statistically (referred to as 'orthogonal' in statistics). These functions will thus complement each other.

Once the possible functions are determined, each of them will let us calculate a score for each case. To determine which function is the most effective, we compare the scores across the response variable's groups. Understandably, different groups are expected to have different scores. Statistically, we test the hypothesis that the group means of the scores, called 'centroids', are all equal. If the probability for the hypothesis to be true is lower than what we preset (0.05 or 0.1, for example), then it is very likely that the groups are very different on the scores, which then suggests that the function is effective.

One should not take the results of such tests as 'final' or 'fixed'. Statistical significance may mislead us to take it as hard evidence of real difference when it is actually a result of strong power of the test. This is especially the case for social science data sets as their sizes are usually very large. For the case of testing the effectiveness of discriminant functions, the statistical significance of group centroids at least partly comes from the large size of each group. In other words, the centroids may not be that different even though the statistical tests indicate so.

A more pragmatic test of the effectiveness of the discriminant functions is to see how many cases have been correctly classified. This is particularly useful given the fact that correct classifications, not the tests of group differences, are our ultimate objective. That is, we would like to have a matrix as presented in Table 9.1.

Table 9.1 A classification matrix for two groups

Actual group	Predicted group 1	2	Actual group size	Correctly classified (%)
1	n_{11}	n_{12}	n_{1+}	n_{11}/n_{1+}
2	n_{21}	n_{22}	n_{2+}	n_{22}/n_{2+}
Predicted group size	n_{+1}	n_{+2}	n_{++}	$(n_{11}+n_{22})/n_{++}$

In this table, n_{11} and n_{22} are the number of correctly classified cases. For the sample as a whole, $(n_{11} + n_{22})/n_{++}$ therefore indicates 'the hit ratio', the overall proportion of correctly classified cases.

To obtain such table, we must know which cases have been classified to each group with the selected discriminant function. The question is: With the score generated by the function for a particular case, in which group should we classify it? Just as setting up a threshold for determining a case's membership with a predicted probability produced by a logistic regression model, here we need to decide on 'a cutting score' so that classification can be made.

To illustrate, take the example of two groups. Intuitively, it makes sense to take the point halfway between the two groups' centres as the cutting score, or more precisely, the mean of the two centroids. This is valid, however, only when the two groups are of the same size. If they are not, the cutting score will fall into the larger group, so we will misclassify some cases that are supposed to be in the small group into the large one. Therefore, we need to take into account of group sizes when defining the cutting score:

$$Z_{CS} = \frac{n_1 Z_2 + n_2 Z_1}{n_1 + n_2} \tag{9.6}$$

Now we can determine each case's group membership by comparing the predicted discriminant score and the cutting core, thereby obtaining the classification matrix. The percentage of correctly classified cases should tell us how well the discriminant function has classified the cases, but how high it should be in order to make us happy? We would be very happy if it is 100%, but it is rarely so. What should be the minimum percentage of correctly classified cases?

The statistical answer is the percentage purely determined by chance. Again, we have to consider the relative sizes of the groups. If there are two groups of the same size, then the minimum hit ratio should be 50%. In general, it is the inverse of the number of groups. Extending this to the situation of several groups of unequal sizes, the criterion should be:

$$C = \sum_{i=1}^{g} p_i^2 \tag{9.7}$$

Here, p_i is the proportion of correctly classified cases for group i and there are g groups. Two equal-sized groups are a special situation: $0.5^2 + 0.5^2 = 0.50$.

Statisticians have developed a relatively sophisticated criterion, the *Press's* Q:

$$Q = \frac{(n - n_c * g)^2}{n(g - 1)} \tag{9.8}$$

The idea of this statistic is to compare the total number of cases (n) with the product of the number of correctly classified cases (n_c) and the number of groups (g). We then compare Q with the chi-square value for one degree of freedom to see whether the discriminant function has done a better job than randomly allocating the cases. Therefore, a larger Q is desirable. But note that Q is sensitive to the sample size.

Note that these are all statistical measures for assessing the effectiveness of classification, and the threshold is always the situation by chance. Whenever possible, researchers should consider other criteria based on substantive knowledge, policy or any institutional considerations.

Once the classifications are found to be acceptable, we attempt to understand which explanatory variable has contributed relatively more than the others in discriminating the cases. However, comparing the coefficients in the discriminant function (the Ws in 9.5) is not a reliable procedure due to collinearities among the explanatory variables. A more reliable procedure is to compare the linear correlations between each explanatory variable and the discriminant function, usually referred to as 'discriminant loadings'. This amounts to treating the discriminant function as a latent or unobservable factor, a concept to be introduced in the next chapter, and the explanatory variables as its manifested effects. If an explanatory variable has made a larger contribution in representing the underlying factor, then its correlation with the discriminant function, i.e. the loading, is expected to be higher than others.

This is only for one discriminant function. When the response variable has three or more groups, there will be two or more discriminant functions (given they are all statistically effective enough), so we need a statistic that measures the relative contribution of explanatory variables across all these functions. The potency index is such measure. The idea is very simple: weight each variance explained by an explanatory variable with the corresponding discriminant function's relative discriminating power and then sum them up. The variance explained is simply the square of the discriminant loading.

The above procedure is a purely descriptive; we cannot really interpret *why* a particular explanatory variable has made the larger chunk of discriminating power. The underlying mechanism remains obscured. Therefore, it is wise to spend more time on the last step – validation – rather than interpretation, because our conclusions will be more robust and thus more useful than speculating on why a particular variable has explained more than others. Most straightforwardly, we can validate our classifications by trying the discriminant functions on the holdout sample – this is why you need to set up a holdout sample at the very beginning. Another, more computing-intensive procedure is the jackknife method: finding the discriminant function with only $(n - 1)$ cases, i.e. leaving one as 'the holdout case'. Once the discriminant function is estimated, we use it to predict the group membership of the holdout case. By doing this repeatedly we can predict the group membership of each case in turn. In the end, we can check how many correct predictions we have made. Clearly, this is especially useful for small size samples due to the amount of computing to be done. No matter which of the two procedures you follow, it is always useful to plot the results and visually examine whether the groups are indeed separated from each other at a satisfactory level.

Multidimensional Scaling (MDS)

Multidimensional scaling is very different from the previous two methods in that it is not about how the cases are grouped together. In most social research projects, individuals or aggregates of human beings, such as the respondents in social surveys are the direct targets of cluster and discriminant analyses but not of MDS.

For MSD, the direct target is 'objects', such as products, services, policies or candidates. MDS is about *how respondents perceive these objects*: How do they see the similarities or dissimilarities between the objects? Do they prefer one object to another? Our objective is to reveal the *perceptual* structure in the respondents' mind. We assume that such structure does exist and can be revealed based on the respondents' evaluations of these objects. The respondents themselves may not actually be aware of such structure, either because their attention cannot focus on the whole set of the objects, or because it is very hard for them to specify how they have compared the objects, or both. We aim to reveal the dimensions along which our respondents have unconsciously employed while comparing the objects. By mapping out the objects along these dimensions and analysing their shared characteristics, we shall be able to understand the meaning of these dimensions. The challenge is to determine the number of dimensions and interpret their meanings.

Our data are the evaluations made by the respondents, i.e. scores of similarity or preference. We are not particularly concerned with the validity of these evaluations, i.e. how well they represent the true characteristics of the objects. They may have missed an important feature of the objects, but if that is how the respondents perceive them, then they are valid data. Our concern is whether the respondents have compared carefully and report truthfully what was in their minds when comparing the objects. We shall have good quality data if the ranking scores truly represent the respondents' perceptions and preferences.

In contrast to discriminant analysis, here we do not aim to find out how each dimension is constructed by calculating a variate. Rather, in collecting the data, we ask respondents to report their perceptions of similarity or preferences with an overall scale but *without asking them how* they have come up with such perceptions. The premise is that the dimensions underlying the comparing process may go beyond simple linear summations of specific attributes, or the respondents may find it very hard to express their perceptions or feelings in concrete terms. Therefore, a more effective strategy is simply to let them put the objects in order and leave the discovery of the underlying dimensions to the researcher.

In essence, MDS is a tool for exploring the meaningful dimensions that respondents rely on when they compare the objects. We may invite the respondents to join the researchers for discovering the dimensions after the analysis is completed, but at the beginning the researcher should let them make their comparisons and choices without a pre-determined framework. To some, the whole process may seem to be too free of control, but that is the very advantage of MDS: respondents can report their perceptions without any constraint. To interpret the results properly is a skill that the researcher has no other choice but to obtain through experience.

Initially, the selection of the objects to be presented to the respondents appears to be a natural process: all the major brands of soft drinks on the market, all types of childcare services, and so on. As long as the empirical boundaries of the research project are well defined, there should be little doubt as to which objects are to be included in the study. The objects should be comparable as well, either they fall into the same category, located in the same geographical area, or created by the same institution.

However, the number of objects to be included could become overwhelming if we consider the actual process of comparing them and figuring out the dimensions. First of all, when we ask respondents to compare a set of objects, they must compare each pair of the objects in order to put the objects in an ordered sequence with regard to either similarity or preference. Suppose there are p objects, then we shall have $\binom{p}{2} = \dfrac{p(p-1)(p-2)!}{(p-2)!2!} = \dfrac{p(p-1)}{2}$ pairs of them. For example, three objects (A, B, C) come in three pairs (AB, AC and BC), but there are 45 pairs in 10 objects. So when the number of objects approaches 10, we may have to worry whether respondents have sufficient cognitive capacity to compare the objective in a reliable way.

This practical concern, however, will be counterbalanced by the desire to have at least 'enough' objects in order to find out a reliable solution to the number of dimensions. The number of dimensions must always be smaller than the number of objects: one dimension is enough for mapping out two or even three objects, and you do not need three dimensions to represent the relative positions of two objects. However, if the number of objects is not substantially larger than the number of dimensions, then we will have the problem of 'over-fitting'. That is, the dimensions found can represent the objects' positions very well, but we cannot confirm whether we shall find the same dimensions with other objects because we do not have additional objects. So, for the purpose of obtaining stable solutions to the question of how many dimensions there are, we want to have more objects. It has been suggested that there should be more than four times as many objects as the desired number of dimensions (Green et al., 1989). This means that we shall need 9 objects if we plan to use 2 dimensions and 13 objects for 3 dimensions. But as shown above, the respondents must compare 45 pairs if there are 10 objects. In practice, it is very hard to include more than 10 objects and/or more than three dimensions in a single study.

The analysis of similarity data is somehow different from that of preference data. Here, we focus on the former. Suppose we have the evaluations from only one respondent. If there are only two objects, then the respondent does not really need to compare anything as there is only one pair. The simplest situation, therefore, is having three objects, say, A, B and C. To put them in an order of similarity, the respondent needs to compare three pairs: AB, AC and BC. If the respondent finds that BC is more similar than AC and AC is more similar than AB, then we can represent the results as BC > AC > AB. We can also assign a number to represent the ranking order; for example, BC = 1, AC = 2 and AB = 3, with a smaller number representing similarity. We can map out their relative positions in one dimension as illustrated in Figure 9.2.

We can do that with two dimensions as well, but there is no need to do that, as the one dimensional solution is equally good.

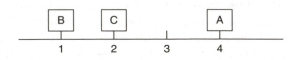

Figure 9.2   Mapping out the relative positions of three cases in one dimension

Now let us move on to the situation of four objects. We can present their relative positions in the following 'similarity matrix', see Table 9.2.

Table 9.2   An illustration of similarity matrix with four objects

Object	A	B	C	D
A	—	3	2	4
B		—	1	5
C			—	6
D				—

Suppose the numbers in the table are the similarity measures reported by a respondent on these six pairs, with 1 indicating most similar and 6 most dissimilar. Here, I purposefully make the relative positions between A, B and C to remain the same as the previous simpler example. With the additional object D, it is difficult for us to find the right place for it: there is simply no such point in this one dimensional space that simultaneously satisfies the conditions that D is about four units away from A, five from B and six from C, even though these numbers only indicate relative positions rather than absolute distances, because we are supposed to have DC > DB > DA, but the order in the previous configuration shows that the order must be DB > DC > DA. This is so because D has only two directions to go but in neither of them D can find the right place. The only solution is to add one more dimension.

It should be clear by now that with more objects the search for the right number of dimensions and the right places for each object in the space will become more difficult and uncertain. The strategy of MDS is to compare the relative positions generated with a particular number of dimensions – starting with two – with the positions reported by the respondent. If they are not close enough, then we try a different configuration in an attempt to close the difference between the two ranking orders. When we reach a satisfactory configuration, we may want to try a higher dimensional configuration and see if we can get a better fit. As with other statistical procedures, we need to set up a criterion as a reference point of fitness. Clearly, this will be a highly interactive process and will involve intensive computing. And it is possible that the computer program simply cannot find 'an optimal configuration' but still generate one that does not represent the observed relations at all (the so-called 'degenerate solution').

Remember that we have discussed how to map out the perceptions of only one respondent. In marketing or psychological studies, there are usually not many respondents. In social research, however, the number could be very large. So how are we going to analyse perceptual rankings by so many people? One intuitively straightforward solution is to take an average score for each object across all respondents and then to analyse the averages as if they were from 'an average respondent'. The question is: can the averages truly represent the rankings of so many people? This will be a serious problem when the rankings are widely different from one respondent to another, making an average a poor overall indicator. In short, this method is valid only when there is only a small amount of variation of rankings across the respondents.

There are some other strategies for summarizing the scores from a large number of respondents, but the researcher has to either impose a restriction or manipulate the data to some extent in order to sum up the results. A method that I have found most natural is 'subjective clustering' or 'confusion data' (Hair et al., 2006: 647). Using this method, we ask each respondent to group similar objects into 'clusters'. Ideally, the number of clusters should come as a natural outcome of the clustering process. However, if the researcher has a particular number of clusters in mind, we can ask the respondents to group the objects into a particular number of clusters. Either way, we then count the number of times that a pair of objects has been clustered together in a same group. The frequency data will serve as the similarity measure of the objects. After settling all these issues, we can use a computer program to produce the results.[5]

The researcher needs to accomplish two more tasks: determine the number of dimensions and interpret them. The two activities are intertwined together: when you determine the number of dimensions you must ensure their interpretability. Again, the researcher must balance the dual demands – statistical and substantive. Statistically, we must consider which configuration – the number of dimensions – can generate the results that are closest to the data, i.e. respondents' rankings of similarity among the objects. The most commonly used measure is 'stress', which aims to measure the proportion of the variance of the differences between the predicted and the observed similarity scores *not* accounted for by the configuration. The smaller the stress, the better the fit.

More than one equation has been created for measuring stress, but they all measure the distance between the predicted similarity (or dissimilarity) score, $\bar{d}_{ij}$, and the original score reported by respondents, d_{ij}, where i and j indicate the two different objects. The following is one such equation:

$$stress = \sqrt{\frac{\sum (d_{ij} - \bar{d}_{ij})^2}{\sum d_{ij}^2}} \qquad (9.9)$$

Other equations usually keep the same numerator but use a different denominator, such as $\bar{d}_{ij}^2$ or $\sum (d_{ij} - \bar{d}_{ij})^2$.

The values of stress for each respective configuration can then be plotted against the number of dimensions, usually called a scree plot, which we shall encounter while learning factor analysis in the next chapter. If, say, there is a big fall in stress from the configuration of two dimensions to that of three dimensions, then the three-dimension solution seems to have generated a better fit. Remember, however, that is not the end of the story. We must think whether the statistically preferable solution makes any substantive sense. To search for the meaning of those dimensions,

---

[5]So far our discussion has concentrated on similarity data. There are a few issues specific to preference data, but I skip those mostly technical points in order not to make this chapter too long. For computer software, Borg and Groenen (2005) reviewed most packages for conducting MDS in Appendix A of their book, but they did not mention SPSS, a very popular package among social science students, which does contain the facilities for MDS.

a common strategy is to compare the objects clustered along a same dimension. Any characteristics shared by these objects should suggest a possible interpretation.

Finally, we need to validate the configurations. Unlike discriminant analysis validation in MDS is less rigorous. We could split the sample and see if the different subsamples generate about the same results. The difficult question is: if the results are very different, which is highly likely, shall we attribute the differences to the true differences in the respondents' perceptions or to the different configurations, or both? It is very hard to tell. In the end, one has to go beyond MDS to validate the results: we have to compare the objects *with regard to their attributes, which are not used in MDS*, and see whether objects clustered along one dimensions are indeed different based on these attributes. As the reader may have seen, this brings us back to discriminant analysis.

Correspondence Analysis (COA)

In MDS, we know either the level of similarity or at least the ranking order of similarity among a set of objects. What MDS does for us is to find a space with a very small number of dimensions in which the objects can be visually represented according to the observed level or order of similarity. This configuration will facilitate the detection of any groupings among the objects and the dimensions along which the groupings are made.

We can think of MDS as an effective tool when the similarity (or distance) among objects is measured at the ordinal or metrical levels. However, what if the objects are described at the nominal level? In contrast to the perceptual data for MDS, data for correspondence analysis involve mostly frequency counts of classifications or typologies, and this is why it can be seen as a special kind of MDS. We will study similarities or distances among them, but measures of similarity or distance are derived later statistically rather than supplied by respondents at the beginning of the data collection process. For this reason, correspondence analysis can go far beyond perceptual data; it can study virtually any set of data of cross-classified objects, such as cities, nations, universities, geographic areas, types of firms or jobs and so on. What it shares with MDS is the logic of analysis, not the type of data: both methods attempt to map out the relative positions among the objects in a very small number of dimensions so that associational patterns can be detected and interpreted.

If the target of correspondence analysis is a cross-tabulation of categorical variables, you may wonder why we don't use methods we learnt before, such as chi-square test, odds ratios and loglinear models. What is the added value of correspondence analysis? The answer is, if the table is quite small with only two or three rows or columns, we could readily study the relationship between the row and the column variables by examining proportions, odds ratios and so on, but it becomes much harder when the size of the table is increasing.

For example, Table 9.3 is an 8×5 table of Internet access and opinions on homosexuality that I have created from the Round 3 of European Social Survey. Even in this relatively small table, it is already hard enough for detecting any clear patterns.

Table 9.3 Personal use of Internet/email/WWW and opinions on homosexuality

		Gays and lesbians free to live life as they wish					
		Agree strongly	Agree	Neither agree nor disagree	Disagree	Disagree strongly	Total
Personal use of Internet	No access	122	368	104	42	22	658
	Never use	78	172	54	25	14	343
	Less than once a month	16	25	9	1	1	52
	Once a month	14	27	6	2	1	50
	Several times a month	24	37	16	7	1	85
	Once a week	29	53	14	10	1	107
	Several times a week	64	113	30	10	1	218
	Everyday	128	168	41	19	11	367
Total		475	963	274	116	52	1880

The major value of correspondence analysis is the ability of visually representing the relations between the row categories and the column categories in a map so that the detection of any patterns can be greatly enhanced.

An advantage of correspondence analysis over MDS is that it goes far beyond perceived similarities between objects. Any cross-tabulated results can be the subject of correspondence analysis, and the table does not have to be a contingency table. That is, the sum of all cell counts may be larger than the total number of respondents, which occurs when the respondents are allowed to choose two or more categories, such as their favourite sports or brands. This is why correspondence analysis is particularly useful for social research.

The major limitation of this method is that it is a tool of exploration or display, not a tool of statistical inference or modelling. After mapping out the categories on a two-dimensional space, we may be able to find some connections among them. Nevertheless, there is no way for us to assess the statistical significance of our findings, as we can with loglinear models.

Now let us discuss the idea of mapping out the categories, which are like the objects in MDS, onto a low-dimensional space. In MDS, the similarities (or distances) between the objects are represented as ordered positions or metrical scores. An important question in correspondence analysis is: how would we represent the similarities between categories? As each cell count in a cross-table connects a row category and a column category, we would naturally use the cell counts as measures of similarity. This is not appropriate, however, because the raw counts vary substantially with the number of categories and the total sample size. We need a standardized measure.

Since the similarity measure is to represent the association between two categories, we can use the chi-square test score:

$$\chi^2 \text{ for a cell } = \frac{(\text{expected count } - \text{ observed count})^2}{\text{expected count}} \tag{9.10}$$

Recall that the null hypothesis for a chi-square test is independence between two categorical variables. It is an overall summarized score. Now, we calculate one for each cell in order to obtain a measure of similarity between a pair of categories. The idea, however, remains the same: a larger chi-square score would indicate interdependence while a smaller one tends to indicate independence among the categories, because an expected count represents the effect of chance. In this sense, the scores can be used as a measure of similarity.

Based on these scores, computer software can help us put the categories on a space (a map, or a biplot) of a particular number of dimensions. Figure 9.3 is the map of two dimensions for the above example.

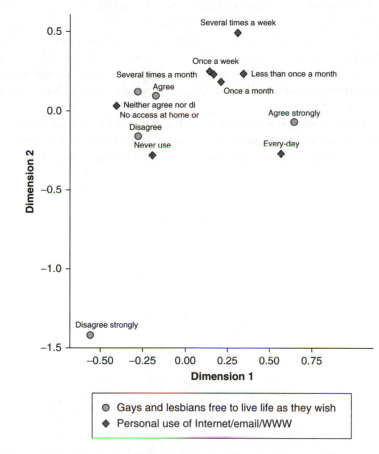

Figure 9.3   A biplot of access to the Internet and opinions on homosexuality

The first thing we notice is that the category 'disagree strongly' is far away from other categories, and it has little connection with any category of Internet access. For other categories, we can see a certain level of association: 'agree strongly' is close to using the Internet 'every day', 'disagree' to 'never use', and other middle-level categories somehow cluster together.

Besides this graphical exploration, further statistics can be produced in order to gain a better sense of how effective this procedure has been. The first question relates to how effective the dimensions are in accounting for the variations among the categories. Statistically, this effect is measured by an 'eigenvalue' (also called 'singular value'), or 'inertia', which is the square of eigenvalue. These are all terms of matrix algebra, from which the proportion of 'explained variances' can be calculated. For the above example, the singular value for dimension 1 is 0.145, so the inertia is 0.021, and it explains about 70% of the variance. Dimension 2 explains another 14%. There has been no consensus as to an acceptable value of eigenvalue or inertia. The exploratory nature of this method suggests that social researchers should not be obsessed with these criteria.

Similarly, we can explore the relative contribution of each category to each variable, which is referred to as 'mass' in statistics. For the variable of using the Internet, 'no access' account for 35% of its variation, followed by 'everyday' (20%) and 'never use' (18%). We can see that it is these extreme categories that carry much heavier weight than those categories in the middle. The situation in the variable of attitude toward homosexuality is rather different: 'agree' and 'strongly agree' account more than 76% of the variation, and the effect of 'disagree strongly' carries almost ignorable weight (2.8%).

Clearly, correspondence analysis is a useful exploratory tool for representing connections among a large number of categories, mainly visually but numerically as well. The results greatly facilitate our examination of regularities in the data.

TEN

Methods for Analysing Latent Variables

Latent Variables in Social Research

After introducing multiple regression models in Chapter 7, we have expanded our discussions in two different directions. First, we added temporality to our analysis in Chapter 8, studying two statistical models that deal with time. Then we enriched our study of cases in Chapter 9 by learning several statistical tools for discovering grouping patterns among the cases. In this chapter we make a third expansion on variables.

So far, when we use variables, we take them as completely true measurements of what they are supposed to measure. In some situations, the gap between what is measured and what is supposed to be measured can be very small, such as variables about factual attributes. For example, there may still be errors in people's reports about their gender, age, weight, whether they voted or not in the last national election, but these errors tend to be very small. More importantly, the errors are mainly due to poor memory or intentional misreporting rather than due to the complex nature of the concept to be measured.

When the concepts are complex, measurement errors become fundamental because the concepts do not lend themselves to direct and clear classification or numeric scaling. For the example of IQ, it is impossible to directly measure the quality of a human brain's information-processing capacity. What we can measure directly is *the outcomes or the representation* of such capacity, such as test scores. IQ is an excellent example of 'latent variable' because it is hiding in a human brain, and the test scores are its 'observed variables' (or 'manifest variables').

From this example, we can see two important features of latent variables. First, they are not directly accessible to scientific measurement, but – and this is important – *they do exist*, at least to the extent that we can justify. Second, they are responsible for some phenomena that we can directly measure, and it is *such a connection* between the latent but unobservable cause and the observable indicators as effects that allows us to make inference about the latent variables. We cannot directly observe how intelligence works because we cannot open a living person's brain and watch how the neurons and cells are working while the person is still alive. Nevertheless, we do know that intelligence is real; not only is it responsible for results, such as exam marks, but also because it has *a tangible carrier*, the brain.

This seems to suggest that latent variables are special targets reserved for psychological and neurological studies. What about latent variables in the social sciences? They have been no less widely used in sociology, political sciences, business and organizational studies. The trouble is, in some occasions, latent variables were confused with other kinds of variables. It is very important to ensure that the variables under study are indeed latent before we employ any statistical tools suitable for analysing them. This, however, is not always the case in the practice of social research.

Take the example of a person's socio-economic status (SES). Is it really a latent variable? How can we be so sure that it actually exists? What is the tangible carrier of SES and what is it responsible for? The answers are elusive. To be sure, SES is an individual person's attribute that is derived from a set of the person's other attributes, such as income, wealth, education, occupation and so forth. It should not be treated as a latent variable such as intelligence, because it does not reside in any natural entity that we definitely know is there; rather, it is a human-made conceptual device. Besides, SES is not responsible for income and other attributes; instead, the opposite is true – it is income and other attributes that define SES. Clearly, SES does not carry the defining characteristics of a latent variable as IQ does.

Here is the source of confusion: SES is *a composite indicator derived from other manifest variables*, so it cannot exist without those manifest variables, but it is sometimes treated as the source, not the outcome, of the manifest variables. In short, latent variables should not be confused with composite scores or indices that are artificially created based on a set of observed variables. Even when we use SES to explain something other than its components, we must remember that it is not an independent entity.

An even more complicated example is social capital. Suppose we plan to study the effect of social capital on another variable, such as poverty, health or democracy. What kind of variable is social capital in such analysis? The answer is not straightforward because social capital is a very complex concept. First, the unit of measurement: is social capital a collective property, an individual property, or both depending on the context? I have answered the question elsewhere (Yang, 2007). Here, suffice it to say that initially we should study it as an individual property and then treat it as a collective property.

More relevant to our discussion is the concept's second complexity: is it a manifest or latent variable, or something else? The most well-known advocate of the concept, Robert Putnam (1994, 2001, 2004), never directly measured social capital in his books. What he used was proxy indicators that he believed to represent the effects of social capital, such as memberships of civic organizations or time spent on watching television. Given that social capital is real, the key question is: what is its relationship with the observed variables? Is it a truly latent variable or is it a composite index determined collectively by the observed variables? If the former, then we must demonstrate that it already exists prior to the observed variables. However, this is not very clear in the current literature. There seem to be several scenarios: sometimes we know social capital is there because people have behaved in a certain way, such as letting children play outside without worrying they will come to harm, but other times social capital is in the making because people are trying to establish mutually beneficial relations, and furthermore we are not sure whether social capital really exists, such as when we find that fewer people go to church but more people are social with friends. In short, we must think carefully about whether the concept under study is a genuine latent variable *before analysing it as such* in our statistical models. *Not all variables that cannot be measured directly are necessarily latent variables.* Some concepts are artefacts that actually do not exist in reality and therefore cannot be responsible for any observed variables.

If the concept under study has been doubtlessly defined as a latent variable, our analysis on this type of variables can enjoy some benefits. First, by incorporating measurement errors into our statistical analyses, we can check whether we should change or modify our substantive conclusions. The other benefit is that latent variables may represent underlying factors responsible for the observed indicators, therefore, allowing us to focus on the more fundamental processes. In addition, relations among latent variables can be expressed with great flexibility in structural equation models, thereby representing more complicated relations among the variables. These models can then be applied to study the effect of time as we shall see later in latent growth curve models.

Exploratory Factor Analysis (EFA)

We want to use factor analysis when we have a large number of variables and find some of them to be highly correlated among themselves but not with others. This can happen in two situations. In the first situation, we do not know why these variables have been created and measured. This is possible when we analyse secondary data or when the inclusion of those variables was dictated by the literature while we were not certain about the relations among the variables. For example, suppose there are eight variables in the data matrix that we are interested in. To explore their relations, we produce a following 'correlation matrix' (Table 10.1).

In such a matrix, all values on the diagonal cells are 1 because a variable is perfectly correlated to itself. Cells in the upper half of the table have been left blank because they are only the mirror image of those in the lower half. Each of the other numbers is the correlation coefficient of the corresponding pair of two variables.

Table 10.1   A hypothetical correlation matrix

	V1	V2	V3	V4	V5	V6	V7	V8
V1	1.00							
V2	0.46	1.00						
V3	0.28	0.88	1.00					
V4	0.51	0.56	0.43	1.00				
V5	0.82	0.55	0.35	0.46	1.00			
V6	0.30	0.61	0.44	0.73	0.35	1.00		
V7	0.44	0.58	0.51	0.72	0.38	0.78	1.00	
V8	0.29	0.89	0.77	0.48	0.28	0.31	0.47	1.00

Even with only eight variables, it is already hard enough to detect any patterns simply by browsing the correlation coefficients. In order to have a clearer picture, we need to re-organize the cells as follows in Table 10.2

Table 10.2   Re-organization of Table 10.1

	V2	V3	V8	V4	V6	V7	V1	V5
V2	1.00							
V3	**0.88**	1.00						
V8	**0.89**	**0.77**	1.00					
V4	0.56	0.43	0.48	1.00				
V6	0.61	0.44	0.31	**0.73**	1.00			
V7	0.58	0.51	0.47	**0.72**	**0.78**	1.00		
V1	0.46	0.28	0.29	0.51	0.30	0.44	1.00	
V5	0.55	0.35	0.28	0.46	0.35	0.38	**0.82**	1.00

In Table 10.2, we regroup the variables together according to the strength of their correlations. We can see that variables 2, 3 and 8 are highly correlated together, so are variables 4, 6 and 7, and variables 1 and 5.

The question is: how are we going to interpret these groupings of correlated variables? When there are only two variables, such as variables 1 and 5 above, one possibility is the existence of a confounding variable, and another possibility is that there is a latent variable (factor). As we cannot determine which possibility it is, it is unwise to claim the existence of a factor with only two correlated variables.

With three or more variables, it is more realistic to claim the existence of a factor. Some statisticians would require five or more observed variables for each factor. For this particular example, there seems to be two factors. Note that this is an exploratory process: we do not know whether factors can be found or not, how many there are, and what they mean. Statistical methods for answering these questions constitute 'exploratory factor analysis', which will be the focus of this section.

The other situation in which we can expect correlations among variables is when we have conceptual or theoretical explanation for the correlations. For example, when psychologists design questions for testing different types of personalities, they have some theories about the types and the indicators of each type. In social research, investigators of social surveys usually create a set of questions for a particular concept based on a current literature, for example, trust, religiousness or political orientation. Researchers would not be surprised if they find the set of variables designed for measuring such a concept are highly correlated; actually, they would be very surprised if the variables are not correlated. Clearly, this is a confirmatory rather than exploratory process: we know beforehand how many factors there should be and what they mean, hence 'confirmatory factor analysis'.

Now let us focus on exploratory factor analysis. You can see from the above that the starting point is the correlation matrix; all the rest of our analysis depends on the quality of this matrix. As we have used correlation coefficients, we assume that all the variables are metrical and normally distributed, at least approximately, and there are no outliers.[1] Sample size should not be a serious problem for the data collected from social surveys. Finally, it rarely occurs but is possible that all correlation coefficients are very small, say below 0.3. In that case, there is no point in carrying on the analysis as the data are too weak to warrant a factor analysis.

Given the correlation matrix is free of the above problems, how can we find out how many factors there are and what they mean? Statisticians study the structure of correlated variables by decomposing and examining different variances, as they give us a broader view of relations among variables than correlations. To illustrate, suppose that four observed variables, A, B, C and D, are correlated and we want to know whether there is a common factor behind them. Their relations can be represented as in Figure 10.1.

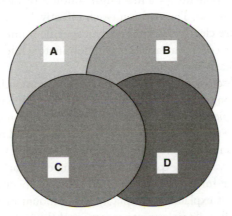

Figure 10.1   An illustration of variances of four observed variables

In Figure 10.1, each circle represents the variance of a particular variable. As they are correlated in pairs, there are some overlapping areas, which represent the common variances or *co*-variances. Each variable has its own non-overlapping area, which is its *unique* variance. Finally, there may be a portion of *error* in each variable's unique variance due to sample variations, which is represented by a white rectangle in each circle. In sum, the total area of a variable's variance can be decomposed into three parts:

Total = common + unique + error

---

[1]There are statistical methods that deal with categorical variables in factor analysis, but as those methods are only different in statistical technicality we shall not discuss in this book.

We distinguish these variances from one another because we can take either of the following two approaches to discovering latent variables (factors). Strictly speaking, the term 'factor analysis' refers to 'common factor analysis', because it studies only the common variances, ignoring the unique and error ones. The rationale is that a factor is only responsible for the common variances, which should make sense because it is exactly due to them that we suspect that a factor may exist. The other approach is to analyse all variances, and the aim is to find a minimum number of factors that can explain the maximum proportion of the total variance. Often, factors found in this way are not called 'factors' but called 'principal components'; hence 'principal component analysis' (PCA).

There is no hard and fast rule for deciding which one to use for a particular study, as each method serves a different function. If your objective is purely exploratory, i.e. you simply want to obtain a small number of components that are behind a large number of observed variables, PCA will do a better job. But if you want to find out the factors that can explain the correlations (or common variances) among the variables, then you should conduct a factor analysis.

A drawback of factor analysis is that it does not generate a single solution – just as we saw in cluster analysis, the researcher's subjectivity has to intervene in order to reach a final solution. PCA, while searching for 'the best solution' (the minimum number of components for a maximum amount of variance explained), will give you a definite answer. The two can reach effectively the same solution if the observed variables are clearly determined by a specific number of factors, because for both methods the common variances will dominate while the unique and error variances become nearly ignorable.

In the following discussions, we shall focus on the common factor approach, since to explain the common variance is what social researchers often want to do. The whole process is highly exploratory as we are searching for a compromised solution in between two extreme situations. On the one hand, there could be only one factor but it will only explain a small proportion of the common variance. On the other hand, we could have all of the variance explained by assigning each variable a factor, but that does not do anything for us. A compromised solution specifies a small 'optimal' number of factors that explain an acceptably large amount of the variance. A small number of factors will facilitate our interpretation of the factors, and a large amount of explained variance will justify the identification of them.

When do we know we have found the compromised solution? A first attempt is to create a plot with a pair of factors as the axes and the observed variables as the dots in the space. The distance between each variable and the origin indicates the strength of correlation – called 'factor loadings' – between the variable and the factor. Ideally, we would like to see that each observed variable is far away from the origin on one axis but near the origin on all the other axes, because that indicates a clear grouping of observed variables into one and only one factor.

The plot for any particular analysis may not show such clear picture. For example, some variables may be somewhere in between two axes, although they are far away from the origin. This is the situation where rotation is needed. Generally, there are two types of rotation. The first is 'orthogonal rotation'. In mathematics, two lines are orthogonal if they form a rectangle (90°). In statistics, two variables are orthogonal if they are independent of each other, that is, they have nothing to do with each other, or their correlation coefficient is 0. In the initial solution of a factor analysis, a pair of factors is represented as two orthogonal axes, meaning they are not correlated with each other at all. If there are more than two factors, you have more pairs of factors. And if such solution does not capture the groupings of variables very well, then we need to rotate the two orthogonal axes around the origin while the variables stay at their positions in order to search for a best position so that the axes can be as close to the variables as possible.

The above assumption of independent factors, however, may not be realistic. Indeed, it is hard to imagine that two factors from the same sample are completely independent of each other. This is why there is another rotation, the oblique rotation. In physics, 'oblique' means diverting from a straight line. Therefore, when we make an oblique rotation of the factors, we do not maintain the 90° angle anymore, as we do for orthogonal rotation. Angles other than 90° indicate dependent relations among the factors.

Two issues arise, however, with this more sensible solution. First, how much do we allow the factors correlate with each other? Recall that our original objective is to separate the observed variables into different groups so that each group represents one factor. If the factors are highly correlated, then it suggests that we have failed to detect distinctive factors. In other words, there should be a limit on how correlated the factors are allowed to be. However, there is no consensus among researchers on what the limit should be. In addition, if we allow the factor axes to form any angle between them, then we can always find factors. Consequently, factor solutions start to become arbitrary and subjective.

Given that we make no rotation or make only orthogonal rotation, a simple but effective way of determining the number of factors is to create and examine a scree plot, with the eigenvalue on the vertical axis, which represents the amount of explained variance, and the number of factors on the horizontal one. Figure 10.2 provides an example.

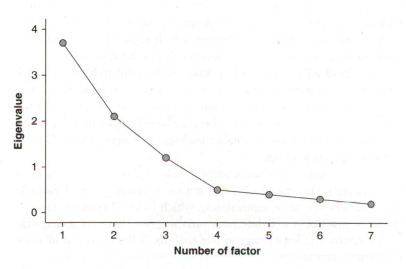

Figure 10.2 An illustration of scree plot

The objective of using a scree plot is to detect a turning point at which an additional factor does not substantially increase the explained variance anymore. Often such turning point is called 'the elbow' because it indicates a relatively sharp turn. In Figure 10.2, the point for four factors seems to be the elbow as the line becomes gradually flat afterwards.

To numerically confirm the pattern found in the scree plot, we could examine the correlation patterns between each factor and the observed variables. If the factors that we have found are truly responsible for their respective observed variables, we would expect that each observed variable is strongly correlated with one and only one factor, and a large proportion of each observed variable's variance has been explained by the solution. If our expectation is correct, then we should have a table similar to Table 10.3.

Table 10.3   An ideal factor loadings table

	Factor				
	1	2	3	4	Communality
V2	0.88				0.90
V3	0.91				0.91
V10	0.90				0.88
V1		0.85			0.87
V5		0.84			0.88
V8		0.92			0.94
V4			0.78		0.87
V11			0.84		0.78
V9			0.90		0.89
V7				0.82	0.85
V12				0.83	0.87
V6				0.89	0.93

This example is hypothetical, but it works in illustrating the point: the numbers in the cells indicate the correlation between each observed variable and its corresponding factor, and each factor has a clearly defined group of observed variables. The last column shows the communality values, which represent the amount of variance accounted for by the whole factor solution for each variable.

In reality, the results of a particular analysis may not turn out to be so clean and tidy. Some loadings may not be as high as those in Table 10.3. Most researchers would agree that a loading has to be 0.5 or more to validate the existence of a factor. But this guide should not be taken rigidly because large samples or a large number of variables will produce relatively smaller loadings, so keeping their effects in mind when interpreting the loadings.

The second 'messy' situation is when a variable is loaded on two or even more factors ('cross-loadings'). This means that it is not clear which group of variables that a variable should belong to or, equivalently, which factor should be responsible for it. The usual practice is to delete such variables, but that may damage the theoretical or substantive underpinnings of our analysis. Is the statistical neatness worth the theoretical sacrifice?

A further messy situation is when we have low communalities for some observed variables, suggesting that the current factor analysis solution does not account for an acceptable amount of the variance of those variables. The usual threshold is 0.5, but again, there is no hard rule on this. We could try different solutions, such as ignoring a variable, using different rotation methods or changing the number of factors allowed, until a satisfactory one is found. Remember, however, you as the researcher must provide theoretical justification for the solution.

Once the factors are determined, researchers need to interpret their meaning. In a fashion similar to cluster analysis, we obtain the meaning of a factor by studying the observed variables under its influence. The common feature of the observed variables usually gives us a useful clue. This process will be much easier if we have orthogonal rotation as we can interpret each factor separately without worrying about its association with other factors. If the rotation is oblique, then interpretation becomes harder as we have to figure out how the factors are meaningfully associated together. We can validate our interpretations by conducting a confirmatory factor analysis on a different sample.

Confirmatory Factor Analysis (CFA)

By definition, the factors in exploratory factor analysis are discovered after we explore the relations among a set of pre-selected observed variables. The researcher is expected to answer a series of questions: Which observed variables are to be selected? How many latent variables there are? How should we interpret them?

In contrast, CFA demands a more explicit and crucial role of theory. Here, theory does not mean a set of logically interconnected statements for explaining a particular phenomenon. It simply refers to any sensible explanation of the relationship between a factor and its indicators. For example, assuming that an adult has an established orientation toward most political affairs, say liberal, or conservative or independent, we would expect some stable responses from that person to a series of questions related to politics. We collect data to confirm such expectation, but before doing that we already had an idea about the connection between the concept (political orientation) and its indicators (represented as survey questions about taxation, immigration or abortion). If we have several factors in mind and have a theory about their relations among them, then we have a theory about the relations of these factors, then we have a structural equation model, which we shall introduce in the next section.

Besides confirming the expected relation between factors and their indicators, another important function of CFA is to take into account of measurement errors. Many statistical methods and analyses, including those that we have learnt in the previous chapters, do not take into account measurement errors. However, it is very important for social researches to take measurement errors seriously because the errors will affect our substantive conclusions.

Willem Saris forcefully demonstrated the effect of measurement errors in a workshop sponsored by the European Science Foundation by using the results from an experiment conducted as a part of the first round of European Social Survey in 2002. In the experiment, conducted in the UK on 500 respondents, two scales, one having four points and the other 11, with a bigger number indicating higher level of trust, were used for measuring the correlation of political trust and social trust, each having three indicators. Tables 10.4 and 10.5 present the two correlation matrices.

Table 10.4   Correlations of the indicators measured with a four-point scale

Social trust	Political trust		
	V1	V2	V3
V1	−0.147*	−0.030	0.094
V2	−0.060	−0.070	−0.005
V3	−0.074	−0.064	0.041

Table 10.5   Correlations of the indicators measured with an 11-point scale

Social trust	Political trust		
	V1	V2	V3
V1	0.291*	0.225*	0.208*
V2	0.313*	0.285*	0.328*
V3	0.265*	0.242*	0.227*

The difference between the two sets of results cannot be more striking: simply by changing the number of points of the scale, the correlations between the same pair of indicators have changed dramatically with regards to sign, magnitude and statistical significance. Our subsequent analysis and substantive conclusions rely on these correlation coefficients; therefore, we cannot afford to ignore measurement errors.

Analysis such as the above is impossible if a factor has only one indicator. We have no way of knowing whether it truly represents the concept we want to measure because there are no other indicators to permit a comparison. This is why we usually need multiple indicators, especially for complicated concepts.

The above discussion can be summarized as follows: any observed variable (indicator) can be seen as a response to two explanatory variables, the unseen factor and the measurement errors (here we lump all kinds of measurement errors into one term). Graphically, this conceptualization can be represented in Figure 10.3, in which there are four observed variables (OB1 to OB4) and there is also an error term (ET1 to ET4) for each of observed variable.

We could have two or more factors, each with its own indicators – we do not hypothesize cross-loadings (an observed variable is loaded or explained by two or more factors) as it will suggest that the factors are not clearly defined. In measurement models, we hypothesize that all factors are mutually correlated; otherwise, either we should have separate measurement models if the factors are not correlated, or we must have structural equation models that will specify how the factors are connected with each other in a more specific way. For the example of two factors, one

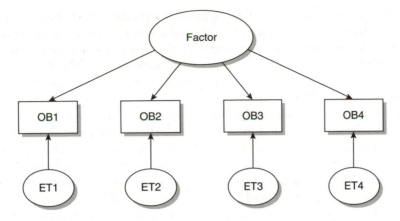

Figure 10.3   A confirmatory factor model with four observed variables

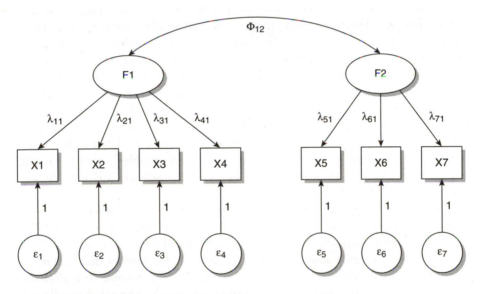

Figure 10.4   A two-factor measurement model

with four indicators and the other with three, we can present the measurement model as shown in Figure 10.4.

The model hypothesizes that the first four observed variables are counted for by the first factor and the other three by the second factor. The two factors are assumed to be correlated with each other with the correlation coefficient Φ_{12}. The λs represent the loadings of each observed variable onto its factor. Epsilon represents the error terms, and it is assumed that an error term explains all the effects on a particular observed variable after the factor's effect has been accounted for.

An important question is: given a measurement model like this, how can we know it is 'confirmed'? The idea is to check how well the model has done what it is meant to do. Statistically, the model is supposed to reproduce the variance–covariance matrix of the observed variables. Therefore, we aim to test the null hypothesis that the variance–covariance matrix produced by the model is equal to the observed one.[2] Statisticians have created several candidate statistics for testing it.

One can start with the most straightforward one, the chi-square test, which basically compares the two sets of elements by summing up their squared differences. Its degree of freedom is the difference between the number of distinctive items (the diagonal items and those below it in the matrix) and the number of estimated parameters. Here we have a problem that is very similar to the chi-square test for a contingency table, i.e. the test statistic is heavily influenced by the size of the table. For the case of comparing variance–covariance matrices, the chi-square value is clearly influenced by the number of variables involved: more variables lead to a larger matrix with more items to compare. Less obvious is the effect of sample size on such chi-square value: larger samples tend to have larger variances, thereby leading to a larger chi-square value.

It is important for those new to measurement models to note that our expectations here are directly opposite to our expectation when we test a hypothesis on the relationship between two or more categorical variables in a contingency table. When studying a contingency table, we would expect to see a large chi-square value or a corresponding small p-value (usually smaller than 0.05) as we expect strong evidence for the variables' associations. Here, our expectation is the opposite: we would expect to have a small chi-square value or a corresponding large p-value because we expect the two sets of variance items are close enough, which will indicate fitness of the model to the data. The trouble with a test on a large sample or a large number of observed variables is that the results may indicate poor fit when actually the two variance matrices are quite close to each other.

It is to correct those effects that statisticians have invented other measures of the model's fitness to the data, such as the Root Means Square Residual (RMSR) or its standard version, the incremental fit indices and the parsimony fit indices. They all share the same objective of neutralizing the effects other than that of the variables' relations. There is no agreement on which one is 'the best'. It is often recommended that researchers use different types of measures together in a flexible way (Hair et al., 2006: 752–3).

Just as we should not completely rely on a single number of the chi-square value when studying a contingency table, nor should we rely on any of the above measures alone. Even when all measures indicate good fit of the model to the data, we need to read all available information in order to check the validity and the reliability of the model. For example, all factor loadings should be high (usually above 0.7) and statistically significant. If there are two or more factors, the direction and the size of their correlation coefficients should make substantive sense. Further, the factor should explain at least more than half of each variable's variance. Finally, each of the factors should make distinct contribution to the explanation of the observed

---

[2]Two matrices are equal if all their corresponding elements are equal.

variables, and they should not have cross-explanations of the indicators. In short, conducting a confirmatory factor analysis involves a lot of work.

Structural Equation Models (SEM)

A confirmatory factor model has two main functions: (1) to confirm the relationship between each factor and the set of observed variables it is responsible for; (2) take into account of measurement errors. However, it assumes that all factors are correlated with each other. If we have any theoretical expectations of the relationships among the factors and would like to see whether the data support our expectations, then CFA models are of little help as no specific relationship is represented in such models.

Structural equation models (SEM) are special cases of CFA models because they contain only a subset of specific relations. For example, in a structural equation model, only some factors are hypothesized to be connected to each other, and these connections are usually recursive, represented by one-way arrows, rather than non-recursive (double-ended arrows or loops). When two factors are assumed to have no association at all, there will be no arrow between them in the diagram. Which factors are connected to other factors and how they are connected, including the sign and the absolute value of the coefficient from one factor to another, are theoretical rather than statistical questions. Answers to these questions are the hypotheses that are proposed by the researcher based on preferred theories, the literature or knowledge of any substantive field.

The capacity to represent and test the relations among a set of variables (latent and observed) based on some theories is the most attractive feature of SEM to social researchers. All regression models, no matter how complicated, usually allow only one response variable, while in SEM there can be as many response variables as deemed necessary, and a variable can be a response variable (endogenous) as well as an explanatory variable (exogenous) at the same time, thereby being able to represent more complicated relations among the variables.[3] It is thus tempting to think SEM as a collection of interconnected regression models, with one model's response variable being included in another as an explanatory variable. That is the basic idea of path analysis.

Path analysis aims to connect a set of relationships together so they can be represented by a path diagram. If all variables in a path model truly represent what they are supposed to represent, in other words, if they all have high validity and reliability, then there is no need to use SEM. However, as illustrated above, most variables in social sciences do have measurement errors, and sometimes the errors can be very serious and thus have great impact on our conclusions. Therefore, it is necessary to introduce measurement models into path analysis. By combining confirmatory

---

[3]The word 'exogenous' is more precise because it refers to variables that are not explained by any variable *in the model*; other variables that explain them may exist outside the model. Similarly, 'endogenous' variables are the response variables in the model under study.

factor analysis and path analysis, we have structural question models. This is why an SEM has two components: the measurement component and the structural component. Putting the two components together into a single model (a set of interconnected equations) brings about further statistical complications, and to test such model requires more stringent conditions.

Before discussing those statistical issues, however, I must point out that the importance of specifying the relations of the variables *in theoretical terms* can never be overestimated. First of all, more often than not, the statistical issues would have to be resolved in an arbitrary fashion. As we have seen before, statistical criteria should be applied with caution when answering a particular question, such as determining the number of clusters, factors or testing the statistical significance of a coefficient. Statistical principles should be used as a guide, not hard-and-fast rules. It is unwise to completely rely on statistical evidence for accepting or reject-ing a particular structural equation model. Similar to the effect of sample size on statistical significance, the statistical evidence for supporting a structural model could be heavily influenced by the number of observed variables for each latent variable, the total number of factors, interaction terms and the total sample size. That is, statistical indicators may be more an effect of all these artefacts than an effect of the consistency between the model and the data.

Even when statistical indicators consistently support the proposed model, it only means that the model has gained statistically significant support from the data; it does not mean that the model is the only correct model, because other models may have equivalent or even stronger support from the data *in statistical terms*. This is an inherent limitation of all statistical models: their value is justified based on indicators of fitness to the data rather than on any specific theories on how things work, but *there is no necessary connection between statistical fitness and theoretical sensibility*. These theories are *outside* the models, and the models repre-sent the theories only in the sense of what would happen to the variables *if those theories are correct*. This limitation is due to the fact that the theories in statistical models are understood as a systematic set of relationships among the selected observed variables. As discussed in Chapter 7, some prominent social scientists have found such approach very problematic.

It is particularly important to keep this limitation in mind when taking a struc-tural equation model as 'a causal model', as many researchers do in practice. Actually, SEM is often referred to as 'causal model'. We shall discuss this issue with more details in the next chapter. Put simply here, we must realize that the causal relations among the variables, either latent or observed, *have already been argued and specified before a structural equation model is tested*. That is, the model cannot tell us why and how the variables should be connected in the way repre-sented by the model. All it can do is to show the level of support from the data for the proposed relations.

Given that the researcher is highly confident of the theoretical sensibility of the model, now let us learn the basic ideas of SEM. It starts with the variance–covariance matrix of the selected variables. Covariance rather than correlation is recommended because: (1) correlations can lend to errors in standard error computations; (2) correlations do not have information related to the scale or magnitude of values; and (3) any comparison between samples requires that covariance be used. To illustrate, Table 10.6 provides a covariance matrix of five variables.

Table 10.6   A generic covariance matrix of five variables

	V1	V2	V3	V4	V5
V1	V1 variance				
V2	V2–1 covariance	V2 variance			
V3	V3–1 covariance	V3–2 covariance	V3 variance		
V4	V4–1 covariance	V4–2 covariance	V4–2 covariance	V4 variance	
V5	V5–1 covariance	V5–2 covariance	V5–2 covariance	V5–4 covariance	V5 variance

We can turn this table into a correlation matrix because the correlation coefficient can be defined as:

$$\frac{\text{Covariance of } X \text{ and } Y}{(\text{Standard deviation of } X)(\text{Standard deviation of } Y)}$$

That is, if we divide the items under the diagonal in Table 10.6 by the product of the standard deviations of X and Y, then we obtain their correlation coefficient. If we do the same to the diagonal items, they will become 1 because the product of two identical standard deviations – there is only variable for the diagonal items – will be the variable's variance. So we have now have Table 10.7.

Table 10.7   A generic correlation matrix of five variables

	V1	V2	V3	V4	V5
V1	1				
V2	V2–1 correlation	1			
V3	V3–1 correlation	V3–2 correlation	1		
V4	V4–1 correlation	V4–2 correlation	V4–2 correlation	1	
V5	V5–1 correlation	V5–2 correlation	V5–2 correlation	V5–4 correlation	1

It should be clear by now that if we have a covariance matrix and divide all the cells with the variance of each variable, the covariance matrix will turn into a correlation matrix. The reader may have noticed that the production of such matrices requires the variables to be measured at the metrical level. If some variables are ordinal or binary, correlation coefficients specially created for such variables are available and should be used. If some variables are multi-nominal, then the researcher could transform them into a set of binary variables.

With such a matrix ready for analysis, the researcher aims to produce a model that would be able to reproduce the covariance matrix at a satisfactory level of fitness. In this light, structural equation models follow exactly the same logic as regression models. More specifically, after selecting a set of variables out of theoretical considerations, we can produce a covariance or correlation matrix of these variables. This matrix will then be used for estimating the coefficients in the model, which specifies how the variables are connected to each other. Next, the estimated coefficients will be plugged back into the model to produce an estimated covariance or correlation matrix. Finally, we compare the two matrices to see if the estimated one is close to the original one at a satisfactory level. The fitness indicators used for SEM are almost the same as those for CFA. It is a common practice to modify the model in order to achieve a better fit. However, researchers must justify that the modifications made are theoretically sensible.

Finally, the researcher should be aware of a practical issue. Too large a sample size (more than 500) may cause a problem as the method becomes very sensitive and almost any difference is detected, making goodness-of-fit measures too often suggest poor fit. Conversely, 'Studies show that larger sample sizes are required as communalities become smaller … models containing multiple constructs with communalities less than 0.5 (i.e., standardized loading estimates less than 0.7) also require larger sizes for convergence and model stability. The problem is exaggerated when models have one or two item factors' (Hair et al., 2006: 741). In social science data sets, it is the former situation that worries us.

Latent Growth Curve Models (LGCM)

When learning methods for analysing longitudinal data in Chapter 8, we understood the correlation of measurements taken repeatedly at different time points as an effect of grouping under the same case. After reading the previous sections of this chapter, the reader may realize that we could understand these highly correlated measurements as the observed variables of a latent factor. This means that we could apply methods introduced in the previous sections to analyse longitudinal data.

The most important conceptual issue in making such application is: what do the latent factors mean? It is quite straightforward to establish the meanings of the latent factors when they have a specific and substantive meaning, such as political participation, socio-economic status or attitude toward immigrants. The observed variables of such factors are expected to be strongly correlated because they collectively measure different aspects of the same factor.

Such conceptual basis, however, does not necessarily exist for longitudinal data: the observed variables are correlated not because of a shared common factor, but purely because they are measured on the same individual case. This is a significant change because we may not know what exactly in an individual case is responsible for the correlations of the observed measurements. The only general and sensible explanation is that a same case's characteristics should tend to be stable or to change in a regular way such that earlier observations should help us expect what later ones look like.

Therefore, the exact conceptual meanings of the latent factors in using SEM for analysing longitudinal data are much less clearly specified than they are in cross-sectional studies. It is very important for social researches to realize this because *the latent factors here do not have direct correspondence to any concepts used in the social sciences*. Rather, *the latent factors should be understood as the dominant features of the unobservable pattern of change*, which are often referred to as 'chronometric common factors'. In other words, we hypothesize that there exists an underlying pattern of change throughout the time period in which the measurements were made. Furthermore, it is the features of this pattern of change, such as its starting point, shape of change and rate of change, that are responsible for the strong correlations among the observed variables. The pattern does not have to be a curve of 'growth', of course. The phrase 'growth curve' should not be understood restrictively as an upward or progressive trend; rather, it means *any* pattern of change.

What social researchers must do before specifying a latent growth curve model is explore whether any growth curve seems to exist in the data. In other words, a model of change can be constructed only when *there is indeed change over time*. The implication of this requirement for data collection is that there are three or more time points on which cases are measured; clearly, it is impossible to represent any curve-linear shape with only two time points. Conversely, a large number of measures may not necessarily be an advantage. As Preacher and his colleagues have found that 'parsimonious linear models often have trouble adequately fitting more than six repeated measures ... LGM is best suited for modelling trends measured over a limited number of occasions in large samples' (2008: 12). Beyond a certain number of observations over time, the trajectory is unlikely to be strictly linear and may not show any clear pattern at all. In those situations, GCMs will struggle to fit the data based on the assumption of linearity.

Other design issues in longitudinal studies also apply, including the frequency of observations, whether the time gap between two consecutive measures remains constant, and whether the cases were measured at the same time points, and so forth. It is not our objective to discuss the effects of these designs on subsequent statistical models;[4] we introduce these issues here because, as shown below, how time is defined will influence the factor loadings in the model.

Once the temporal change is established, the next question relates to the shape of change. This is especially important when the researcher would propose that the shape of change is curve-linear rather than straight-linear. All these explorations and considerations will lead to the specification of a particular LGCM.

Assuming the shape of change is linear, two factors are usually assumed if change is identified: the intercept factor representing the effect of the starting point (time is set to 0) and the slope factor representing the rate of change. If there is no change, the model would only include the intercept, but we do not have much substantive interest in such 'null model' and use it only for the purpose of comparing with other models. If change does exist, the simplest LGCM would be a two-factor model, while the observed variables, like those in ordinary structural equation models, will have their variance–covariance matrix, which will be the starting point of analysis and the reference point for assessing the performance of a model. As with many other models, our objective is to find a model with the smallest number of parameters that can produce a variance–covariance matrix closest to the observed matrix.

The general model with the intercept and the slope factors could be presented graphically as shown in Figure 10.5.

It is a random intercept and random slope model because it is assumed that both are responsible for the observed temporal correlations among the repeated

---

[4]Interested readers could consult Biesanz et al. (2004), Hancock and Choi (2006) and Stoolemiller (1995), for more detailed and technical discussions.

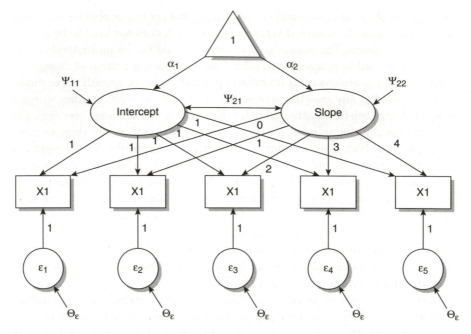

Figure 10.5   A random intercept and random slope latent growth curve model

measurements. If, for example, we hypothesize that the slope does not have an effect, then it will not appear in the graph at all. In this model, we hypothesize that the effect of the intercept is constant over time, hence all the ones on the regression loadings. In contrast, the effect of the slope is assumed to change over time, which is shown by 0, 1, 2, 3 and 4. Such assignment of time scale can change, depending on how we perceive its effect (see more below). We also hypothesize that the intercept and the slope are correlated; that is, the rate of change is connected with where a case starts at the initial time point. All the other symbols are simply the parameters needed for estimating the model.

If we ignore the loadings on the above graph, we can see the above model as a general model. At the conceptual level, it actually includes several models, each having its own specifications (hypotheses) with regard to the nature of the factors' effect on the observed variables. Such effect could be fixed or random. For example, when the intercept factor's effect is fixed, we hypothesize that all cases have the same starting point (the same value at time 0). If we hypothesize that it is random, the cases will have different starting points, obviously a more realistic assumption. The same logic applies to the slope factor as well, depending on whether we would think that the cases experience different or the same rate of change.

A more realistic model is usually more complicated; that is, it contains more parameters to be estimated. For example, if our hypothesis is that both intercept and the slope effects are fixed, then we only need to estimate three parameters (the mean intercept, the mean slope, and the error variance, which is assumed to be the same for all observed variables). If we relax the model to allow both factors' effects to be random, then we will have to estimate three more parameters (each factor's variance and their covariance).

Besides the nature of the factor's effect on the observed variables, we also need to specify how the slope factor's effect is represented over time. A major difference between a cross-sectional SEM and a LGCM is that the factor loadings need to reflect the change over time, and how this is done is a more substantive than statistical issue. It is straightforward to define the loadings on the intercept factor – as no change needs to be reflected in this factor, the loadings are fixed as 1 for all observed variables.

More care needs to be taken when scaling time for the slope factor because the loadings should represent the temporal pattern, and how the time points are defined and scaled will determine the interpretation of the model parameters related to the slope factor. In contrast, the same time points can be scaled in different ways that are mathematically equivalent (linear transformations); therefore, any particular scaling will not affect overall model fit. For example, suppose there are five time points on which the cases were measured: 1992, 1994, 1996, 1998 and 2000. The loadings of the slope factor on the observed variable at each point can be scaled, respectively, as 0, 2, 4, 6 and 8. This is alright if the researcher believes that it is meaningful to take 1992 as the reference point. If the year 1996 is deemed as the meaningful reference, then the time should be scaled as –4, –2, 0, 2 and 4, respectively.

Note that if the researcher does not have a strong theory or hypothesis on the shape of change, the specific type of the trajectory can be left unspecified. This means that one or more loading of the slope factor are to be estimated by the data. In this situation, the model is used essentially as an exploratory rather than confirmatory tool.

As usual, we leave the matter of estimating the parameters to statisticians and computer software programs[5] but focus our attention to the interpretations. The mean of the intercept factor only indicates the average starting point, given the hypothesis that the cases have different starting points, and as long as it makes sense substantively, it is not very interesting to us.

Most interesting to us is the mean of the slope factor and its relationship with the intercept factor. Note that we can study such relationship only after we allow the intercept as well as the slope factors to be random (or their parameters to be freely estimated). The former shows the direction (indicated by its sign) and the rate of change, given that the cases have different rates of change and all changes are linear. Their relationship is measured by the covariance, from which we can tell whether cases starting high or low will experience a lower or higher speed of change and in which direction (up or down). The variance terms (the variance of each factor plus the variance of the error term of each observed variable) tell us how much variation remains after the effects of the factors have been taken into account, thus suggesting whether further explanation is needed in order to improve the performance of the model.

As a common practice in statistical modelling, several models are usually estimated, evaluated, and compared. Like other structural equation models, the models will be

---

[5] Besides the most widely used programs for SEM (AMOS, EQS, LISREL and Mplus), Mx (Neale et al., 2003) is a public domain software (free for download) especially written for estimating LGCMs. For a guide on how to fit and evaluate LGCMs with different software programs, see Ferrer et al. (2004).

evaluated based on a set of fitness indicators. Recall that in the previous section, it was recommended that several indicators should be used together in order to ensure a high level of consistency. The fitness indicators for LGCMs are similar to those used for other SEMs but with some changes and extensions. Here, we shall not present the equations and mathematical justifications for each indicator. Suffice it to show that the most popular indicators are all based on the chi-square idea of comparing the fitted values and the observed values of the variance–covariance matrix, with the alternative indicators attempting to take into account of the effects of degrees of freedom, the number of parameters, or the sample size.

As users of these indicators, social researchers, however, must understand what each of them suggests for a particular model. Duncan et al. (2006: 15, Table 1.1) have produced a table showing the fit indices used by the four most popular software programs (AMOS, EQS, LISREL and Mplus). They have also pointed out that besides the chi-square indicators, Comparative Fit Index (CFI), Non-Normed Fit Index (NNFI) and Root Mean Square Error of Approximation (RMSEA) are the mostly widely acceptable ones. This is basically consistent with what Preacher et al. (2008: 18–20) have suggested, except that they replace CFI with standard root mean square residual (SRMR). RMSEA is a so-called 'negative' indicator as it shows misfit rather that fit of a model; therefore, a smaller RMSEA represents better fit. SRMR is also such negative indicator but based on standardized residuals. The advantage of NNFI is its robustness to violations of distribution assumptions (mostly multivariate normality).

Built on these relatively simple models, we can have many other extended models to represent different hypotheses, expectations, and theories. Very briefly, we could have the following extensions of the above basic models:

- If we are interested in comparing different samples or subgroups with regard to the same changing pattern, we could fit the same model to different samples or subgroups and compare whether the model fits each sample or subgroup differently.
- Similarly, we could have the same model on different latent factors and see whether the same temporal pattern applies to different factors. We can do it separately or put them in the same model while assuming the two factors are correlated.
- If we plan a regression-type of analysis, that is, to explain the observed changing pattern with another variable, we could introduce a time-varying variable that temporally changes with the previously selected variables.
- If we believe that the changing trajectory is curve-linear and we can specify its form, such as quadratic, we could introduce another slope factor. Note that usually the lower order factor must be included when a higher order one is included.
- If we believe that the factors may have levels, that is, one slope factor is responsible for several other slope factors, we could include all the factors in a model at different levels.
- There are also LGCMs that aim to neutralize the cohort effect by fitting the same model to several sequential cohorts.

By now it should be clear that the latent growth curve approach is highly flexible, being able to incorporate many effects. Besides the above capacities, such models could also include categorical variables and cope with missing values. The reader can find details of these extensions by consulting the excellent text by Duncan et al. (2006).

ELEVEN

Causal Analysis

Statistics and the Challenge of Studying Causal Relations

Establishing causal relations between two phenomena in the English philosophical tradition is a mission impossible (Hume, 1975[1777]; Russell, 1963). In contrast, social scientists see the study of causal relations as the most important achievement (MacIver, 1942; Abbott, 2004; Stinchcombe, 2005; Cartwright, 2007), and their desire to find causality is motivated by at least three potential benefits. First, causal explanation is believed to transcend time and space and therefore has a much wider scope of applications. Second, causal connections constitute the foundation of good control of the interested phenomena, which is especially important for policy and decision-making. Third, most causal statements are subject to the laws of logic and therefore at least sound more rigorous than they would have been if no logic were involved.

Perhaps aiming to reconcile the fundamental difficulty and the desire to study causation, Herbert Simon (1953) proposed a modest and realistic approach. He suggested that discussions of causality be restricted to our model of the reality rather than to the reality per se. We shall follow Simon's pragmatic approach in this book. We leave all the difficult issues to philosophers to resolve. We take causal models as analytical tools, which are to be used appropriately only for a particular purpose or in a specific context. Therefore, we take the results as temporary representations of specific causal relations in reality, which are subject to further modifications and rejections if there is a more convincing model and empirical evidence.

In this chapter we review some statistical methods in light of their utility and the logic of causal analysis. I aim to show that statistics should be a tool in social researcher's toolbox. It is too radical to claim that statistical methods are inherently incompetent of modelling causal relations and therefore should be distanced from causal analysis. Statistics can do something with causal analysis. First of all, statistical studies can help us establish the phenomenon and even suggest clues for causal explanations. Second, some statistical models (structural equation models or counterfactual models) can represent causal theories. Third, the size of a causal factor's effect is very important as by evaluating it we can decide how much serious attention we should pay to it, and for this purpose statistical methods can be of great use.

Conversely, we must keep in mind that it is only when the conditions have been satisfied that statistical methods can be useful for studying causal relations. One condition is that the research was designed properly to allow causal inference in the subsequent analysis of the data. Another is that we must already have a theory of causal relations and only use statistics to support such theory. As Jon Elster points out, 'Statistical explanations are incomplete by themselves, however, since they ultimately have to rely on intuitions about plausible causal mechanisms' (2007: 8). In short, *statistical methods cannot do causal analysis on their own*; they must join forces with other research activities.

This is a key point that social researchers should keep in mind. The identification of causal mechanisms and processes is not a task for statistical models and for empirical observations in general. To discover or identify causal mechanisms is a task for heuristics and research design. Causal mechanisms are either found through heuristic methods, such as experiment or observation, or simply derived from current theories and knowledge. It is only after the causal relationship is proposed that statistical methods can be brought into the analysis. Statistical models are most effective of representing, measuring and validating the identified processes. It is therefore unwise and even counterproductive to use these models to prove the correct identification of causal mechanisms.

Some Basic Concepts and Issues in Causal Analysis

Causality implies a force of production. When we say X causes Y, we mean the connection has a one-way direction, going from X to Y. A causal relationship is thus asymmetric. Sometimes, the term 'reciprocal causality' is used, meaning X causes Y and Y causes X as well. Although that relationship is possible, very often it indicates that a temporary order or an underlying causal mechanism has not been clearly identified. To make our discussion focused on the concepts and the logic, we shall only examine the following simplest scenario and take it as the starting point: a directed (non-recursive) causal relationship with only one cause and one outcome.

The first question is: What makes us think that X is a cause of Y? For example, how come do we want to study the effect of family types, such as single- or both-parent families, on mental health? The answer to such question is not part of normal causal analysis. *To theorize or hypothesize the causal relationship cannot be achieved by statistical work.* We may have observed the connection between the two variables in anecdotal cases, either our own or other people's experience reported in the media. Or, it simply sounds sensible for us to make such observation. As Stinchcombe (1968) pointed out many years ago in the Preface of his well-read *Constructing Social Theories*, to be able to propose several sensible explanations is a basic skill for sociology students. It is the researcher's task to ensure the logical or substantive sensibility of the hypothetical causal relationship before it is tested with data.

This should not leave us an impression that discovering the cause is either very easy or not as important as other activities. Instead, the discovery – at least the suspicion or the hypothesis – of an important cause is no less, perhaps even more, important than modelling and measuring the causal connection. We the researchers must explain how we come up with a particular cause and why it is important to study it. However, this kind of work is not a part of statistical analysis. Our statistical work starts after the causal mechanisms have been identified and the causal relations have been proposed. Statistical research is concerned with the confirmation, the representation and the measurement of causal relations.

It is only after the above is done that we can come to the next question: How can we establish the causal relationship with as much confidence as we can? In theory, causal relationships are best established when two conditions are satisfied. Suppose that the cause X takes only two values, 'exists 'or 'does not exist', and for the outcome Y, 'has happened' or 'has not happened.' Then we have four possible scenarios (Table 11.1).

Table 11.1   Scenarios of cause and outcome

| | | Outcome (Y) | |
		Has happened	Has not happened
Cause (X)	Exists	Scenario 1	Scenario 2
	Does not exist	Scenario 3	Scenario 4

For example, consider whether taking a personal tutorial would improve a student's exam results. The tutorial does not help if the student takes it but no improvement follows (scenario 2) or if the student does not take it but improvement is still achieved (scenario 3). We can say that the tutorial is a causal factor of improvement only when *both* scenarios 1 and 4 are true, that is, if the student takes the tutorial and improvement follows and if not, no improvement. Note that *in principle*, the two scenarios must happen *at the same time*; otherwise, we have to assume that the situations at two different time points are exactly the same, which is a very strong assumption. It is likely that something that happened between the two scenarios may interfere with the interested process and mislead our understanding of the true causal process. A simple example is that the student has become used to the way the tutorial is conducted and thus improved his or her performance. Therefore, it is extremely hard to justify the equivalence of events that have taken place at different time points.

It is obviously impossible to satisfy the requirement of observing two different processes at the same time; for the above particular example, a student either has taken the tutorial or has not taken it; it is impossible to have taken and have not taken a tutorial at the same time. That is, either scenario 1 or scenario 4 is counter-factual at a particular time point. This is the so-called 'the fundamental problem of causation' (Holland, 1986). People interested in a particular study may find it acceptable to assume that nothing important to the interested phenomena has happened, so the studied events could be treated as if they had happened at the same time. Such situation, however, merely indicates the agreement among the people involved rather than an effective solution of the problem.

Here comes a paradox: the *ideal but impractical* condition for establishing causal relationship is that the expected outcome happens with the cause present and does not happen without the cause *at the same time and on the same set of cases*. These conditions are necessary for dismissing any potential interfering effects from the events in between the times of observation or from the observed character-istics of the cases. As it is impossible to satisfy these conditions in practice, we have to find alternative but unavoidably compromised ways of studying causal relations. This reinforces a point made previously: *causal analysis is more a research design problem rather than a problem for data analysis*.

The best solution to this fundamental problem is to design an experiment. There are a great variety of experiments, of course, but with regard to establishing causal connections, they follow about the same logic. For the above simple situation, the cause has two values, having tutorial and not having tutorial. Because we cannot let the same cases, such as the same group of students, experience the two values at the same time, we break the cases into two subgroups, experiencing a different situ-ation of the cause, respectively; that is, one subgroup having the tutorial – usually referred to as 'the treatment group' in the literature of experiment design – while the other not ('the control group'). Compared with the ideal situation, this is a compromised solution because we are taking the risk of letting a third factor inter-fere with the interested process. For example, it is likely that the treatment group happens to include most of the smarter students, so it is their intelligence, not the tutorial, that explains their better performance.

It is therefore critically important to ensure that the two groups are *the same except for their exposure to different causal conditions* (having tutorial or not). This is why we need randomization: as the cases will always be different in a certain aspect, we let an almost completely objective process to determine the formation of the subgroups; otherwise, any formation of groups created either by the investigator or the respondents will likely bring in an interfering factor. There is a chance that the subgroups randomly formed may still be different in a way that will confound the interested causal relationship, and the adopted randomizing procedure can never be completely random – there are rules for creating random numbers, but the similarity between the two subgroups has been maximized.

The key advantage of randomization is that it provides us with the best possi-ble opportunity to see the two groups *as if they were actually one group experienc-ing two different values of the cause at the same time*. It is purely by chance that some members of this one group have ended up in the treatment subgroup while the rest ending up in the control group, but the two are *effectively substitutable*.

The unfeasibility of carrying out experiments in social science studies is well known. One difficulty is that for ethical and practical reasons, we cannot randomly assign human beings, for example, to a particular socio-economic status (SES) and ask them to live like that for a certain period of time. Besides, experiments have their own limitations as well. A major problem is their low external validity – usually they are conducted in artificial settings, making it very hard to generalize the conclusions beyond the studied context.

In social research, most data are collected in observational studies, in which it is unclear how a particular treatment (one of the two values of the cause) has been assigned to some cases but not to others. That is, we do not know whether the cases are under different conditions because they are there by chance, i.e. similar to an experiment condition, or there is a mechanism unknown to us that put them in a particular condition. Without such knowledge, obviously it is very difficult to establish causal relationships because we are unable to isolate the effect of the hypothesized cause from that of the unknown mechanism. Note that this is an inherent problem with research design in all social science studies, not a particular problem with statistical methods. It is confusing and unfair to criticize statistics for being unable to properly establishing causation simply because statistics is used for analysing the data collected from observational studies not designed for establishing causal relations.

Given these difficulties, statisticians have adopted three criteria that originated from David Hume for inferring a causal relationship (Agresti and Finlay, 2008: 302): (1) covariation between the presumed cause and outcome; (2) temporal precedence of the cause; and (3) exclusion of alternative explanations for cause–outcome connections. All three have to be satisfied *at the same time* in order for causality to be derived. It is worth emphasizing that even when that is achieved, causal relations still cannot be completely established; it is just that we have collected the strongest evidence available for supporting our causal hypothesis.

The first is the starting point and the easiest to establish. It is possible that one event causes another but we do not observe any association between them if the causal effect has been cancelled out by another, unobserved effect. But such processes are very rare and will not draw our attention in the first place – we will not be motivated to study their causal relations if we do not observe any kind of association between them. Any causal analysis must start with some kind of association. We have learnt before in this book some statistical tools for measuring the association, such as the Pearson correlation coefficient, the chi-square and the odds ratio. However, correlation is not enough for establishing causation because it is much less informative than causation. *Causation can be seen as a subset of correlation when the direction of a relationship is specified.* The establishment of causal relations is therefore one step ahead of correlation, but to take that step demands further information.

The second criterion is more complicated and difficult to satisfy. The main problem lies in the uncertain relationship between *temporal* order and *logical* order. A cause must *both temporally and logically* precede an outcome, but a precedent event may or may not be a logical cause. Temporal connection is a special type of covariation and, therefore, does not necessarily lead to causal connection. For example, people acquire several fixed attributes at birth, such as sex, age, ethnicity and order among siblings, but it makes little sense to take them as direct causes of other attributes that are developed at later stages of life, such as political affiliation. In addition, it can even be very difficult to determine the temporal order of two variables. The relationship between political interest and political participation is a good example: do people become interested in politics after participating in political activities, such as election campaigns, or do they participate in political activities because they are interested in politics? Or do these two processes take place concurrently?

The last criterion is perhaps the most difficult to satisfy. It has become common sense now that the objective of this criterion is to avoid confusing a spurious relationship, which will disappear if an underlying common cause is taken into account, with a genuine causal one. The difficulty of satisfying it stems from the requirement that all possible common causes have been included in order to claim that the interested causal relationship is not a spurious one. Any important cause missed by the research behind a paper submitted to an academic journal could be easily picked up by its reviewers. To avoid rejection, some authors have tried to include as many variables as possible, consequently making the model excessively complicated without any justification other than the purpose of sifting out spurious relations. The most undesirable consequence is that to select a model or to test theories in general becomes a process of identifying statistically insignificant variables and the original theoretical models are usually abandoned purely for statistical reasons (Lieberson, 1985).

In sum, it is quite difficult to meet at least the last two criteria, thereby making it even more difficult to satisfy all three of them at the same time. Even the simultaneous satisfaction of these three criteria cannot actually guarantee causal connections. They are simply all what researchers can do in an attempt to increase the level of robustness of the claimed causal connection by showing empirical regularities repeatedly ('causation as robust dependence', Goldthorpe [2000: 138–42]). Data collected in longitudinal surveys may to a certain extent enhance the robustness by better satisfying the temporal order criterion, but that is not a fundamental solution.

This does not mean, however, that we should stop doing causal analysis. The logic holds for all statistical analysis: although we cannot prove that something is true, we can measure the likelihood that something is not true by analysing the available information. Especially for statistical studies, causal relationship is probabilistic rather than deterministic. Deterministic causality applies to all cases under study without any exception. In the sciences of human beings, researchers can only hope to measure the probability of a causal connection for a particular case, or they have to work at an aggregate level. Exceptional deviant cases should not be taken as evidence of disproof. If currently no information casts a serious doubt on the proposed causal relationship, we keep it. Further consistent results will increase the level of our confidence, while new inconsistent evidence will help us modify or even abandon the previous findings.

Linear Regression Models and Causal Relations

Let us start with the simple linear regression model as it corresponds to the simplest situation of causation. There is only one cause X and one outcome Y; for example, father's SES is deemed as the cause of children's academic performance at school.

It is important to point out that what we would ask statistical models to represent is *not the actual causal process but a measurable consequence* of the proposed causal process. It is very likely that we have already had a causal mechanism in mind when making such observation, but it is very difficult, if not impossible at all, to mathematically include the causal mechanism in a statistical model. Therefore, *it does not make sense to ask a statistical model to represent the proposed theory of causal process itself*. For this example, it does not make sense to claim that a father's SES could cause his children's academic performance. As a person, a father can have an effect on his children – a father of higher SES is capable of sending his children to a better school or living in a neighbourhood where better schools are located, but his SES, as an attribute of a person, cannot be causal.

However, that does not mean that studying attributes is of no use for analysis of causal relations. It is true that we cannot directly model the process that fathers influence their children's academic performance, but if we think that is the causal process in reality, we would expect to find statistically significant effect of father's SES on their children's academic performance. Statistical models are not direct representations of the causal processes; rather, they represent what we would observe if the proposed causal process is valid. To ensure that the statistical model is a valid representation of the observed outcomes of the causal process is the whole business of translating the theory into a statistical model that can 'best' represent what would happen if the theory is right.

Let us be a bit more specific about what we are doing with a linear regression model. When we hypothesize that father's SES is a cause of his children's performance, we mean that the children's performance will improve if the father's SES goes up and their performance will deteriorate if the father's SES goes down. As pointed out above, we should observe these two processes taking place at the same time period to avoid potential interfering effects. But because it is impossible to do that, we may want to carry out an experiment on a sample of fathers and their children. Given that these people are absolutely comparable in all other aspects, we would, first, measure the fathers' SES and their children's academic performance, second, we would randomly select some fathers and increase their SES to a higher level, and finally we measure all the children's performance again to see if those whose fathers' SES have been promoted have performed better than those whose fathers' SES have not been promoted.

Strictly speaking, it is only in such context that a simple linear regression model $Y_i = \beta_0 + \beta_1 X_i + \varepsilon_i$ is a valid representation of the causal relationship, because the model compares the means of academic performance of the two groups of children given that (1) the effect of father's SES has been singled out as the only cause at work and (2) the father's SES can be manipulated so that the change of children's performance can be measured. It is only a representation because the model itself does not contain any information about how the cause has produced the outcome. Given that the identified causal relationship is valid, the model has estimated the causal effect of X on Y using the difference of two values of Y when X takes two different values. In other words, the model is *not a device for confirming* the validity of the causal relationship; it is only *a tool for estimating* the size of the causal relationship. As Berk aptly summarizes: 'There is nothing in simple linear regression that, by itself, will lead to causal inferences. One needs clear definitions of the relevant concepts and then good information about how the data were generated before causal inference can be drawn' (2004: 101).

In observational studies, none of the conditions can be satisfied – we cannot neutralize the effects of possible confounding factors by keeping them 'constant', nor can we manipulate the level of the explanatory variable (father's SES in this case). The usual practice is to draw a random sample of families, asking the selected respondents to report their father's SES and children's academic performance. We may produce a regression model exactly the same as the above one derived from an experiment, but the underlying processes that produced the data are fundamentally different. Even when the key regression coefficient β_1 is statistically significant and the model fits the data very well (say, $R^2 = 0.90$), we are still unable to say that β_1 represents the causal effect of X on Y because of the way in which the data were collected. This reinforces the point that establishing causal connections is essentially an issue of research design, not of statistical modelling.

In light of the three criteria of causation listed above for observational studies, this example satisfies the first two without much difficulty: the correlation between X and Y could be big in size and statistically significant (very low chance of being 0), and X precedes Y in time (father's SES comes before children go to school). But it is difficult to meet the third one: alternative explanations have been dismissed. The analysis is relatively easy if the researcher knows what the alternative explanations are. Statistically, this means to include the possible confounding variables in the model so that their effects are 'controlled'. This is why we need multiple linear regression models. For this example, we may believe that we must take into account father's education, because it is reasonable to hypothesize that a father's education is responsible for both the father's SES – better education helps the father get better job and higher income – and his children's academic performance – fathers with better education may encourage their children perform better or help their children study more effectively.

It is important to note that the meaning of such 'control variables' should be understood statistically rather than experimentally. That is, we did not literally control the effects of such variables by holding their values constant, as setting the lights in a room at a particular level of brightness. In observational studies, there is no actual process of controlling anything. The meaning of 'control variables' has to be understood in the comparative sense; that is, we study the interested causal relationship *at a certain level of a control variable*. For the above example, we measure the effect of father's SES on their children's performance when all the fathers under investigation have the same level of education. What the model has done is equivalent to the following process: suppose there are four level of education, we select four groups of fathers, each at a different level of education, and then we study the effect of father's SES on their children's performance in each group. If the conclusion remains the same across all four groups, then the proposed causal relationship is supported; otherwise, it has to be modified or even rejected. All we hope to find is that the interested causal relationship does not have to be seriously modified when an additional variable is introduced in the model. Again, this is what John Goldthorpe refers to as 'causation as robust dependence' (2000: 138–42), as opposed to 'causation as consequential manipulation' in experiments.

Useful as the above notions are, they do not offer a solution for overcoming the limitations of 'causation as robust dependence'. First, most of the time the researcher cannot be completely certain about what the alternative explanations are, that is, which variables' effects must be controlled. Ultimately, it is all down to the researcher's justification and the agreement with other researchers. Second, even when the first issue is settled, it is hard to know how robust the interested causal relationship has to be and whether such robustness is meaningful in theoretical or conceptual terms. It has become a common practice in social science research for the researcher to include as many control variables as possible simply for the sake of ensuring the robustness of the hypotheses. Third, it is very unlikely that the hypothesized causal relationship will be completely robust – always standing firm no matter how many and which variables are introduced. In such situation, it is unclear whether the researcher should throw away the causal statement or ignore a few occasions in which the causal hypothesis does not hold.

We can sum up the above discussion with three important points. First, we can use linear regression models and all their extensions to represent measurable outcomes of any hypothesized causal mechanisms and processes, although we cannot use statistical methods to study the mechanisms and processes directly. Social researchers must keep in mind that it is their job to ensure the consistency of the statistical model and the proposed causal relationship. Second, statistical methods are best at *measuring the causal effect*, but the measurement – achieved through statistical models – is only valid provided that the causal relationship is already established, not a task for statistical models to accomplish. Third, measuring and testing the robustness of a causal effect should not be a completely statistical matter. Both statistically significant and statistically non-significant results should inform our analysis of the interested causal process.

All these points are applicable to structural equation models (SEM) as well. SEM can be seen as extended linear regression models in two senses. Their most relevant property to causal analysis is their flexibility of representing complicated causal relations. This is a major advantage over other regression models because the latter can only represent causal relations in which there is only one outcome. With SEM, in theory we can include as many outcomes as deemed necessary and a variable can be both a cause and an outcome in the same model. Consequently, they can represent causal chains, indirect causes, multiple causes and so on. The other advantage of SEM is that they explicitly include measurement errors, thereby making our estimates of causal effects more accurate.

Unfortunately, these capacities cannot offer much help to overcome the inherent limitations of linear regression models for the purpose of studying causal relations.

If the data are collected in a sample survey rather than an experiment, then most statistical models cannot help for establishing casual relations. SEM has been referred to as 'causal models' not because it can single out the unique effect of a cause in an experimental setting but because they can represent a variety of causal hypotheses. In experiments, the studied causal relation is usually much simpler than that represented by a structural equation model, but the evidence offered by an experiment is much stronger. For SEM, causal relations are argued or hypothesized. About 25 years ago when they taught junior researchers to use SEM as causal models, Saris and Stronkhorst put it very clearly: 'The formulation of a structural equation model requires that the researcher plays an active role in specifying the causal mechanism which might have produced the observed data' (1984: 62). Today, this warning is repeated again by other statistical experts: 'Ultimately, SEM alone cannot establish causality. It can, however, provide some evidence necessary to support a causal inference' (Hair et al., 2006: 721). The arrows in an SEM model should only indicate causal effect in the regression sense.

Counterfactual Model for Causal Analysis of Observational Data

The difficulties in isolating the effect of the interested cause make it impossible to measure the genuine causal effect with observational data. During the past three decades, statisticians have developed a logically sound statistical procedure to solve this problem.[1] Obviously, this approach is very useful for social research due to the wide availability of observational data from sample surveys.

The overall idea is to find out what observational studies do not have, in comparison with the idealized conditions for establishing causal associations, and then to devise statistical tools to overcome such limitations. As shown above, the major problem is that the cases cannot be put under different causal conditions at the same time, but our estimate of the causal effect would be the most reliable if we had the results from these causal conditions. Our objective is to find procedures that would allow us to have the best approximation of the ideal situation so that we can make the best estimate of causal effect. Since it is the absence of the counterfactuals that prevent us from deriving a reliable estimate, we need procedures that can help us overcome that difficulty. This is why this approach is called 'counterfactual' or 'potential outcome'. After setting up the situation, I shall introduce two procedures: matching and instrumental variable.

Before discussing them, it is important to remind the reader that they are not complete or final solutions to the causation problem in social sciences as they have two

---

[1]The leading statisticians in this area are Donald Rubin (1974, 1990), P. Holland (1986), Holland and Rubin (1988) and P. R. Rosenbaum (2002). Michael Sobel (1995) has summarized the logic from a sociological perspective. The literature, however, is mostly very technical. For readers who would like to read more, I strongly recommend starting with Steven Morgen and Christopher Winship's (2007) recent book *Counterfactuals and Causal Inference*.

major limitations: (1) they work only under a series of assumptions, some of which can be quite strong; (2) the causal relationship under study is usually very simple.

To specify the problem, let us start with the ideal situation for estimating causal effect (Figure 11.1).

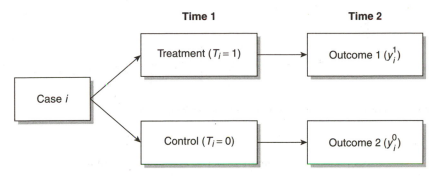

Figure 11.1   The ideal situation for inferring causal effect

In such situation, each case experiences the two causal conditions – treatment and control – at the same time (Time 1). We use T_i to represent the variable with only two values, i.e. the two conditions. For each condition, there will be a corresponding outcome after a period of time (to Time 2). The difference between the two outcomes, y_i^1 and y_i^0, will be the causal effect δ_i (delta):

$$\delta_i = y_i^1 - y_i^0 \tag{11.1}$$

Note that such definition works only when the interested cause is the sole source of the different outcomes. If there is another source, it will not work. One possibility is that the cases in different causal conditions interfere with each other through interactions or communications. If this is the situation, then our identification of the cause has been contaminated by another one. The assumption of no interference among the cases is called 'the stable unit treatment value assumption' (SUTVA). As Goldthorpe (2000: 146–8) has pointed out, the counterfactual notion of causation has missed out 'the agency effect', that is, the observed difference may not be a result of 'the treatment' but a result of the actions initiated by the respondents under study. I doubt that SUTVA will be seriously compromised in large-scale social surveys – how often do we have evidence that interactions among our respondents have changed their answers? Nevertheless, we should not take for granted that SUVTA always holds. At least, researchers should keep this assumption in mind when using this method.

Even SUTVA holds, the reality is far from this ideal situation, of course. The major gap is the fact that each case can experience only one causal condition at a particular time point (Figures 11.2 and 11.3).

The broken lines indicate the unrealized situation; as a result, the corresponding outcome is potential rather than real. In either situation, we cannot use (11.1) to calculate the causal effect anymore because either y_i^1 or y_i^0 is missing. Therefore,

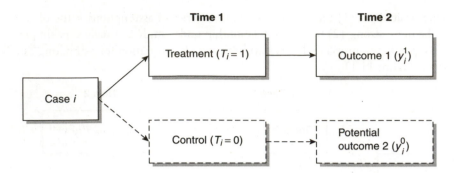

Figure 11.2 Observation available for treatment but not for control

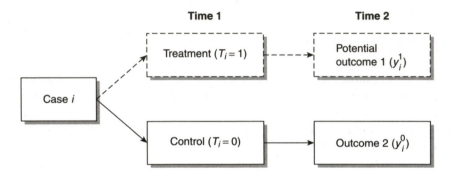

Figure 11.3 Observation available for control but not for treatment

the fundamental difficulty for establishing causal relations *at the individual level* is the impossibility of collecting information on the potential outcomes.

If it is impossible to study causation at the individual level, we may be able to do that *at the group level*. That is, we define the causal effect – more precisely, the mean of the causal effect – as the difference between the means of the two groups on the interested variable:

$$\bar{\delta} = \bar{Y}^t - \bar{Y}^c \tag{11.2}$$

In statistics, this is usually expressed in terms of the expected value:

$$E[\delta] = E[Y^t - Y^c] = E[Y^t] - E[Y^c] \tag{11.3}$$

Conceptually, the two equations are the same.

Note that (11.2) is for the population. In observational studies, we often only have a sample. It is therefore attempting for us to use the sample means (indicated by the hat on top of each term below) to estimate the means in the population:

$$\hat{\bar{\delta}} = \bar{Y}^t_{i \in T} - \bar{Y}^c_{i \in C} \tag{11.4}$$

On the right-hand side, $\overline{Y}^t_{i \in T}$ is the estimated mean of the treatment group while $\overline{Y}^c_{i \in C}$ is the estimated mean of the control group. Therefore, their difference is the estimated mean difference between the two groups based on the sample, which we can call 'the sample average causal effect'.

The question is: is it sensible for us to use $\hat{\delta}$ for estimating $\hat{\delta}$. It can be easily proved that we can do that if the following two assumptions can hold: $\overline{Y}^t_{i \in T} = \overline{Y}^t_{i \in C}$ and $\overline{Y}^c_{i \in T} = \overline{Y}^t_{i \in C}$ (see Winship and Morgan, 1999: 665–6, for details). In plain English, the assumptions mean that *the treatment group and the control group are the same with regard to the mean of* Y. So if we can somehow show that the two groups are equivalent or substitutable, then we can use the average sample causal effect (11.4) as an acceptable estimator of the targeted population average causal effect (11.2).

The best, albeit not certain, way of satisfying these assumptions is to assign the cases randomly into different causal conditions. The idea is that randomization will virtually eliminate any possible systematic differences between the two groups (treatment and control) so that they can be deemed as substitutable. This reaffirms the advantage of using random allocations.

The above discussion also highlights the difficulty with using the data collected from observational studies to estimate causal effect: the groups under different causal conditions are not comparable, at least we cannot dismiss the potential risk, and a common reason is that the cases assign themselves to a particular condition. Now, the challenge is *to ensure the comparability of the groups even though they are not formed through a random-assignment process*. The main objective of the counterfactual methods developed so far is to solve this problem.

Because the cases have not been assigned to different causal conditions randomly, we need to take such assignment mechanisms into our models so that their effect has been neutralized. This is the standard regression approach. The logic is that if we think that the cases have selected themselves for different causal conditions because of a particular attribute, then we can divide the cases into groups according to the levels of that attribute. As the cases within each level are the same, or at least very comparable, the effect of self-selection on the studied causal relationship has been eliminated or minimized. In the counterfactual literature, this procedure is referred to as 'ignorability':

$$(Y^t, Y^c) \perp T | S \qquad (11.5)$$

In the above statement, the vertical bar is a symbol for 'given' and $\perp$ means 'independent', so it reads 'given S, Y^t and Y^c are independent of T'. This comes from a more relaxed situation in which we assume that the values that each group takes have nothing to do with how they are assigned to each causal condition, that is:

$$(Y^t, Y^c) \perp T \qquad (11.6)$$

But later as we know or suspect that they are not actually independent because the assignment process is influenced by a set of variables S. So now we bring S into the analysis: at each level of S, Y and T become independent again. *It is at each particular level of S that its effect becomes ignorable.* Morgan and Winship refer to the effect of S as 'back-door path' to Y, and to make the effect ignorable is to block those back-door paths.

The regression strategy has two major limitations. First, how do we know we have blocked all the back-door paths? To ask the same question in the statistical language: how can be certain that S has included all the variables so that their effects become ignorable? For an individual researcher, this is a serious problem: as we mentioned before when discussing control variables in regression models, if you have missed a variable that your anonymous reviewer thinks important, your paper is doomed to be rejected. From the perspective of the whole scientific community and the development of science, this is absolutely fine because it is the very nature of scientific research that we miss something at a particular time point but discover it later on.

A second limitation is that even when there is no problem with regard to the selection of variables in S, practically we may not be able to calculate the causal effect at *a particular level of* S. When there are p variables and each of them has j values, S will have $p \times j$ levels, which will become very large even when p and j are only moderately large. Unless we have a huge sample size, very likely we do not have enough cases at each level, especially for both treatment and control groups, for estimating the causal effect. It is likely that at a certain level there are only treatment group cases or control group cases. In the end, we cannot calculate the overall causal effect as a weighted average across all the levels.

Matching

How can we eliminate all the differences that are deemed related to the assignment process between the treatment and the control groups? Paul Rosenbaum and Donald Rubin (1983, 1984, 1985; Rubin, 1991; Rosenbaum, 2002) have developed the propensity score. For an individual case, its propensity score is the probability that it will be assigned to the treatment group instead of the control group given that it carries a set of observed characteristics. The idea is to estimate such score by using a binary logistic regression model:

$$\Pr[D = 1|S] = \frac{\exp(\beta S)}{1 + \exp(\beta S)} \tag{11.7}$$

Albeit a very simple idea, it has solved the sparse data problem that we had before. With only one dimension, i.e. the propensity score, now we can make the cases under treatment and control as comparable as they could be, because the single score has absorbed all the important information for blocking the back-door paths. If no important observed variables have been missed out, here are the steps we need to follow:

(1) Carefully select the variables to be included in S based on current knowledge and theories to ensure that all the important variables related to the assignment process have been selected.
(2) Calculate the propensity score with a binary logistic regression model.
(3) Pick up a case in the treatment group randomly.

(4) Look for a case in the control group that has the same or the closest propensity score as the case selected in step 3, which is called 'matching'.[2]

(5) Repeat the matching process for the rest of the cases in the treatment group.[3]

Once the matching is done, we will be able to calculate the estimated causal effect based on the means of the two groups.

Using an Instrumental Variable

Another strategy for dealing with non-random selection of cases into different causal conditions is to use an instrumental variable. To learn its basic logic, let us start with the non-random situation, which is represented by Figure 11.4.

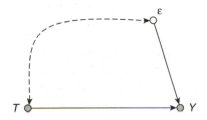

Figure 11.4   Association of the error term with assignment

This diagram illustrates why it is inappropriate to blindly use the following regression model:

$$Y_i = \alpha + \delta T_i + \varepsilon_i \tag{11.8}$$

Again, T is the binary variable representing the two causal conditions: 1 for treatment and 0 for control. Simply by looking at this equation, we may not be aware of the correlation between the error term ε and T. But if they are correlated, then it is misleading to use δ to represent the causal effect, because some of its effect has been explained by ε.

An instrumental variable could be used to solve this problem. It helps to illustrate this with Figure 11.5.

You can see that the difference between Figure 11.4 and Figure 11.5 is the newly added instrumental variable Z in the latter figure. It is instrumental because it can help us estimate the causal effect of T on Y while T is still correlated with the error term.

---

[2]There are a few methods for determining a matched pair, including exact matching, nearest-neighbour matching and so on.

[3]The number of cases under treatment is usually smaller than that under control because it is harder to obtain treated cases, especially in medical research. In the social sciences, this may not be a problem, but the two groups are rarely of the same size. Obviously, we start with the smaller one and find matching cases in the bigger group.

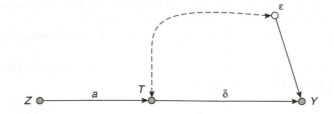

Figure 11.5   Use of an instrumental variable

In order to understand why it can do this, we need to clearly define its relations with other terms. To be an instrumental variable, it has to satisfy three criteria: (1) it has an effect on the treatment assignment variable; that is, it affects how cases are assigned to a particular causal condition; (2) it does not have a direct effect on Y, the variable that we use for calculating the causal effect; in other words, the instrumental variable has only an indirect effect on Y, which is referred to as 'exclusion restriction' in the literature; (3) it is not correlated with the error term.

Once these conditions are satisfied, the idea is to produce a new estimate of T and Y, respectively, and to use these statistics to estimate the causal effect. More specifically, there are three steps of achieving this (Winship and Morgan, 1999: 682):

(1) Regress Y_i on Z_i to obtain $\hat{Y}_i$.
(2) Regress T_i on Z_i to obtain $\hat{T}_i$.
(3) Estimate the causal effect with $\hat{Y}_i = \bar{\delta}\hat{T}_i + \varpi_i$.

The whole process can also be represented as a ratio, which is referred to as 'the Wald estimate':

$$\hat{\delta}_{IV,Wald} = \frac{E[\overline{Y}_i|Z_i = 1] - E[\overline{Y}_i|Z_i = 0]}{E[\overline{T}_i|Z_i = 1] - E[\overline{T}_i|Z_i = 0]} \tag{11.9}$$

The idea remains the same as the numerator is the standard estimator for the effect of Z on Y, while the denominator is the estimator for the effect of Z on T, and the ratio thus represents the effect of T on Y.

It is not easy to find instrumental variables. If we can collect our own data, we may purposefully create an instrumental variable that satisfies the above conditions. However, if we use secondary data, very likely the primary investigators did not know we were interested in a particular causal relationship and therefore did not include a usable instrumental variable. We might be able to find one if we are lucky enough, but it is clearly difficult to find one that is only associated with treatment assignment while not associated with Y at all. This, however, is only a practical reason why an instrumental variable may not be a widely used strategy. As Morgan and Winship (2007: 197–200) point out, there are some other statistical problems with 'the traditional IV (instrumental variable) estimation', such as biased estimates with finite samples and the loss of information and thus statistical power.

Another important limitation of the traditional instrumental variable is that it assumes that every individual case responds to the instrumental variable in the same way. Clearly, it is hard to hold such assumption in reality. For example, Gelman and Hill (2007: 215–25) used an example of children watching a particular television programme on their learning of English letters. Because researchers could not assign children to a particular causal condition (watching the programme or not) by force, they asked the teachers to encourage their children to watch it. Therefore, encouraging or not became an instrumental variable. However, a teacher's encouragement might or might not work. That is, there is no direct connection between the instrumental variable and the assignment. Actually, there are four possible scenarios (Table 11.2).

Table 11.2   Four scenarios of an instrumental variable and assignment

		Would watch?	
		Yes	No
If encouraged?	Yes	Compliers	Never takers
	No	Always takers	Defiers

The benefit of distinguishing these scenarios is that we allow our causal estimate to vary according to each scenario, thereby taking into account the 'local variation' of the causal effect. This is why the effect derived this way is called 'the local average treatment effect' (LATE). Such improvement, however, is limited as it cannot relax the stringent conditions for an instrumental variable.

In this book we have studied the concepts behind a variety of statistical procedures and methods. I sincerely hope that the discussions have given you an insight into why particular methods are suitable for specific purposes and help you in choosing the most appropriate method for your own research. Due to the limited space, my explanations may have been too brief on a few topics for some readers. If this is indeed the case, please move on by consulting the works cited in the discussion and the bibliography in general.

Bibliography

Abbott, A. (1988) 'Transcending general linear reality', *Sociological Theory*, 6: 169–86.

Abbott, A. (1992) 'What do cases do? Some notes on activity in sociological analysis', in Charles C. Ragin and Howard S. Becker (eds), *What Is a Case? Exploring the Foundations of Social Inquiry*. Cambridge: Cambridge University Press. pp. 53–82.

Abbott, A. (2001) *Time Matters: On Theory and Method*, 2nd edn. Chicago, IL: University of Chicago Press.

Abbott, A. (2004) *Methods of Discovery: Heuristics for the Social Sciences*. London: W.W. Norton.

Agresti, A. (2007) *An Introduction to Categorical Data Analysis, 2nd edn*. Hoboken, NJ: WileyBlackwell.

Agresti, A. and Finlay, B. (2008) *Statistical Methods for the Social Sciences, 4th edn*. Upper Saddle River, NJ: Pearson Education.

Alison, P. D. (1990), 'Change scores as dependent variables in regression analysis.' *Sociological Methodology*, 20: 93–114.

Anscombe, F.J. (1973) 'Graphs in statistical analysis', *The American Statistician*, 27 (1): 17–21.

Babbie, E. (2007) *The Practice of Social Research*. Florence, KY: Wadsworth.

Berk, R. (2003) *Regression Analysis: A Constructive Critique*. Thousand Oaks, CA: Sage.

Berry, W.D. (1993) *Understanding Regression Assumptions*. London: Sage.

Biesanz, J.C., Deeb-Sossa, N., Papadakis, A.A., Bollen, K.A. and Curran, P.J. (2004) 'The role of coding time in estimating and interpreting growth curve models', *Psychological Methods*, 9 (1): 30–52.

Blossfeld, H. P. Rohwer, G. and Golsch, K. (2007) *Event History Analysis with Stata*. Mahwah, NJ: Lawrence Erlbaum Associates.

Blumer, H. (1956) 'Sociological analysis and the "variable"', *American Sociological Review*, 21: 683–90.

Borg, I. and Groenen, P.J.F. (2005) *Modern Multidimensional Scaling*. New York: Springer.

Bourdieu, P. (1986) 'The forms of capital', in J.G. Richardson (ed.), *Handbook of Theory and Research for the Sociology of Education*. New York: Greenwood Press. pp. 241–58.

Bowker, G.C. and Star, S.L. (1999) *Sorting Things Out: Classification and Its Consequences*. Cambridge, MA: MIT Press.

Box-Steffensmeier, J.M. (2004) *Event History Modeling: A Guide for Social Scientists*. Cambridge: Cambridge University Press.

Bradley, W.B. and Schaefer, K. (1998) *The Uses and Misuses of Data and Models: The Mathematization of the Human Sciences*. London: Sage.

Byrne, D. and Ragin, C.C. (2009) *The SAGE Handbook of Case-Based Methods*. London: Sage.

Caramani, D. (2009) *Introduction to the Comparative Method with Boolean Algebra*. London: Sage.

Carrington, P., Scott, J. and Wasserman, S. (2005) *Models and Methods in Social Network Analysis*. Cambridge: Cambridge University Press.

Cartwright, N. (2007) *Hunting Causes and Using Them: Approaches in Philosophy and Economics*. Cambridge: Cambridge University Press.

Chamberlayne, P., Bornat, J. and Wengraf, T. (2000) *The Turn to Biographical Methods in Social Science: The Comparative Issues and Examples*. Florence, KY: Routledge.

Chatfield, C. (2003) *The Analysis of Time Series: An Introduction,* 6th edn. Boca Raton, FL: Chapman & Hall/CRC.

Chatterjee, S.A.S. Hadi and Price, B. (2000) *Regression Analysis by Example*, 3rd edn. New York, NY: John Wiley & Sons.

Cochran, W. (1977) *Sampling Techniques,* 3rd edn. New York, NY: John Wiley & Sons.

Coleman, J.S. (1990) *Equality and Achievement in Education*. Boulder, CO: Westview Press.

Cox, D.R. (1972) 'Regression models and life tables', *Journal of the Royal Statistical Society*, 34: 187–202.

Cox, D.R. (1975) 'Partial likelihood', *Biometrika*, 62: 269–76.

Diamond, I. (2006) 'Tackling the social science problem', *RSS NEWS* 33 (10).

Dorofeev, S. and Grant, P. (2006) *Statistics for Real-Life Sample Surveys: Non-Simple-Random Samples and Weighted Data*. Cambridge: Cambridge University Press.

Duncan, T., Duncan, S. and Strycker, L.A. (2006) *An Introduction to Latent Variable Growth Curve Modeling: Concepts, Issues and Applications*, 2nd rev. edn. Mahwah, NJ: Lawrence Erlbaum Associates.

Esser, H. (1996) 'What is wrong with "Variable Sociology?"', *European Sociological Review*, 12 (2): 159–66.

Ferrer, E., Hamagami, F. and McArdle, J.J. (2004) 'Modeling latent growth curves with incomplete data using different types of structural equation modeling and multilevel software', *Structural Equation Modeling*, 11: 452–83.

Fink, A. (2003) *How to Manage, Analyze, and Interpret Survey Data*, 2nd edn. London: Sage.

Freudenburg, W. (1986) 'Social impact assessment', *Annual Review of Sociology*, 12: 451–78.

Geertz, C. (1973) *The Interpretation of Cultures*. New York: Basic Books.

Gelman, A.J. and Hill, J. (2007) *Data Analysis Using Regression and Multilevel/ Hierarchical Models*. Cambridge: Cambridge University Press.

Gill, J. (2007) *Bayesian Methods: A Social and Behavioral Sciences Approach*. Boca Raton, FL: Chapman & Hall.

Goldthorpe, J. (2000) *On Sociology: Numbers, Narratives, and the Integration of Research and Theory: Numbers, Narratives and the Integration of Research and Theory*. Oxford: Oxford University Press.

Goodman, L. (2007) 'Statistical magic and/or statistical serendipity: an age of progress in the analysis of categorical data', *Annual Review of Sociology*, 33: 1–19.

Goyder, J. (1987) *The Silent Minority: Nonrespondents on Sample Surveys*. Boulder, CO: Westview Press.

Green, P.E., Carmone, F. and Smith, S.M. (1989) *Multidimensional Scaling: Concept and Applications*. Boston, MA: Allyn & Bacon.

Groves, R.M., Fowler Jr., F.J., Couper, M.P. and Lepkowski, J.M. (2004) *Survey Methodology*. Hoboken, NJ: WileyBlackwell.

Hair, J.F. Jr., Black, W.C., Babin, B.J., Anderson, R.E. and Tatham, R.L. (2006) *Multivariate Data Analysis*, 6th edn. Upper Saddle River, NJ: Pearson Education.

Hancock, G.R. and Choi, J. (2006) 'A vernacular for linear latent growth models', *Structural Equation Modeling: A Multidisciplinary Journal*, 13: 352–77.

Harkness, H., van de Vijver, F.J.R. and Mohler, P. Ph. (2002) *Cross-cultural Survey Methods*. London: WileyBlackwell.

Holland, P. W. (1986) 'Statistics and causal inference', *Journal of the American Statistical Association*, 81: 945-70.

Holland, P. W. and Rubin, D. (1988) 'Causal inference in retrospective studies', *Evaluation Review*, 12 (3): 203–31

Hume, D. (1975[1777]) *Enquiries Concerning Human Understanding and Concerning the Principles of Morals*. Reprinted from the posthumous edition of 1777 and edited by L.A. Selby-Bigge. Oxford: Clarendon Press.

Kader, G. and Perry. M. (2007) 'Variability for categorical variables', *Journal of Statistics Education*, 15 (2).

Kalton, G., Kasprzyk, D. and McMillen, D.B. (1989) 'Nonsampling errors in panel survey', in D. Kasprzyk, G.J. Duncan, G. Kalton and M.P. Singh (eds), *Panel Surveys*. New York: John Wiley. pp. 249–70.

Kennedy, P. (2008) *A Guide to Econometrics,* 6th edn. Oxford: Blackwell.

Kish, L. (1965) *Survey Sampling*. London: John Wiley & Sons.

Knoke, D., Bohrnstedt, G. and Mee, A. (2002) *Statistics for Social Data Analysis*, 4th edn. Itasca, IL: F E Peacock.

Knoke, D. and Yang, S. (2008) *Social Network Analysis*, 2nd edn. Thousand Oaks, CA: Sage.

Koehly, L. and Pattison, P.E. (2005) 'Random graph models for social networks: multiple relations or multiple raters', in P. Carrington, J. Scott, and S. Wasserman (eds), *Models and Methods in Social Network Analysis*. New York: Cambridge University Press. pp. 162–91.

Kruskal, W.H. and Mosteller, F. (1980) 'Representative sampling. IV. The history of the concept in statistics, 1895–1939', *International Statistical Review*, 48: 169–95.

Krzanowski, W. (2007) *Statistical Principles and Techniques in Scientific and Social Research*. Oxford: Oxford University Press.

Liao, T. (2002) *Statistical Group Comparison*. London: WileyBlackwell.

Lieberson, S. (1985) *Making it Count: The Improvement of Social Research and Theory*. Berkeley, CA: University of California Press.

Lieberson, S. (1992) 'Einstein, Renoir, and Greeley: some thoughts about evidence in sociology', *American Sociological Review*, 57: 1–15.

Lieberson, S. (2001) 'Review essay on *Fuzzy Set Social Science*, by Charles C. Ragin', *Contemporary Sociology*, 30: 331–4.

Lieberson, S. (2004) 'Comments on the use and utility of QCA', *Qualitative Methods*, 2 (2): 13–14. And 'Response to reassurances and rebuttals', *Qualitative Methods*, 2 (2): 25.

Little, R. and Rubin, D.B. (2002) *Statistical Analysis with Missing Data*, 2nd rev. edn. New York: John Wiley & Sons.

Lohr, S. (1997) *Sampling: Design and Analysis*, 2nd edn. Florence, KT: Brooks/Cole.

Lutkepohl, H. (2007) *New Introduction to Multiple Time Series Analysis*. Berlin: Springer-Verlag.

Lynn, P. and Jowell, R. (1996) 'How might opinion polls be improved? The case for probability sampling', *Journal of the Royal Statistical Society, Series A*, 159: 21–8.

MacIver, R.M. (1942) *Social Causation*. Oxford: Ginn and Company.

Mahoney, J. and Rueschemeyer. D. (2003) *Comparative Historical Analysis in the Social Sciences*. New York: Cambridge University Press.

McKnight, P., McKnight, K.M., Sidani, S. and Figueredo, A.J. (2007) *Missing Data: A Gentle Introduction*. New York: Guilford Press.

Merton, Robert K. (1987) 'Three fragments from a sociologist's notebooks: establishing the phenomenon, specified ignorance, and strategic research materials', *Annual Review of Sociology*, 13: 1–28.

Morgan, S. and Winship, C. (2007) *Counterfactuals and Causal Inference: Methods and Principles for Social Research*. New York: Cambridge University Press.

Moore, D.S. and McCabe, G.P. (2006) *Introduction to the Practice of Statistics,* 5th edn. New York: W.H. Freeman and Company.

Moore, D.S. and Notz, W.I. (2006) *Statistics: Concepts and Controversies*, 6th edn. New York: W.H. Freeman & Co

Moore, M. (2004) *Researching Life Stories: Method, Theory and Analyses in a Biographical Age*. London: Routledge.

Moser, C. and Kalton, G. (1980) *Survey Methods in Social Investigation*, 2nd rev. edn. Sudbury, MA: Dartmouth Publishing.

Mueller, J.H. and Schuessler, K.F. (1961) *Statistical Reasoning in Sociology*. Boston, MA: Houghton Mifflin.

Neale, M., Boker, S.M., Xie, G. and Maes, H. (2003) *Mx: Statistical Modeling*. Richmond, VA: Department of Psychiatry.

Preacher, K., Wichman, A.L., McCullam, R.C. and Briggs, N.E. (2008) *Latent Growth Curve Modelling*. Thousand Oaks, CA: Sage.

Putnam, R. (1993) *Making Democracy Work: Civic Traditions in Modern Italy*. Princeton, NJ: Princeton University Press.

Putman, R. (2001) *Bowling Alone: The Collapse and Revival of American Community*. New York: Simon & Schuster.

Putman, R. (2004) *Democracies in Flux: The Evolution of Social Capital in Contemporary Society*. New York: Oxford University Press.

Putman, R., Leonardi, R. and Nanetti, R.Y. (1994) *Making Democracy Work: Civic Traditions in Modern Italy*. Princeton, NJ: Princeton University Press.

Raftery, A. (2001) 'Statistics in sociology, 1950–2000', in A. E. Raftery, M. A. Tanner and M. T. Wells (eds), *Statistics in the 21st Century*. New York: Chapman & Hall. pp. 156–70.

Ragin, C. (1992) *The Comparative Method: Moving Beyond Qualitative and Quantitative Strategies*. Berkeley, CA: University of California Press.

Ragin, C. (2000) *Fuzzy-Set Social Science*. Chicago, IL: Chicago University Press.

Ragin, C. (2008) *Redesigning Social Inquiry: Fuzzy Sets and Beyond*. Chicago, IL: Chicago University Press.

Rihoux, B. and Ragin, C.C. (eds) (2009) *Configurational Comparative Methods: Qualitative Comparative Analysis (QCA) and Related Techniques*. Thousand Oaks, CA: Sage.

Roberts, B. (2001) *Biographical Research*. Buckingham: Open University Press.

Rosenbaum, R. (2002) *Observational Studies*, 2nd edn. New York: Springer.

Rosenbaum, R. and Rubin, D. (1983) 'The central role of the propensity score in observational studies for causal effects', *Biometrika*, 70: 41–55.

Rosenbaum, R. and Rubin, D. (1984) 'Reducing bias in observational studies using subclassification on the propensity score', *Journal of the American Statistical Association*, 79: 516–24.

Rosenbaum, R. and Rubin, D. (1985) 'Constructing a control group using multivariate matched sampling methods', *American Statistician*, 39: 33–8.

Rossi, P. H. and Wright, J.D. (1984) 'Evaluation research: an assessment', *Annual Review of Sociology*, 10: 331–52.

Rossi, P. H. and Wright, J.D. (1991) 'Practical implications of modes of statistical inference for causal effects and the critical role of the assignment mechanism', *Biometrics*, 47: 1213–34.

Russell, B. (1963) *Mysticism and Logic and Other Essays*. London: Allen & Unwin.

Salant, P. and Dillman, D.A. (1994) *Conducting Surveys: A Step-by-step Guide to Getting the Information You Need*. New York: John Wiley & Sons.

Saris, W. and Stronkhorst, H. (1984) *Causal Modelling in Nonexperimental Research: An introduction to the LISREL approach*. Amsterdam: Sociometric Research Foundation.

Scott, J. (2000) *Social Network Analysis: A Handbook*, 2nd edn. Thousand Oaks, CA: Sage.

Simon, H. (1953) 'Causal ordering and identifiability', in W. C. Hood and T. Koopmans (eds), *Studies in Econometric Method*. New York: Wiley. pp. 49–74.

Singer, J.D. and Willett, J.B. (2003) *Applied Longitudinal Data Analysis: Modelling Change and Event Occurrence*. New York: Oxford University Press.

Snijders T. (2005) 'Models for longitudinal network data', in P. Carrington, J. Scott and S. Wasserman (eds), *Models and Methods in Social Network Analysis*. New York: Cambridge University Press. Chapter 11.

Sobel, M. (1995) 'Causal inference in the social and behavioral sciences', in G. Arminger, C.C. Clogg and M.E. Sobel (eds), *Handbook of Statistical Modeling for the Social and Behavioral Sciences*. New York: Plenum Press. pp. 1–38.

Sorensen, A.B. (1998) 'Theoretical mechanisms and the empirical study of social processes', in P. Hedström and R. Swedberg (eds), *Social Mechanisms: An Analytical Approach to Social Theory*. New York: Cambridge University Press. pp. 238–66.

Stinchcombe, A. (1968) *Constructing Social Theories*. New York: Harcourt, Brace & World.

Stinchcombe, A. (2005) *The Logic of Social Research*. Chicago, IL: Chicago University Press.

Stoolmiller, M. (1995) 'Using latent growth curve models to study developmental processes', in J.M. Gottman and G. Sackett (eds), *The Analysis of Change*. Hillsdale, NJ: Lawrence Erlbaum Associates. pp. 105–38.

Stoop, I., Billiet, J. Koch, A. and Fitzgerald, R. (2008) *Reducing Survey Nonresponse*. New York: John Wiley & Sons.

Tabachnick, B.G. and Fidell, L.S. (2001) *Using Multivariate Statistics*, 4th edn. London: Allyn & Bacon.

Taris, T.W. (2000) *A Primer in Longitudinal Data Analysis*. London: Sage.

Thompson, S. (2002) *Sampling*, 2nd edn. New York: WileyBlackwell.

Tilly, C. (1972) 'The modernization of political conflict in france', in E.B. Harvey (ed.), *Perspectives in Modernization*. Toronto: University of Toronto Press. pp. 51–95.

Tilly, C. (1992) *Coercion, Capital, and European States, AD 990–1992*. Oxford: Blackwell.

Tilly, C. (1997) 'Parliamentarization of popular contention in great Britain, 1758–1834', in C. Tilly (ed.), *Roads from Past to Future*. New York: Rowan & Littlefield Publishers. pp. 217–44.

van Belle, G. (2002) *Statistical Rules of Thumb*. New York: John Wiley & Sons.

Walker, A., Maher, J., Coulthard, M., Goddard, E. and Thomas, M. (2002) *Living in Britain*. London: The Stationery Office.

Warner, R. (1999) *Spectral Analysis of Time Series Data*. New York: Guilford Press.

Wasserman, S. and Faust, K. (1994) *Social Network Analysis: Methods and Applications*. New York: Cambridge University Press.

Winship, C. and Morgan, S. (1999) 'The estimation of causal effects from observational data', *American Review of Sociology*, 25: 659–706.

Yamaguchi, K. (1991) *Event History Analysis*. Thousand Oaks, CA: Sage.

Yang, K. (2007) 'Individual social capital and its measurement in social surveys', *Survey Research Methods*, 1 (1): 19–27.

Index

scree plot 148, 159
secondary data 16, 22, 24, 35, 155, 188
significance level 69, 78, 87, 97
similarity matrix 146–7
Simon, Herbert 173
simple random sampling (see sampling)
social capital 52–3, 154–5
social indicators 52–3
social network analysis (SNA) 8, 23, 133
Socio-Economic Panel 115
socio-economic status (SES) 154, 177,
   179–80
sociology 1, 2, 7, 52, 154, 175
Sorenson, Aage 1, 111
specification error 92
spread, see variation
SPSS 148f
spurious relationship 178
stable unit treatment value assumption
   (SUTVA) 183
standard deviation 57, 63, 66, 80, 106, 167
standard error, 96
statistical inference 5, 16, 34–5, 37, 61–3, 97
statistical models 19–20
Stinchcombe, Arthur 51, 174
stratified sampling (see sampling)
stratification factor 46
stress 148
structural equation models (SEM) 6, 43, 112,
   162, 165–8,
subjective clustering 148
Surveys of Consumers 36
survival 122–3, 128
survivor function 128

tables 17–9, 75–6
Tau c 82–3
test of hypothesis 50, 66–70, 120
  one-way 67
  two-way 67
test statistic 68
Tilly, Charles 116
time series 115–6

UK 2, 46, 55, 86, 162
UK Household Longitudinal Study
   (UKHLS) 115

unbalanced data 118
unconditional means model 119
unconditional growth model 119–20
univariate statistics 13
USA 46, 100, 107

validation 139, 144, 149, 174
variables 4, 9, 32–3, 132
  absolute 26, 28
  categorical, 17, 28, 58, 86, 99, 102, 149,
    172
  centre of 16–7, 54–61
  confounding 156, 180
  continuous 28
  control 111–2, 180–1
  discrete 28
  endogenous 165
  exogenous 165
  expected value of 110
  interval-ratio 28
  instrumental 187–9
  metrical 28–9, 55–6, 157, 167
  nominal 27–9, 58
  ordinal 27–9, 56, 81–3, 167
  random 24
  time-variant 118, 121
  time-invariant 118, 121
  transformations of 29
  variation of 17, 54–61, 109
  vs. cases 29–33
variance 17, 48–9, 57–8, 63, 106, 121–2,
   157–60
variance-covariance matrix 141, 164, 166–7,
   169, 172

Wald estimate 188
Ward's method 136
Weber, Max 7, 52
Weibull model 130
weight 16, 49–50, 56, 58, 137
Wilks' Lambda, 141

Yule's Q 78

z score 64, 136

The Qualitative Research Kit

Edited by Uwe Flick

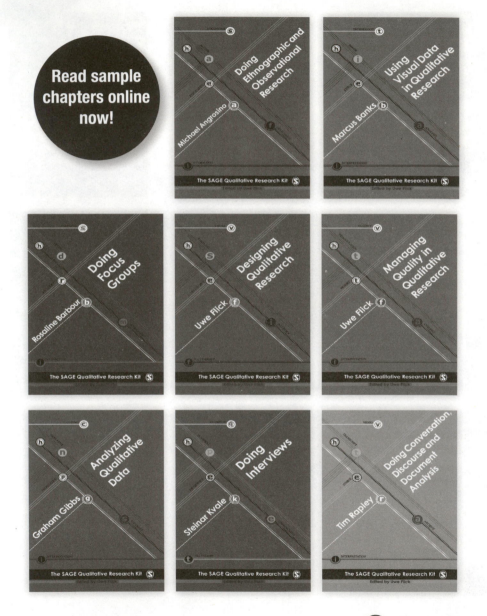

Read sample chapters online now!

Doing Ethnographic and Observational Research — Michael Angrosino
The SAGE Qualitative Research Kit

Using Visual Data in Qualitative Research — Marcus Banks
The SAGE Qualitative Research Kit

Doing Focus Groups — Rosaline Barbour
The SAGE Qualitative Research Kit

Designing Qualitative Research — Uwe Flick
The SAGE Qualitative Research Kit

Managing Quality in Qualitative Research — Uwe Flick
The SAGE Qualitative Research Kit

Analyzing Qualitative Data — Graham Gibbs
The SAGE Qualitative Research Kit

Doing Interviews — Steinar Kvale
The SAGE Qualitative Research Kit

Doing Conversation, Discourse and Document Analysis — Tim Rapley
The SAGE Qualitative Research Kit

www.sagepub.co.uk